Challenging Trafficking in Persons

Sector Project against Trafficking in Women (Eds.)

Challenging Trafficking in Persons

Theoretical Debate & Practical Approaches

gtz
Deutsche Gesellschaft für
Technische Zusammenarbeit (GTZ) GmbH

commissioned by:

Federal Ministry
for Economic Cooperation
and Development

Nomos

The Deutsche Gesellschaft für Technische Zusammenarbeit (GTZ) GmbH is implementing the Sector Project against Trafficking in Women on the basis of a commission from the German Federal Ministry for Economic Cooperation and Development (BMZ).

The opinions and analyses expressed in this book do not necessarily reflect the views and official policies of the Sector Project against Trafficking in Women.

Die Deutsche Bibliothek – CIP Cataloguing-in-Publication-Data

Die Deutsche Bibliothek lists this publication in the Deutsche Nationalbibliografie; detailed bibliographic data is available in the Internet at http://dnb.ddb.de.

ISBN 3-8329-1687-3

Deutsche Gesellschaft für Technische Zusammenarbeit (GTZ) GmbH
Division 42 Governance and Democracy
Bernd Hoffmann
P.O.Box 51 80
65726 Eschborn
Germany
www.gtz.de und www.gtz.de/traffickinginwomen

Editorial Team:
Anna Erdelmann (Director) | Staff Members: Kerstin Brunner, Astrid Niehaus, Johanna Willems | Advisors: Elaine Pearson, Gabriele Reiter
Copy Editor: Sabine Weeke

1. Edition 2005
© Nomos Verlagsgesellschaft, Baden-Baden 2005. Printed in Germany. This work is subject to copyright. All rights are reserved, whether the whole or part of the material is concerned, specifically those of translation, reprinting, re-use of illustrations, broadcasting, reproduction by photocopying machine or similar means, and storage in data banks. Under § 54 of the German Copyright Law where copies are made for other than private use a fee is payable to »Verwertungsgesellschaft Wort«, Munich.

Foreword

It is uncontested that every year tens or even hundreds of thousands of people – most of them women and children but also a growing number of men – are exploited, sold and forced into situations of exploitations from which there is almost no escape. Trafficking in human beings is one of the most globalised and lucrative criminal businesses in the world today, one that almost no country is immune from. Profits from this criminal industry are enormous, generating tens of billions of dollars annually to criminals and organised crime groups.

While in Europe, mainly women and children have been trafficked for sexual exploitation and for the market of pornography, many people in other parts of the world, but increasingly also in Europe, end up being exploited as domestic servants, as bonded or coerced workers in sweatshops, on construction sites, in agriculture and textile and garment factories, in the transportation industry and in restaurant chains, on plantations and in mines.

Admittedly there are signs of progress in the fight against human trafficking, especially when it comes to institutional mechanisms that did not exist several years ago, but there is little evidence that we have succeeded in curbing this crime. Consequently we must reflect on these facts and use them to evaluate our strategies and efforts and improve upon them.

In this context the OSCE warmly welcomes the Sector Project Against Trafficking in Women, commissioned by the German Federal Ministry for Economic Cooperation and Development (BMZ) as a highly commendable effort designed to give new impetus to combating trafficking in persons. This all the more so, as it is now being realised that effective action against human trafficking is going to require more comprehensive and integrated approaches. Currently, the key challenge for countries around the world is to craft and implement sounder and more effective responses that produce meaningful results. More sophisticated understanding of human trafficking is needed to improve the operational effectiveness of the implementation of appropriate anti-trafficking laws, policies and practices utilised in the fight against trafficking in human beings around the world.

Against this background, the present comprehensive publication which highlights broad theoretical debates and showcases practical anti-trafficking interventions is a most valuable tool in finding the very responses and meaningful approaches we stand in need of, if we wish to be successful in our fight against human trafficking.

Helga Konrad
OSCE Special Representative
on Combating Trafficking in Human Beings

Table of Contents

Foreword
Helga Konrad, Special Representative of the OSCE — 5

Directory of Legal Instruments and Policy Documents — 9

Abbreviations — 12

Introduction — 15

Theoretical Debate — 20

    Historical Development of Trafficking – The Legal Framework for Anti-Trafficking Interventions
    Elaine Pearson — 20

    The Victim Perspective – A Neglected Dimension
    Barbara Limanowska — 27

    Highlighting Economic Aspects of Trafficking in Human Beings
    Sebastian Baumeister & Helen Santiago Fink — 32

    Undocumented Migration, Labour Exploitation and Trafficking
    Nivedita Prasad & Babette Rohner — 39

    Forced and Bonded Labour
    Mary Cunneen — 44

    Trafficking in Children
    Mike Dottridge — 50

    Organ Trafficking – Challenges and Perspectives
    Elaine Pearson — 58

    Linkages between Trafficking and HIV/AIDS
    Jane Gronow & Deborah McWhinney — 63

Trafficking in Armed and Post-Conflict Situations
Martina E. Vandenberg 69

Practical Approaches 76

Approaches to Prevention 76

    The Role of the Private Sector in Developing Youth Careers
    Sebastian Baumeister & Susie Maley 81

    Empowerment of Orphans
    Lora Beltcheva, Maria Petrova & Maria Tchomarova 86

    Potentials of Community-Based Approaches
    Lilijana Vasić 90

    Hotlines – An Effective Tool for Outreach Work
    Kateryna Cherepakha & Olga Kalashnyk 94

    Non-Discriminatory Approaches to Address Clients in Prostitution
    Christiane Howe 98

Approaches to Victim Support 104

    Cooperation for Protection – National Referral Mechanisms
    Liliana Sorrentino 108

    A Victim-Centred Approach – The Italian Model
    Isabella Orfano 114

    Specialised Service Centres – The Belgian Model
    Bruno Moens 119

    Sustainable Social and Professional Reintegration
    Iana Matei 123

    Self-Empowerment of Migrant Women
    Warunee Chaiwongkam & Theera Srila 127

Approaches to Capacity and Institution Building   130

   Local Agenda for Community Security
   Diana Segovia   133

   Improving Media Coverage through Journalist Training
   Bronwyn Jones   137

   Addressing Labour Market Dimensions
   Beate Andrees   141

   Incorporating Gender Issues into Police Reform Processes
   Johanna Willems   146

   Developing Training Modules for Peacekeeping Operations
   Gabriele Reiter   149

Approaches to Advocacy Work   153

   Lobbying in Europe
   Mary Cunneen   156

   Strengthening Advocacy through Providing Baseline Studies
   Victoria Nwogu   161

Conclusions and Recommendations   165

Directory of Authors   170

Directory of Organisations   174

References   179

Directory of Legal Instruments and Policy Documents

Selected International and Regional Treaties (in Chronological Order)

The International Agreement for the Suppression of the White Slave Traffic (1904)

International Convention for the Suppression of the White Slave Traffic (1910)

League of Nations Convention for the Suppression of Traffic in Women and Children (1921)

League of Nations Slavery Convention (1926)

ILO Convention No. 29 concerning Forced or Compulsory Labour (1930)
short: ILO Forced Labour Convention No. 29

League of Nations International Convention for the Suppression of the Traffic in Women of Full Age (1933)

United Nations Universal Declaration of Human Rights (1948)

United Nations Convention for the Suppression of the Traffic in Persons and of the Exploitation of the Prostitution of Others (1949)
short: 1949 Convention

United Nations Convention relating to the Status of Refugees (1951)
short: Geneva Convention

United Nations Supplementary Convention on the Abolition of Slavery, the Slave Trade, and Institutions and Practices Similar to Slavery (1956)

ILO Convention No. 105 concerning the Abolition of Forced Labour (1957)
short: ILO Convention No. 105

United Nations International Covenant on Civil and Political Rights (1966)
short: ICCPR

United Nations International Covenant on Economic, Social and Cultural Rights (1966)
short: ICESCR

United Nations Convention on the Elimination of All Forms of Discrimination Against Women (1979)
short: CEDAW

United Nations Convention on the Rights of the Child (1989)
short: CRC or Child Rights Convention

United Nations Convention on the Protection of the Rights of All Migrant Workers and Members of Their Families (1990)
short: (UN) Migrant Workers' Convention

European Convention for the Protection of Human Rights and Dignity of the Human Beings with regard to the Application of Biology and Medicine (1997)

Rome Statute of the International Criminal Court (1998)
short: Rome Statute

ILO Convention No. 182 on the Elimination of the Worst Forms of Child Labour (1999)
short: ILO Convention No. 182

United Nations Optional Protocol to the Convention on the Rights of the Child on the Sale of Children, Child Prostitution and Child Pornography (2000)
short: Optional Protocol to the CRC

United Nations Convention against Transnational Organized Crime (2000)
short: TOC Convention

United Nations Protocol to Prevent, Suppress and Punish Trafficking in Persons, especially Women and Children (2000)
short: (UN) Trafficking Protocol or Palermo Protocol

United Nations Optional Protocol to the Convention on the Rights of the Child on the Involvement of Children in Armed Conflict (2000)

EU Council Framework Decision of 19 July 2002 on Combating Trafficking in Human Beings
short: EU Council Framework Decision (2002)

Additional Protocol to the European Convention on Human Rights and Biomedicine concerning Transplantation of Organs and Tissues of Human Origin (2002)

Council of Europe Convention on Action against Trafficking in Human Beings (2005)
short: Council of Europe Trafficking Convention

Relevant Policy Documents (in Chronological Order)

Beijing Declaration and Platform for Action, Fourth World Conference on Women (1995)
  short: Beijing Platform for Action

BMZ Concept for the Promotion of Equal Participation by Women and Men in the Development Process (2001)

German Government's Program of Action The German Government's Contribution Towards Halving Extreme Poverty Worldwide (2001)

UNOHCHR Recommended Principles and Guidelines on Human Rights and Human Trafficking (2002)
  short: UNOHCHR Recommended Principles

EU Brussels Declaration on Preventing and Combating Trafficking in Human Beings (2002)
  short: Brussels Declaration

UNICEF Guidelines for the Protection of the Rights of Child Victims of Trafficking in South Eastern Europe (2003)
  short: UNICEF Guidelines

OSCE Action Plan to Combat Trafficking in Human Beings (2003)
  short: OSCE Action Plan

WHO Ethical and Safety Recommendations for Interviewing Trafficked Women (2003)

Council of Europe's Recommendation 1611 (2003)

German Government's Development Policy Action Plan on Human Rights 2004 – 2007 (2004)

UNDPKO Policy Paper on Human Trafficking and United Nations Peacekeeping (2004)

NATO Policy on Combating Trafficking in Human Beings (2004)

UNICEF Principles for Ethical Reporting on Children (undated)

Abbreviations

AAF	Animus Association Foundation
AIDS	Acquired Immune Deficiency Syndrome
BiH	Bosnia and Herzegovina
BMFSFJ	Bundesministerium für Familie, Senioren, Frauen und Jugend (German Federal Ministry for Family, Senior Citizens, Women and Youth)
BMZ	Bundesministerium für wirtschaftliche Zusammenarbeit und Entwicklung (German Federal Ministry for Economic Cooperation and Development)
CCF	Christian Children's Fund
CEE	Central and Eastern Europe
CIMIC	Civil-Military Cooperation
CIS	Commonwealth of Independent States
CoC	Code of Conduct
CSR	Corporate Social Responsibility
EAPC	Euro-Atlantic Partnership Council
EU	European Union
FRY	Federal Republic of Yugoslavia
GCSP	Geneva Centre for Security Policy
GTZ	Deutsche Gesellschaft für Technische Zusammenarbeit (GmbH) (German Agency for Technical Cooperation)
HIV	Human Immunodeficiency Virus
IBLF	The Prince of Wales International Business Leaders Forum
ICLEI	Local Governments for Sustainability
ICTR	International Criminal Tribunal for Rwanda
ICTY	International Criminal Tribunal for the Former Yugoslavia
IGO	Intergovernmental Organisation
ILADH	Latin American Institute for Human Rights

ILO	International Labour Organization
ILO - PATWA	ILO Action Programme against Human Trafficking and Forced Labour in West Africa
INGO	International Non-Governmental Organization
IO	International Organisation
IOM	International Organization for Migration
IPTF	Pakistani International Police Task Force
IREX	International Research & Exchanges Board
LOST	Local Strategies to Prevent Trafficking in Persons
MADI	Media and Development International
MDC	Media Development Centre
MDG	Millennium Development Goals
NAC	North Atlantic Council
NAP	National Action Plan
NATO	North Atlantic Treaty Organisation
NGO	Non-Governmental Organisation
NRM	National Referral Mechanism
OCEEA	Office of the Co-Ordinator of OSCE Economic and Environmental Activities
ODIHR	Office for Democratic Institutions and Human Rights
OFER	Roma Youth NGO
OSCE	Organization for Security and Co-operation in Europe
OTR	Associazione On The Road
PACE	Parliamentary Assembly of the Council of Europe
PRA	Participatory Rural Appraisal
ROR	Reaching Out Romania
SEE	South Eastern Europe
SEE RIGHTs	South East European Regional Initiative aGainst Human Trafficking
SEPOM	Self-Empowerment Program for Migrant Women
SPTF	Stability Pact Task Force for South Eastern Europe
STD	Sexual Transmitted Diseases
STI	Sexual Transmitted Infections
STP	*Straniero Temporaneamente Presente* Card

TDF	Terre des Femmes
UN	United Nations
UNAIDS	Joint United Nations Programme on HIV/AIDS
UNDP	United Nations Development Programme
UNDPKO	United Nations Department of Peacekeeping Operations
UNEP	United Nations Environment Program
UNGASS	United Nations General Assembly Special Session on HIV/AIDS
UNHCHR	United Nations High Commissioner for Human Rights
UNICEF	United Nations Children's Fund
UNIFEM	United Nations Development Fund for Women
UNMIK	United Nations Mission in Kosovo
UNODC	United Nations Office on Drugs and Crime
UNOHCHR	United Nations Office of the High Commissioner for Human Rights
WHO	World Health Organization
YCDP	Youth Career Development Programme
YCI	Youth Career Initiative

Introduction

> No one shall be held in slavery or servitude; slavery and the slave trade shall be prohibited in all their forms. (Universal Declaration of Human Rights 1948: Art. 4)

Despite this long-formulated universal claim, in the era of globalisation, modern forms of slavery and slavery-like practices are on the rise and human trafficking is taking on global dimensions. Estimates range from 700,000 and 2,000,000 people who are bought and sold every year, the vast majority of them women and children.

Many of the countries from where people are trafficked are going through a transition phase marked by social upheaval or war. As a result of destitution, violence, unemployment and unstable societal structures, more and more people without any prospects see migration as their best option. The proportion of females among migrants has risen to more than fifty percent over the last two decades. Often, they carry sole responsibility for the household income in their countries of origin. Many female migrants are more vulnerable to human rights abuses and exploitation than their male counterparts since they tend to work in gender-segregated, often unregulated and unprotected sectors of the economy. Furthermore, they work in unskilled jobs, earn low wages and have no job security or social benefits. Female migrants often lack access to networks that enable them to migrate without being subjected to traffickers.

Traffickers frequently exploit the willingness of people to leave their country and their ignorance in how to go about this by organising illegal entry into another country for them; this makes their victims easy targets for blackmail. It is difficult for migrants to obtain legal status because of the restrictive immigration and border control policy of Western states.

The readiness to migrate and the unscrupulousness of traffickers pair up with increasing demand in destination countries for:

- cheap labour as domestic help, in the cleaning sector, restaurants and hotels, in construction and agriculture, as well as for commercial begging;
- sexual services of all sorts (HIV/AIDS has boosted demand for ever younger girls and boys who give an illusion of good health);
- mail-order brides, for whom prospective grooms are willing to pay high fees;
- organ donors, especially for kidneys.

The definition of trafficking in human beings as used throughout this publication is based on the definition of the UN Trafficking Protocol supplementing the United Nations Convention against Transnational Organised Crime. Article 3 of the Protocol defines trafficking as

[...] the recruitment, transportation, transfer, harbouring or receipt of persons, by means of the threat or use of force or other forms of coercion, of abduction, of fraud, of deception, of the abuse of power or of a position of vulnerability or of the giving or receiving of payments or benefits to achieve the consent of a person having control over another person, for the purpose of exploitation. Exploitation shall include, at a minimum, the exploitation of the prostitution of others or other forms of sexual exploitation, forced labour or services, slavery or practices similar to slavery, servitude or the removal of organs.

(b) The consent of a victim of trafficking in persons to the intended exploitation set forth in subparagraph (a) of this article shall be irrelevant where any of the means set forth in subparagraph (a) have been used.

(c) The recruitment, transportation, transfer, harbouring or receipt of a child for the purpose of exploitation shall be considered "trafficking in persons" even if this does not involve any of the means set forth in subparagraph (a) of this article. (UN 2000: Art. 3)

The UN Trafficking Protocol was the result of intense discussions and laid ground for further developments, such as the recent coming into force of the Council of Europe Convention on Action against Trafficking in Human Beings in 2005. The Convention is open for signature for all 46 member states of the Council of Europe. It further emphasises the need for the victims' rights protection including necessary standards for the monitoring of anti-trafficking measures.

Relevance for International Development and Cooperation

Many of the underlying causes for trafficking, such as poverty, gender inequality and weak institutional state structures are addressed by international development cooperation. Furthermore, anti-trafficking interventions also have strong linkages to several crosscutting issues such as HIV/AIDS prevention or the development of social and labour standards. Hence, development cooperation in general can be seen as a contribution to trafficking prevention. It is therefore of great importance to incorporate a comprehensive and integrative anti-trafficking perspective into development projects in the areas of poverty reduction, promotion of gender equality, health and good governance.

Sector Project against Trafficking in Women

In 2003, the German Federal Ministry for Economic Cooperation and Development (BMZ) has established the supra-regional Sector Project against Trafficking in Women. The project represents one step towards fulfilling the German commitment to reach the Millennium Development Goals and the goals set forth in the Programme of Action 2015, the German Government's contribution to reducing poverty worldwide. The Sector Project is being implemented by the Deutsche Gesellschaft für Technische Zusammenarbeit (GTZ) GmbH.

Since its beginning, the Sector Project has worked with local, regional and international partners, both state and non-governmental, active in the countries of origin, transit and destination, with the aim to prevent the phenomenon of trafficking and to protect the rights of (potential) victims. On this basis the Sector Project assists its partner organisations to conceptualise and implement innovative measures taking into account a holistic and human rights based approach. This is in line with the BMZ policy to reach the different development goals by applying a consistent human rights approach. BMZ's human rights approach, specified in the Development Policy Action Plan on Human Rights 2004–2007, is based on the internationally agreed standards. Using the following human rights principles, it also provides useful criteria and mechanisms for the realisation of human rights:

- One key principle is empowerment: people's ability to organise themselves and thus influence the political environment and institutions in a way that will improve their own lives.
- BMZ is focusing its development policy more systematically on people's rights, thus contributing to greater participation and equality of opportunity as well as freedom from discrimination.
- Another focus is to strengthen transparency and accountability by identifying what concrete duties exist in the development process and who is responsible for them. (BMZ 2004: 7)

Another aim of the Sector Project is to facilitate networking and the exchange of experience and to mainstream an anti-trafficking perspective into development cooperation.

As the majority of victims in Germany originate from Eastern European countries, this region has become the focus of the Sector Project's work. However, innovative approaches in other regions such as Latin America, Africa and Asia are also supported.

Aim of the Publication

The publication is directed at local, national, regional and international actors, especially in the field of development cooperation and human and women's rights activists. The aim of the publication is to contribute to the international debate on trafficking in human beings, to highlight neglected or critical aspects of the discussion in the anti-trafficking movement and to illustrate practical examples of how to tackle the problem.

Even though more than half of the practical approaches portrayed in the publication were supported by the Sector Project, it is not the intention of this publication to merely present its funded projects, but to provide an example of practical work and lessons learned in different areas of anti-trafficking interventions in order to illustrate possible approaches. The selection of examples is footed on a human rights based approach. The regional focus of the publication reflects the working areas of the Sector Project.

The methodology for generating the practical experiences was not driven by scientific evaluations, but through reports and narratives of project partners. Therefore, the presentations of the individual projects are based on the perception and observation of the organisations and authors themselves: they attempt to reflect their experiences and to draw lessons out of them in order to allow other individuals or organisations to build upon these results. Hence, the opinions and analyses expressed in this publication do not necessarily reflect the views and official policies of the Sector Project.

To make the reading process more enjoyable, some references are quoted in the articles. The sources for these quotes can be found at the end of the book. Furthermore, a list of legal instruments referred to in the publication gives an overview of the relevant international and legal texts on the context of trafficking in persons.

Content Overview of the Publication

The content of the publication is divided into two areas. The first part focuses on the various facets of trafficking highlighting different underrepresented or critical questions concerning anti-trafficking interventions.

To start with, Elaine Pearson describes the historical development of the international legal framework concerning trafficking as well as the responses from organisations working in the field.

The second chapter written by Barbara Limanowska highlights the need to incorporate the victim's perspective into anti-trafficking interventions.

Sebastian Baumeister and Helen Santiago Fink focus on the economic dimensions of trafficking as a global business as well as the role the private sector can play in anti-trafficking responses.

In the chapter on undocumented migration and labour exploitation, Nivedita Prasad and Babette Rohner analyse the connections between the two phenomena and the global trafficking movements as well as links between the concepts of possible interventions.

Mary Cunneen examines the challenges of addressing forced and bonded labour and the connections between approaches focusing on these two phenomena and anti-trafficking interventions.

As the special vulnerabilities and needs of children are often neglected in interventions, Mike Dottridge reflects these and highlights necessary steps when addressing minors.

Organ trafficking is included in the definition of the UN Trafficking Protocol. However, it is an often-ignored field, analysed by Elaine Pearson in her chapter.

The interconnections between trafficking and HIV/AIDS prevention in the areas of prevention and victim support are specified by Jane Gronow and Deborah McWhinney.

Martina Vandenberg concludes the theoretical debate by drawing attention to the trafficking in armed and post-conflict situations and by listing recommendations to tackle the phenomenon in such situations.

The second part of the book portrays selected approaches in the areas of prevention, victim support, capacity and institution building as well as advocacy work. These are the areas in which most anti-trafficking measures are located. Each section is preceded by an introductory article by the editorial team of the Sector Project highlighting relevant aspects, key concerns and concepts in the respective intervention field. The practical examples were assigned to these intervention areas according to their primary focus, even though the work they describe might tackle more than just one area. Summarising the articles the editorial team extracted standards and key recommendations made by the authors; we hope that they will serve as a sound orientation for future anti-trafficking work.

Acknowledgements

The editors were pleased by the positive response and feedback authors and like-minded organisations gave throughout the process on the value of the publication. They wish to take the opportunity to express sincere thanks to all the authors and organisations involved, without whose contributions this publication would not have been possible. Special thanks are due to Gabriele Reiter for her input and efforts to coordinate this process and to Elaine Pearson for her conceptual support. The production of the publication and the exchange with the authors led to a valuable reflection process on the work and cooperations of the Sector Project.

The editors hope that this publication will provide insights and perspectives to stimulate further discussion on how to tackle trafficking in human beings by taking a comprehensive and holistic approach.

Anna Erdelmann
Project Director
Sector Project against Trafficking in Women, GTZ

Theoretical Debate

Historical Development of Trafficking – The Legal Framework for Anti-Trafficking Interventions

Elaine Pearson

Introduction

The term 'trafficking' and especially 'trafficking in women' has a long history appearing in various international instruments, though it has had multiple and conflicting interpretations. Only with the UN Trafficking Protocol in 2000 has 'trafficking' been defined in international law. On the basis of that definition, states have swung into action as never before: adopting and changing criminal laws and policies, developing anti-trafficking programmes and mobilising communities. The global anti-trafficking effort has probably peaked early in the 21st Century. It is fitting then to remind ourselves, as anti-trafficking actors and advocates, how we arrived at this point where trafficking is an issue of priority and concern on the international development agenda. Why did we coin this term 'trafficking' in connection with people? Why was 'slavery' and 'forced labour' deemed insufficient or inappropriate to deal with this particular abuse? How has civil society, especially women's rights advocates, been instrumental in shaping our contemporary understanding of the issue?

This chapter traces how the legal concept of human trafficking has developed from its roots in the 'white slave' trade of women to its current legal definition concerned with grave exploitation of people for different purposes, from domestic work to factory work, for marriage and removal of organs. By examining the context of debate concerning the term 'trafficking', particularly leading up to the UN Trafficking Protocol definition, we can gain a better understanding of where complexities in the anti-trafficking discourse come from, and hopefully an understanding of how complex situations and challenges might best be solved.

Historical Concepts of Trafficking and Prostitution

Historically, the concept of human trafficking has been closely linked with women and children being sold into prostitution. The term 'trafficking' was first used in international instruments in connection to the so-called 'white slave trade'. The image of the white European women being forced, or indeed, simply moving, into prostitution in the East and Middle East was too much for both puritans and feminists, such as Josephine Butler, to bear. The previous UN Special Rapporteur on Violence against Women notes:

> [...] historically, anti-trafficking movements have been driven by perceived threats to the 'purity' or chastity of certain populations of women, notably white women. (Coomaraswamy 2000)

The International Agreement for the Suppression of the White Slave Traffic in 1904 (between mainly European countries) was followed by an International Convention of the same name in 1910. Both instruments stated their concern with the movement of women and girls across borders for 'immoral purposes'. The 1910 Convention went further than the 1903 Agreement by punishing acts involved in procuring women or girls for immoral purposes. Building on these early international instruments, another two treaties were consolidated under the League of Nations: in 1921 concerning women and children and in 1933 concerning women alone (International Convention for the Suppression of the Traffic in Women of Full Age).

1949 Convention on Trafficking and Exploitation of Prostitution

All of these early conventions formed the basis for the United Nations Convention on Suppression of Trafficking and Exploitation of Prostitution adopted in 1949. The 1949 Convention uses a similar moralistic tone describing prostitution as an 'evil' and like the preceding conventions reinforces a crime control approach to prostitution. Under the 1949 Convention, all third party acts in exploiting prostitution of others such as brothel keeping are punishable offences, regardless of the woman's age or consent. Trafficking is therefore synonymous with exploitation of prostitution under this Convention.

None of these so-called 'anti-trafficking' instruments were very effective in combating either trafficking or exploitation of prostitution. The 1949 Convention has been ratified by few countries (74 to date) and has weak enforcement mechanisms. Some countries were reluctant to ratify the Convention because of its abolitionist stance towards prostitution and some because control over prostitution was seen as a domestic rather than international matter. Furthermore, many countries that did adopt laws in line with the convention such as Italy, found these laws were ineffective in combating trafficking and forced prostitution, especially of migrant women. Anti-prostitution laws in fact tended to be enforced against women in prostitution themselves rather than those 'exploiting' them. This has been the main criticism of the 1949 Convention, that though it does not criminalize prostitution per se, neither does it condemn punishment of women in prostitution. In short, it is not a convention that protects human rights of women.

Feminist Discord over Trafficking

Throughout the twentieth century, a growing number of feminist activists felt that the so-called 'abolitionist' approach to prostitution associated with the 1949 Convention was ineffective in curbing the more severe abuses associated with women's migration, namely forced prostitution, debt bondage and slavery. In the 1980s and 1990s, a new picture of trafficking emerged of victims from Asia, Latin America or Eastern Europe, being deceived and coerced into prostitution in developed and mainly Western countries (Wijers and Chew 1997). Researchers such as Wijers and Chew found that not all of such migrating women in prostitution were held in slavery-like conditions, and furthermore slavery-like conditions were not confined to prostitution alone, but to other situations in which women migrated or worked, such as in domestic labour or marriage.

Wijers and Chew propounded that the concept of trafficking in women was closely connected to forced labour and slavery-like practices. The group of feminists and activists that concurred with Wijers and Chew's perspective became known as the Human Rights Caucus during the Trafficking Protocol negotiations. They felt that the 1949 Convention approach was failing to protect the rights of women in prostitution, by failing to distinguish between enslaved women and those who voluntarily chose to work in the sex industry. The Human Rights Caucus, which included sex workers, made a distinction between forced and consensual prostitution and argued that only forced prostitution should be the subject of criminal sanction.

Other feminists, the 'abolitionists', staunchly defended the position of the 1949 Convention, maintaining that no form of prostitution should be tolerated as prostitution itself in all forms is violence against women and therefore of women's rights. This group believed that ineffective enforcement was to blame for the 1949 Convention's inadequate response to combating trafficking and exploitation of (all) prostitution. They sought to continue the link between prostitution and trafficking, rather than expanding trafficking to areas of labour or including men as victims.

While those advocating abolition of prostitution found precedent in the historical 'trafficking' conventions, more recent human rights instruments in the 1990s began to expound the broader view of trafficking in women not necessarily limited to prostitution. Documents such as the Beijing Platform for Action and reports by the UN Special Rapporteur on Violence against Women recognised women to be trafficked into slavery-like conditions in different sectors, as prostitutes, domestic workers, sweatshop labourers or wives (Coomaraswamy 1997).

The UN Protocol: The New Perspective of Organised Crime

Against this background or perhaps in spite of it, states began discussions to develop a new international instrument on trafficking, the UN Trafficking Protocol in the late1990s. The Protocol was developed in a context of governments' fear about the rapid growth and power of organised crime worldwide, rather than a particular concern about women in prostitution or slavery-like practices and forced labour. Particularly developed, and therefore destination countries were concerned about the rise of organised crime. These states were fearful about growing irregular migration as a direct result of the involvement of organised criminal networks, and the inability of current national laws to control such irregular migration. There was also concern about the huge profits being generated by such groups, undermining both national and international laws (IOM 2000). States acknowledged that organised crime generated enormous profits not only through moving people illegally, but also through subsequently exploiting such persons in various clandestine activities, including prostitution and other forms of forced labour. Hence the development of two distinct protocols to a new Convention Against Transnational Organised Crime: one protocol deals with smuggling of migrants and the other concerns trafficking in persons, especially women and children. The Protocol and Crime Convention sought, at the outset at least, purely to harmonise criminal laws of different countries on trafficking, smuggling and other aspects of organised crime.

Thus the Protocol attempted to fill a gap in states' existing criminal laws. All anti-trafficking activists agreed – though for different reasons – that the 1949 Convention had been ineffective in combating trafficking. Thus civil society and especially women's rights advocates saw the emergence of the Trafficking Protocol as a unique opportunity to influence the first internationally-accepted definition of trafficking and ensure that any anti-trafficking instrument considered protection of rights of trafficked persons. The abolitionists sought a definition that would criminalize all forms of recruitment into prostitution regardless of deception and coercion.

The other group, represented by the Human Rights Caucus, sought a definition that would criminalise only those types of exploitation involving coercion and deception and that prostitution should not be treated differently to other types of labour (Doezema 2002). Part of the reason the Human Rights Caucus was concerned with entering the Trafficking Protocol negotiations was to address the repressive impacts of an abolitionist stance to prostitution upon sex workers and victims of trafficking, and therefore block attempts to continue in the same vein as the 1949 Convention.

The final definition of trafficking in the Protocol is one that is broader in scope than exploitation of prostitution (see p. 16 for the full definition). This long and complex definition considers trafficking to be the facilitated movement of a person via deceptive or coercive means into any form of exploitation, including sexual exploitation, forced labour or slavery-like practices. Playing it diplomatically safe, 'exploitation of prostitution' and 'sexual exploitation' are left undefined as a matter for the domestic policies of individual states. The Protocol further states that consent of a victim of trafficking to the intended exploitation is irrelevant where deception, coercion or other means have been used. Therefore this means even if a person consents to migrate they may still be trafficked if they are subsequently held in conditions of 'exploitation', such as forced labour. In terms of children, the Protocol distinguishes that the various means of deception, coercion, etc. do not need to be proven. Thus the evidentiary burden is lower for children; one only has to prove the facilitation *plus* exploitation to prove the crime of trafficking to be committed.

The long-winded definition of trafficking in the Trafficking Protocol covers all aspects of exploitative migration in which traffickers are involved, from initial recruitment through to the subsequent receipt and exploitation. This is needed to ensure that all parties to the crime are brought to justice. Yet it has been somewhat difficult for states in practice to use national laws with this definition against traffickers. This is due to the complex evidentiary requirements to prove the crime of trafficking. As a result, the individual elements of exploitation under the Protocol, in particular forced labour and contemporary manifestations of slavery are receiving a new resurgence. For example, in the USA, the new definition of the crime of forced labour is used more commonly to prosecute traffickers than the one of the crime of trafficking (Pearson 2002: 125).

Dealing with situations of forced labour and severe exploitation of migrants as 'trafficking' was an enormous opportunity under the Protocol. Certainly there are many other instruments on slavery and forced labour that have simpler definitions and are easier to understand. However, these instruments were not being applied to the situation of migrants in severe exploitation. The Protocol incorporates forced labour in such a way that it is to be taken seriously by governments and acted upon.

Incorporating Human Rights

The influence of civil society in the drafting of the Protocol is not confined to the definition of trafficking alone. Civil society activists with differing ideologies around prostitution reminded states during the negotiations that trafficking involves severe violations of the rights of victims involved. Thus, a rights-based approach is required to protect and assist victims of trafficking. Advocates were successful in that protection of victims' rights in accordance with international standards is established as one of the three main aims of the Protocol under Article 2, alongside preventing and combating trafficking and strengthening international cooperation.

The Protocol specifies some measures for states to undertake to prevent trafficking, for example engaging in information campaigns and social and economic initiatives. It further identifies key areas of protection for victims such as the right to appropriate services for the physical and psychological recovery of victims, rights to privacy, information and redress as well as the right to temporary or permanent residency in countries upon humanitarian or compassionate grounds.

The actual wording of such protections in the Protocol is relatively weak when compared with the law enforcement provisions, i.e. 'States shall consider in appropriate cases' rather than the unequivocal 'States shall'. Therefore some state and regional agreements adopted in the wake of the Protocol, such as the European Union Framework Decision on Combating Trafficking in Human Beings, have focused on harmonising law and law enforcement, neglecting human rights protection.

Despite this weakness, the inclusion of these areas in the Protocol has had an enormous impact in shaping anti-trafficking programmes and policies, especially those funded by the international development community. It is now virtually taken for granted that comprehensive anti-trafficking initiatives must cover the key areas of prevention, protection of rights, law enforcement and international cooperation. International agencies and civil society have analysed the Protocol in line with international human rights standards to know what gaps remain and how these can be addressed. For instance, to compensate for weak protection of victims' rights in the Protocol, the United Nations Office of the High Commissioner for Human Rights (UNOHCHR) issued recommended principles and guidelines on human rights and human trafficking. These have proven an effective guide to states and anti-trafficking activists in their advocacy for victims at national, regional and international levels. Some regional initiatives have further developed the broad standards articulated in the Protocol. For example in Europe, the development of the Council of Europe's Convention on Action against Trafficking in Human Beings (2005) specifies concrete measures for victim protection between states (including a temporary residence during a reflection period of 30 days for victims). This Convention also establishes that an independent group of experts will monitor state compliance with the Convention.

Remaining Challenges: The Issue of Migration

The Protocol has been successful in placing comprehensive anti-trafficking strategies much higher on international and national agendas. At the same time new threats have emerged to jeopardise the success of anti-trafficking interventions. One of these is the agenda of controlling irregular migration.

The two protocols clearly distinguish between smuggling in migrants and trafficking in persons – smuggling concerns facilitation of illegal migration in return for profit or a material benefit, trafficking concerns facilitation of migration (internal or cross-border, legal or illegal) into conditions of exploitation. As such the protocols distinguish between smuggled migrants and victims of trafficking. This distinction is a necessary one, because victims of trafficking do have distinct needs for protection different from smuggled migrants. However at the same time, it creates a binary opposition between those identified as 'smuggled' as opposed to those identified as 'trafficked'. This has been noted with concern by the UNOHCHR former Advisor on Trafficking who states:

> The regime created by the two protocols, (whereby trafficked persons are accorded greater protection and therefore impose a greater financial and administrative burden on States Parties than smuggled migrants) creates a clear incentive for national authorities to identify irregular migrants as having been smuggled rather than trafficked. (Gallagher 2002: 27)

Gallagher further notes that the differences between smuggled and trafficked migrants are not as clean-cut as the two protocols may make them seem. Trafficked migrants may start off being smuggled and end up being trafficked. Similarly, many trafficked migrants who escape an exploitative situation through their own means rather than through law enforcement may then stay on and work illegally in a country. Such victims would find their status changes from 'victim' to 'illegal migrant' and as such are not deemed fit for the extensive protections under the Trafficking Protocol. This is despite the fact they have had the courage to leave the situation on their own, and may have the same needs for services and access to information and justice as other trafficked persons.

Advocates were certainly correct to point out that not all migrant women are victims, however the danger of the water-tight definition of the Protocol is that on an operational level, many victims risk being not identified as such and thus lack protection under the law and fall outside the rubric of anti-trafficking programmes designed to help them. This problem stems from the reality that states are more concerned with controlling all forms of irregular migration than with protecting victims of trafficking. There have been attempts to address this, for example the Council of Europe Trafficking Convention contains procedures to ensure accurate identification of victims. However, it is a crucial aspect which should be considered in more anti-trafficking interventions.

What is needed in fact is a more comprehensive migration policy that includes trafficking as an issue of concern, rather than taking trafficking as the only human rights concern in migration. Smuggled migrants also have rights to be protected, some of which are covered under the Smuggling Protocol, but whereas sensationalism around 'sex slaves' has generated attention on trafficking, smuggled migrants rights have been largely ignored. There is a danger that some anti-trafficking interventions, which have been guided by the Trafficking Protocol in isolation, do fall into the trap of affording rights to victims of trafficking at the expense, and greater harm, of other migrants. The Trafficking Protocol needs to be considered in its context as essentially a tool for defining a crime (trafficking). However, this crime and human rights violation is not the only one that is committed against migrants.

Civil society is aware and active on this issue by calling for more attention to be placed on protection of all migrants, as under the framework of the UN Migrant Workers' Convention. Concurrently, a practical approach concerned with improving labour protection to all workers, migrant and local, in formal and informal areas of work requires further development. These are new frameworks currently being applied by civil society and some states. It requires a shift which governments particularly of destination countries may be unwilling to accept. However, the successes made by the anti-trafficking movement in the past years suggest that it is possible. The role of international development needs to be clearer on this aspect too. Rather than only funding anti-trafficking programmes in countries of origin, perhaps donors should consider more anti-trafficking programmes at destination concerned with protecting migrants' and workers' rights. A framework of criminal repression, in conjunction with extensive labour and migrant protection will be most effective in combating trafficking.

The Victim-Perspective – A Neglected Dimension

Barbara Limanowska

Present Pitfalls of Anti-Trafficking Programmes

The process following the adoption of the UN Trafficking Protocol has motivated anti-trafficking actors to develop intervention strategies in the area of prevention, victim assistance and protection, law enforcement and legislative reform. All countries of South Eastern Europe (SEE) designed and adopted National Plans of Action to prevent and combat trafficking in human beings. Interagency working groups and appointed National Coordinators formed part of a coordinated approach, working together alongside agreed standard procedures and necessary infrastructure to implement specific programmes. The success of a country's anti-trafficking response can be measured against indicators that describe at least two different approaches in anti-trafficking work.

On the one hand, the effectiveness of anti-trafficking measures relies on the real impact of these programmes on trafficked persons, especially in the areas of identification, assistance and reintegration. This implies that the starting point for any intervention is safeguarding the best interest of the victim. The success of such an intervention should be assessed by indicators based on the well being of the victim.

On the other hand, successes in anti-trafficking responses are most commonly described by the functioning of well-developed institutions and the available infrastructure in place to combat trafficking in human beings. This, however, does not necessarily lead to the creation of a well-functioning system of identification or to better assistance for trafficked persons. There are many examples of problematic results of anti-trafficking interventions, which show that the existing system on the operational level could be greatly improved while the implementation is not properly monitored and evaluated.

The examples quoted here are drawn from research carried out in the framework of the SEE RIGHTs (South East European Regional Initiative aGainst Human Trafficking) project; however, these experiences will most probably apply to other regions as well:

- While according to the police, only one person was registered as trafficked in 2004, according to NGOs there were more than 70 assisted victims of trafficking.
- With just few identified and known cases of trafficking and, at the same time, a well-developed anti-trafficking mechanism, authorities for more than two years regarded a young woman from the Roma minority (the only trafficked person assisted in a long time), identified by NGOs as victim of trafficking to be a stateless alien, who could not receive documents regularising her status.

- An NGO tries for more than half a year to officially register a child, victim of trafficking, in their custody. Again the fact that the child is from the Roma minority overshadows its victim status.
- In another case, a foreign woman was assisted by an NGO for more than a year, while authorities continue to ignore her case. The legal status of the woman is not clear; she does not have documents and is simply tolerated on the territory of the country, without any rights and indications about the outcome of her case.
- Police promised a woman who decided to testify against her traffickers that, two to three months after giving her testimonies she could be resettled to a third country. Five months later she is still locked up in a shelter (for her own protection) and cannot leave the country.
- Information about the results of HIV/AIDS tests is not kept confidential but is rather shared with the media and becomes common knowledge. The name and the photograph of an HIV positive woman was publicised widely.
- In many countries, while taking part in anti-trafficking training and claiming good understanding of the issue, police sends only those, who agree to testify, to shelters. Moreover, police demand unconditional access to shelters, or even request permanent police presence in the shelters.

While the majority of the above-mentioned problems have their roots in the lack of cooperation between different institutions and the lack of practical implementation of anti-trafficking measures, some of them are also the result of gaps in the anti-trafficking response.

Identification

In 2002, according to law enforcement agencies and NGO assessments, not more than 35% of trafficked persons (Limanowska 2002: 142) in the countries of the Western Balkans were identified as such and received assistance. Recently, the number of successful identifications and assisted cases was drastically reduced leading to an even smaller percentage of trafficked persons being identified as such and offered assistance. While this is mainly caused by the change in trafficking patterns in the region and probably by the fall in the number of cases of trafficking in general, there is also a growing number of cases of trafficked women who refuse to be identified as victims of trafficking due to the very limited options offered to them by the assisting agencies. Even worse, there are still cases of identified victims of trafficking that have been placed in detention centres or deported, instead of being referred to shelters and assisted. Hence, support organisations visit detention centres to look for trafficked women and offer them assistance. Police still tend to regard only those persons as victims of trafficking who are willing to testify against traffickers and who are in possession of information that can lead to prosecution.

In many countries, regardless signed agreements, police do not involve NGOs or social workers in the process of identification. Identification is still carried out by police only, without any clear procedures in place. Usually NGOs offering services to trafficked persons are informed post factum about a police action (usually a bar raid) and are requested to accept some presumed trafficked persons to the shelter. There they learn that the referred persons themselves do not know why only some of them were taken to the shelter and what happened to the others.

In most cases identified victims are not provided with any information on the procedure or the consequences of their identification. There is often no proper translation available so that women literally do not understand what is happening around them. There is also no proper legal information available and trafficked women do not understand the consequences of their decisions, for example the consequences of going to a shelter or signing the voluntary return form. Accepting assistance usually also means for women to be immediately removed from a bar without any opportunity to collect overdue salaries or even time to collect their belongings.

However, the main problem related to identification remains the fact that women themselves usually do not want to be identified or do not see themselves as trafficking victims. They know that being identified as victims of trafficking usually means a lack of any choices other than to return to their home country (or to be deported in the case that they refuse assistance). Thus being identified as a victim of trafficking, in a situation of limited choices and limited assistance, might not be in the interest of victims but rather in the interest of law enforcement and migration authorities. This is often being ignored and questions about the real needs and expectations of trafficked persons are rarely addressed.

Assistance

Judging from the decreased number of referred victims of trafficking in South East Europe (Limanowska 2005: 49), the assisting agencies seem to have been less effective in reaching trafficked persons in the last two years, 2004 and 2005. The drop in the number of referred cases is not only the result of using problematic or ineffective identification methods but also of limited provision of assistance. Many trafficked women and children are not willing to accept assistance on the conditions under which it is offered. According to research among trafficked persons who were assisted by German NGOs (Kroger, Malkoc, Uhl 2004) the three main concerns of returning trafficked persons are confidentiality, security and real, long-term psychological and economic support. These concerns are rarely met by assisting organisations.

The assisting agencies (international as well as governmental) focus primarily on the legal status of trafficked persons as irregular migrants and seek solutions through the provision of documents and the organisation of return, instead of focusing on their status as victims of trafficking and offering necessary support. What is needed, though, is the provision of assistance in a secure but friendly and open environment, the focus on stabilisation of mental, psychological and physical conditions, the provision of social, economic and medical help, seeking long-term solutions to their problems, including the possibility to stay in the country of destination, etc. The lack of those provisions is often criticised by local NGOs because it fails to address the real needs of trafficked persons: from their perspective an immediate return procedure is perceived as an additional punishment rather than assistance. Furthermore, the return is often not treated confidentially – authorities in countries of origin, who are informed about the return of trafficked persons, request statements and testimonies in trafficking cases without properly protecting the victims from traffickers. Lack of further protection and limited assistance after the return to countries of origin do not offer long-term solutions. Therefore the needs of trafficked persons for confidentiality, security and effective, long-term psychological and economic support are usually not met.

There is a need to reorientate the system of assistance and to shift the focus clearly on the protection of victims' rights and the well being of trafficked persons, instead of concentrating solely on their status as illegal migrants. In addition to that the lingering conflict should be resolved that exists between the best interests of trafficked persons and the interests of law enforcement agencies (collecting intelligence, taking testimonies) and migration policy (lack of legal provisions that allows at least a temporary stay in the country of destination and an alternative to return to the country of origin).

Reintegration

Although the return of trafficked persons to their countries of origin is seen as the main assistance tool by governments of destination countries and by international agencies, policy makers and implementing agencies in SEE countries have still not developed clear standards or even an understanding of what should and could be done to ensure "reintegration" (or: social inclusion) of returned victims of trafficking. Neither do they make it obligatory for governments of countries of origin to provide returning victims with the possibility of social inclusion.

It seems that the theory and practice of reintegration is still not understood across the region. With exception of the documents produced by the Stability Pact Task Force for South Eastern Europe (SPTF) from 2002, there is little information about the meaning of reintegration and the obligations of states to support trafficked persons upon their return. Strategies mentioned in SPTF documents are very general and relate rather to general assistance than to reintegration, such as actively preventing stigmatisation, legal assistance, social, medical and psychological care, the provision of shelter, counselling, material assistance, skills training and job counselling. Only skills training and job counselling elements can indicate that assistance should be long-term and aim at social inclusion for the returned trafficked persons.

In practice the reintegration assistance is usually limited to some training and re-schooling, which often does not lead to employment. Effective support in finding housing, job placement, micro-grants, scholarships, etc. is rather an exception than the rule. It also has to be added that such programmes are usually only short-term, not sustainable, entirely dependant on external donors and very expensive. NGOs are struggling to offer to traumatised women, with often very low education and low self-esteem, some life options in the situation of general unemployment, poverty and discrimination against women, also on the labour market.

Some NGOs are carrying out combined prevention and reintegration programmes. The programmes are aimed at young women from high-risk groups (ethnic minorities, girls leaving orphanages, girls leaving schools in areas with high unemployment or high levels of trafficking) and at women who have returned and were (or still are) supported by assisting agencies. By mixing prevention and reintegration components, accepting persons from different groups and with different experiences and not calling the programmes 'anti-trafficking programmes' but rather 'empowerment' programmes, these agencies try to avoid stigmatising returned women. This approach is supported through the fact that victims of trafficking are included in courses designed for persons with similar levels of education, which increases their chances of employment and social inclusion.

Recommendations

Looking at the problematic outcomes of many anti-trafficking actions in SEE, several basic questions should be asked: Namely – is the identification, assistance and social integration of trafficked persons in its current forms focussed on the needs of victims of trafficking? Which programmes are effective and for what reason? Is the system organised in a way to ensure the effectiveness of programmes? What can be done to ensure better protection of the rights of trafficked persons in the process of identification, assistance and reintegration?

Those issues are often addressed by local NGOs from SEE. NGOs offer innovative approaches and programmes which are designed to be effective and use the principle of 'do no harm to victims in the process of assistance'. However, such programmes are still rarely mainstreamed into anti-trafficking strategies of governments.

It seems that without better understanding of the real needs of trafficked persons, learning from innovative projects designed and implemented by local NGOs, and without taking them into account while creating identification, assistance and reintegration programmes, those programmes will not become more effective, regardless of the number of new structures, initiatives and all the efforts of governmental and international organisations.

Highlighting Economic Aspects of Trafficking in Human Beings

Sebastian Baumeister & Helen Santiago Fink

Economic Mechanisms of Trafficking

In 2003, during the course of the Dutch Chairmanship, trafficking in human beings was given higher priority on the political agenda of the Organization for Security and Co-operation in Europe (OSCE). Throughout that year trafficking was examined from the economic perspective, which culminated in a number of recommendations for OSCE participating states. These contributed to raising awareness of the economic root causes, issues of supply and demand and the importance of economic development and multi-stakeholder cooperation in the prevention of trafficking.

The nature of trafficking as a criminal business thwarts the collection of reliable information including quantitative data on economic costs obscuring the full ramifications of the problem. Being aware of these restrictions, this article focuses on the economic mechanisms of trafficking: What are the economic factors that make trafficking work? What are its economic implications for the countries of origin and destination? What are the gender aspects that contribute to the particular vulnerability of women and children? And what is the role of the private sector?

The Business of Trafficking

Trafficking in human beings is a criminal business operated by individuals, networks, and/or mafias driven by the motivation of economic gain through the exploitation of persons. According to the Trafficking Protocol a key feature of trafficking is that it occurs "for the purpose of exploitation", with exploitation being defined as:

> [...] the exploitation or the prostitution of others or other forms of sexual exploitation, forced labour or services, slavery or practices similar to slavery, servitude or the removal of organs.

Trafficking is fuelled by the generation of tremendous profits. It is estimated that these profits are only rivalled by those of trafficking in drugs. Yet, the profit margins may even be greater for human trafficking given that in its context individuals are a reusable and resalable commodity compared to the one-time usage of drugs.

Traffickers operate in both the formal and informal sectors. Sophisticated criminal groups may use the services of travel agencies, hotels, language schools, and embassies, to secure the appropriate documentation to traffic an individual under the pretence of a legitimate business activity.

The business of trafficking is (predominately) driven by demand. The greater the distance between countries of origin and destination, the more sophisticated the trafficking operation and the higher the profit margin. Traffickers look for opportunities to exploit, assessing the economic landscape, market demand and local circumstances, to then capitalise on the existing discrepancies among legal, labour and financial systems.

The victims who constitute the supply side of the trafficking business may be generated in a number of ways. Traffickers exploit the opportunities existing in the local environments, often represented by poor socio-economic conditions. Victims may be willing to take a calculated risk of employment abroad, despite only receiving partial information, yet willing to migrate for a job classified as 3-D (dirty, dangerous, and demanding) and then become entrapped in an exploitative situation. In other cases, victims may be blatantly deceived by family members, spouses or acquaintances, or victims may also be kidnapped. Reports have pointed to girls being kidnapped on their way to school in rural Albania and young women being abducted on trains travelling through Romania and Bulgaria, most probably to meet the growing demand for younger victims for the commercial sex trade.

In all situations, the girls and women become the property of the traffickers and are often violently coerced and exploited into performing services for which they receive little to no compensation and have little to no recourse.

Push und Pull Factors

Trafficking occurs in the context of an increasingly globalised world characterised by intensified flows of information, goods and services as well as by a greater mobility of people and an increased penetrability of national borders. Increased economic globalisation has facilitated access to foreign markets and the advantages offered by technological innovations have made many enterprises expand their activities across borders, seeking to develop them on a transnational scale. But the opportunities offered by globalisation and the creation of a new global market have had both positive and negative impacts. Increased economic ties between states and regions have led to increased economic competition among regions and industries, which thrive towards profit maximisation. As globalisation and increased market competition reinforce pressure for cheaper production and thus cheaper labour, workers become more and more vulnerable to insecurities, exploitation, and trafficking. IOM and ILO studies indicate that millions of men, women and children are trafficked worldwide into slavery-like conditions for sexual as well as for non-sexual purposes every year. It is particularly the poor, the unskilled, and women that are the most vulnerable and can find themselves trapped in conditions of bonded labour, servitude, and prostitution in their search of opportunities for economic sustainability.

In the OSCE region, trafficking is fuelled by economic disparities within and among states. The lack of economic opportunities, unsustainable salaries and dissatisfaction with local labour conditions create opportunities for traffickers to operate via legal or illegal channels to meet the demand for services in sectors such as tourism, transportation, entertainment, agriculture, and construction.

In Western European countries, trafficking is increasingly driven by an unmet demand for labour. Low fertility rates coupled by longer life expectancy have created a growing demand for labour in Western countries. It is estimated that by 2050 over 68 million foreign workers will be required to stabilise the working population in the EU countries. This labour imbalance, exacerbated by the demand for cheap labour in the West, versus the lack of opportunities in the East and coupled with increased globalisation and competition forces, continues to fuel economic migration. However, restrictive Western migration policies have to date failed to fully incorporate the needs of the Western labour market, thus creating a demand for illegal migration, which is in turn exploited by criminal elements. Therefore, in Western countries or countries of destination, it is important to perceive trafficking to a certain extent as a labour market failure. In addition, trafficking is facilitated by employment policies and services that do not work properly, by labour inspection services which fail to enforce rules and regulations, by the unwillingness of government and industry to take action against exploitive employers and by trade unions and labour organisations that are unable to reach out to unprotected workers.

In transition countries within the OSCE region, poverty, unemployment and the lack of economic opportunities are main push factors contributing to the vulnerability of persons, including children, to trafficking. Scarce and dismal prospects of earning a living in their home countries regularly force individuals to take risks in search of a better life elsewhere.

The fall of the Soviet Union marked the beginning of a period of severe economic transition and restructuring that resulted in the downsizing or even elimination of many state welfare programmes which largely supported the needs of women and children. Consequently, the new climate and associated burdens have rendered large groups within the post-communist societies vulnerable to trafficking, in particular poor communities and marginalised groups. Lack of or limited economic opportunities drive women, but also men and minors to seek employment elsewhere – despite known risks. The fact that the economic situation of women has been more affected by the ongoing transition process is reflected in the overwhelming majority of female victims. IOM estimates 50% of worldwide migrants are female. In addition, an increasing number of the victims and potential victims are minors. Parents abandon their children in search of economic opportunities abroad. For instance, in Ukraine, children of parents working abroad are seen as an emerging group at risk of being trafficked, with an estimated 100,000 social orphans as a result of parents emigrating to find employment. The ILO Rapid Assessment Survey for Moldova emphasises that minors who are particularly at risk of being trafficked come from either socially vulnerable or dysfunctional families or live in specialised institutions.

The protracted process of transition from command to market economy in many countries of South East and Central Europe and the CIS has resulted in criminal profit motives and economic desperation forming the basis on which the global business of human trafficking has flourished.

The Economic Impact of Trafficking

In countries of origin, the loss and destruction of human capital often associated with trafficking victims has serious implications for the current society as well as future generations. Trafficking is linked to organised crime, corruption, and money laundering. The vast amounts of money generated by trafficking help foster pervasive crime and corruption and undermine the rule of law and economic development of countries. This is particularly true for transition countries where the process of economic reforms is ongoing, and market and public institutions are in the process of evolving. Crime and corruption deter both domestic and foreign investment. They weaken public institutions and can favour the mismanagement of already scarce public resources. In turn, economic failure weakens the state's capacity to create and maintain order and security, thus deteriorating its prospects for development and growth. A sound business environment and good governance are essential preconditions for sustainable economic growth enabling states to reduce poverty and inequality and increase social integration and opportunities for all.

In the Western countries of destination, trafficking negatively impacts the economic and social fabric. Illegal competition based upon the exploitation of unprotected (illegal) migrant workers puts increasing pressure on the legally operating low wage sector and threatens its competitiveness. This unfair competition contributes to further decreasing low wages to the extent that the living standards of the unskilled labour forces decline and initiates the emergence of new poverty. In addition, legal low wage jobs may break away to operate in the informal sector. This development only further reduces the capacities of Western labour markets to absorb unskilled or low educated workers, and thereby puts additional stress on the social welfare systems. In turn, the growth of the informal sector reduces the national tax base and income revenues. Furthermore, it fosters corruption and empowers criminal network groups. Traffickers and criminal elements reinvest their profits into other criminal activities or even legal businesses, commonly using their financial influence to corrupt officials. As such, trafficking weakens the business environment and legitimacy of enterprises.

Gender Aspects of Trafficking

The political and economic transformation still underway in much of the former Soviet Union has impacted the lives of women most significantly. The reduction and elimination of many state welfare and childcare programmes have created difficult socio-economic environments and fostered the feminisation of poverty. Conflict situations have further compounded the difficulties for women, often leaving them as head of household having to care as well as economically provide for their children and families. Women have been further burdened as decreased availability and access to educational and health services have resulted in declining nutritional health indicators among women and children. In education, significant gender disparities have been reported at all levels, with women underrepresented in secondary, tertiary, vocational and university institutions. The lack of adequate education creates an initial disadvantage for women and inhibits their capacity to acquire marketable skills to effectively enter the labour force. Intrinsic cultural traditions and the (re)emergence of conservative values in some parts of the CIS, coupled with existing discriminatory employment practices, deprive women of gainful employment in their home countries.

The political disempowerment of women in the aftermath of the steep economic decline in the former communist countries has also contributed to fostering inequalities of women and indirectly increasing their vulnerability to trafficking. Limited political representation in decision-making organs of governments has reduced their capacities to influence developmental and social agendas and to address the institutional gender prejudices within their local environments. For example, in Bulgaria, the nature of the structural reforms implemented so far has particularly affected women's employment. A Bulgarian woman earns 72 cents for every dollar a Bulgarian man earns. Women are employed in lower paying activities compared to men. 65% of the unemployed are long-term unemployed women, of which 20% are women-heads of households. The resulting impoverishment of women and loss of social cohesion affects to a large extent children and thus the future generation of the country. In Bulgaria, more than 800,000 children are affected by poverty as a result of the severe economic conditions faced by women. UNDP warns, that as an outcome, an underclass may emerge made up of a generation of young people born into poverty and lacking full education and skills to integrate into a modern society (UN/UNDP in Bulgaria 2005).

Also the case of Ukraine exemplifies that women have been the hardest hit by the social and economic crises associated with transformation. In Ukraine, unemployment is rampant. During the period of 1998 to 2002 the real level of women's unemployment in the age group 15 to 69 grew by 10.8 per cent. The youngest working women, aged 15 to 19, experienced the largest unemployment. In addition, the resurgence of negative gender stereotypes and restrictive gender roles in the name of tradition has, as in other countries, resulted in the Ukrainian labour market being divided into two, one for men and another for women. The main difference being that the employed women have lower status and subsequently lower wages than men. The average monthly salary, when it is paid, is insufficient to meet basic living needs. Women are the last hired and the first to be fired. As a result, women are increasingly pushed into the low-wage service sector or seek employment, including secondary employment, in the unregulated informal sector (UN/UNDP in Ukraine 2003).

The Role of the Private Sector

The Brussels Declaration on Preventing and Combating Trafficking in Human Beings addresses the necessity of a global approach to effectively fight trafficking in human beings. Similarly, the OSCE Action Plan to Combat Trafficking in Human Beings that was adopted in July 2003 underscores the need for a multi-sectoral approach that systematically involves the private sector in anti-trafficking initiatives.

Integrating the private sector into the fight against trafficking is essential to address the economic root causes and prevent the perpetuating cycle of poverty and exploitation. The private sector, including enterprises, business associations and trade unions, can play an instrumental role in the prevention of trafficking through awareness raising and self-regulatory efforts. The private sector's knowledge of the formal and informal labour markets can be invaluable in developing initiatives to better enforce government policies and restrict business opportunities for traffickers. Well-targeted preventive measures in cooperation with the private sector can complement economic empowerment programmes operated by the public authorities, NGOs or IOs and help leverage limited public resources to address the supply side of trafficking. In doing so, local ownership and sustainability of economic empowerment measures will be fostered.

There is great potential for the private sector – in particular among transnational or Western companies that have established operations in countries of transition – to contribute to economic empowerment initiatives to the mutual benefit of at-risk groups and the business community in countries of origin. The private sector can support vocational training programmes by creating apprenticeship/internship opportunities within their work environments. This will allow individuals to learn marketable skills and acquire practical experience. In doing so, the business community helps cultivate a qualified labour force and supports local economic development, thereby enhancing the chances of vulnerable groups to have a sustainable future in their home countries.

Corporate Social Responsibility (CSR) activities such as the Youth Career Initiative (YCI), a programme developed by the International Business Leaders Forum (IBLF) in cooperation with the hotel industry (see pp. 82), should be endorsed by all stakeholders and further replicated in other sectors of society and countries of need.

The business community can also play a crucial role in tackling the demand side of trafficking, in particular the demand for sexual services, by adopting self-regulatory practices and making them part of the daily operations. Above all, the travel and tourism industry can help increase the awareness of tourists and business travellers on trafficking and contribute to creating an environment that does not tolerate the exploitation of persons, and in particular of minors.

Conclusion

Trafficking in human beings is a criminal business that will continue to flourish as long as the demand for labour and sexual services is not reconciled with the lack of economic opportunities in developing countries.

Combating trafficking requires a comprehensive approach ranging from adopting and enforcing appropriate legislation, establishing victim protection mechanisms and providing economic alternatives to those at risk of being trafficked.

From an economic perspective in countries of origin, the reduction of poverty and economic empowerment should be a priority for governments in the context of their anti-trafficking strategies. Greater emphasis must be placed on human capital development and supporting children and the family unit. Empowerment and preventive measures must be targeted at improving the economic situation of socially vulnerable families. Long-term and sustainable approaches to combat trafficking must focus on facilitating economic recovery, particularly in disinvested regions, by creating new opportunities for skill building, employment and business development. Government economic empowerment programmes should be designed to have short- and long-term impacts in the prevention of trafficking. In countries of destination, in particular in Western countries, there is an urgent need to address the shortcomings of the labour market, such as insufficient law enforcement, to review migration policies and raise awareness among societies as to the nature and implications of trafficking.

Furthermore, trafficking in human beings is a complex problem, which warrants a multi-sectoral approach involving stakeholders from not only government and civil society but also the private sector. Cooperation with the private sector offers new opportunities in prevention as well as in breaking the cycle of economic desperation. Yet, there is still a persisting lack of adequate awareness among all stakeholders, including the international community and business community itself, as to the benefits the private sector can bring to anti-trafficking efforts and how the private sector can participate in practical terms.

The views expressed in this article are made in personal capacity and do not necessarily reflect the views of the OCEEA or the OSCE.

Undocumented Migration, Labour Exploitation and Trafficking

Nivedita Prasad & Babette Rohner

Distinction between Trafficking and Illegal Residence

The public discourse on undocumented migrants, labour exploitation of migrants and human trafficking often only focuses on the debate around 'illegal immigration'. Yet, concentrating solely on illegal immigration detracts from the real problems associated with these topics. In many cases, labour migrants enter destination countries legally with all required documents. This is usually the case where migration via a land route does not seem possible. Some trafficked people are even citizens of the destination country. For example, in 2003 in Germany about 10% of the trafficked people in the sex industry were German citizens (BKA 2004: 5).

Even in the group of undocumented migrants, a large percentage enters the countries legally, but become illegal residents as a result of regulations imposed by destination countries. This is why concentrating on illegal immigration throughout the entire discussion is too narrow in its focus and does not correspond to reality. It seems the topic of trafficking is used as an instrument for restrictions on migration.

> Policies should clearly stress that trafficking in human beings is a serious crime and human rights violation, which needs to be addressed separate and apart from other forms of illegal activities, in particular illegal migration. (EU Experts Group 2004: 10)

Undoubtedly both, trafficked persons and undocumented migrants, start off as labour migrants who are looking to improve their economic situation. The legal restrictions imposed on foreigners make both groups vulnerable to blackmail and exploitation.

In some cases, there is a grey zone between trafficking and undocumented entry, especially if people become captured in debt bondage as they have to repay smuggling fees. However, it is vital to distinguish the two phenomena. Organising an illegal entry into Western Europe is difficult. Hence, most people who would like to migrate are dependent on the help of migration facilitators or 'smugglers'. While some migrants can pay for this service in advance, others have to be prepared to work off the 'debts' of the journey once they are in the destination country. Some migrants are able to pay these debts at fair terms, others are being exploited. This way undocumented migrants can get trafficked.

Both trafficking and smuggling are criminal offences. Smuggling of human beings or facilitated migration can be considered an offence against the borders or the sovereignty of a state, while trafficking always constitutes a violation of the individual freedoms of a person – predominantly of women. Trafficked people are hardly ever forced to migrate. At Ban Ying, a German counselling centre in Berlin, there has not been a single case of coerced migration in 15 years.

Until the migrants enter the destination country, both groups – smuggled and trafficked persons – assume that they will achieve their migration objectives. This guarantees that the migrant will cooperate during the journey, since it appears to serve his or her own goals. Once they arrive in the destination country, migrants who have been 'smuggled' can generally move around independently from the smugglers, since they have paid for a service that was effectively rendered. For trafficked persons, their dilemma becomes palpable once they successfully enter the destination country and the conditions for working off the 'debts' become clear. An essential means of applying pressure on migrants is their 'voluntary' illegal entry.

Undocumented migrants can generally determine their living and working conditions in the given, albeit very narrow, context. Trafficked people, however, are at the mercy of the traffickers, who not only exploit them but also take advantage of their dilemma or use violence, threats, or deception to force them to work and generally control their lives.

Also the quantitative difference should not be underestimated. In Germany, for example, it is assumed that approx. 1,000,000 people are living as undocumented residents (Alt 2003). For years, about 1,000 trafficked people have been reported in the German Federal Criminal Police statistics. This number only includes trafficked people in the sex industry who have cooperated with the police. So far, the numbers of trafficked people in other employment sectors in Germany were not documented due to the fact that only recent legislative changes consider all forms of trafficking. However, even the highest estimates of the number of trafficked persons fall far short of the assumed number of undocumented migrants.

Both groups risk being deported if they end up in a police raid. A trafficked person can delay her deportation if she reports that she is a victim of crime and is prepared to testify as a witness. Generally, in all European destination countries she is then granted a temporary residence permit for the duration of the legal proceedings. However, Germany for example does not offer non-trafficked undocumented migrants this option. Suing for unpaid wages is generally not an option for undocumented migrants, because there is no guarantee that filing a claim will not lead to deportation. Yet trafficked workers do in fact have the theoretical option of suing for unpaid wages.

A closer analysis of the two phenomena of trafficking and undocumented migration reveals that they are very different criminal offences. These differences can only be tackled appropriately if they are considered to be separate phenomena.

Distinction between Trafficking and Labour Exploitation

New policy and legislative documents, which seek to concur with the complex UN Trafficking Protocol, contribute to an increasing confusion when it comes to distinguishing between trafficking and labour exploitation. While NGOs on the one hand were strongly lobbying for an expansion of the definition, they on the other hand fear that the capacities of their counselling and support centres would be quickly exhausted.

While trafficking always entails the exploitation of a work force, including sexual or other services demanded outside of employment arrangements, the reverse is not necessarily true. The term trafficking can only be used if the situation includes elements of contemporary forms of slavery, debt bondage, serfdom or forced labour. Although today not every form of trafficking in Europe can be identified as serfdom or debt bondage some core elements can legally be proven such as considering a person as property, selling and purchasing a human being, restricting the freedom of a human being, imposing de facto rightlessness or using deception or coercion. The first report of the EU Experts Group on Trafficking in Human Beings stresses:

> [...] the element of coercion makes it clear that, in order to qualify as trafficking, the exploitative outcome must be such that it constitutes forced labour or services, slavery or slavery-like practices. (EU Experts Group 2004: 49)

A problematic aspect is the fact that many people in this situation do not understand that they are trafficked persons because they may have originally agreed to work under certain circumstances. However, according to the EU Experts Group, this original agreement is only significant if the party in question was provided with detailed information about the working conditions – based on the concept of 'informed consent'.

Keeping this in mind, it is obvious, that people can decide to migrate – even without documents – and to work as sex workers, and then still get trafficked. They can state that they are willing to work under exploitative conditions, but by definition, they cannot consent to forced labour or agree to slavery-like practices. Of course, not every underpaid undocumented woman labour migrant – even sex workers – is a trafficked person.

The term 'exploitation' is problematic since it is not uniformly defined. Some countries do not determine minimum wages, which could give the labour migrant an idea of what work is well paid, poorly paid, or even paid at a rate that is considered to be exploitative. This leads international conventions to rather use the term 'forced labour', which is defined in ILO Convention 29 as:

> [...] all work or service which is extracted from any person under the menace of any penalty and for which the said person has not offered himself voluntarily. (ILO 1930: art. 2)

Potential Dangers of the Trafficking Discourse

In recent years, more and more critical voices state that the trafficking discourse damages both, the migration discourse and the international sex workers movement. It is feared that governments will use the topic of trafficking as an instrument to make national borders impenetrable and restrict the freedom of movement of women. Another point that is continuously being brought up is the apparent privileged treatment of trafficked people compared to other vulnerable groups. Bangladesh can serve as an example when it comes to restricting the freedom of movement for women. The government of Bangladesh uses trafficking to legitimise the massive restriction of the freedom of movement of its female citizens (Jana 2002). Such measures that violate human rights are only conceivable in a discourse that makes no distinction between trafficking and smuggling. If distinctions were made between the two concepts, it would be apparent that migration restrictions cannot prevent trafficking.

In fact, the opposite is true. An adequate way to prevent trafficking is to create regular labour opportunities for migrants. Conversely, the view also exists that increasingly stringent immigration restrictions are responsible for the increase of trafficking. The EU Experts Group states:

> State policies in promoting immigration restrictions and reducing opportunities for regular migration have not been effective in preventing migration. Rather they have created a market for irregular migration, often as organised serious crime, through trafficking and smuggling of people. (EU Expert Group 2004: 11)

The sex workers movement fears that the trafficking discourse will compromise a woman's voluntary decision to work in the area of prostitution, as has happened so often throughout history (Doezema 2002). The opportunity for migrants to be legally employed must therefore obviously include employment in the prostitution sector. The need for employees in both the prostitution sector and the low wage sector is undisputed. People, who are prepared to do this work, will migrate voluntarily, so states could consider supporting this potential.

The fear that the human trafficking discourse may be instrumentalised to restrict immigration is not unfounded. In Germany, it is currently discussed how a liberalisation of German visa policies in the Ukraine has affected human trafficking. The media presentation suggests that visa liberalisation has led to an increase of trafficking victims from Ukraine. However, there is no proof that these policies did indeed promote human trafficking. The only proven fact is that several labour immigrants received visas and used them to enter Germany safely in order to work voluntarily without the required documents. According to Ban Ying's information, there is only one trafficked victim who entered Germany during the liberalisation phase. This particular case is continually cited in the press, hence, giving the wrong public impression on the dimension of the impact of more liberal visa policies.

In many countries, migration channels for highly skilled workers have been opened up, but for labourers in the low wage sector or prostitution hardly any migration opportunities exist. If the low wage sector were to be opened to migrants entering the country, it must be ensured that they cannot be exploited. There must be minimum standards required by employment laws that labour migrants can use to orientate themselves. The trafficking discourse can serve as a good basis. The International Labour Office believes:

> [...] that the global movement against trafficking has certainly given an impetus to the understanding of, and action against, forced labour [...]. (ILO 2005: 7)

This has been proven true in practice. For example, Ban Ying was able to implement minimum standards for domestic staff employed by diplomats. This group of female labour migrants lives and works in an extremely precarious situation. Their residence in Germany is tied to their work in the household of a certain diplomat. Additionally because of their diplomatic immunity, these employers cannot be arrested under German jurisdiction. This special legal construct makes this group of women an extremely vulnerable group in the context of trafficking. By sensitising the responsible authorities on the basis of the trafficking discourse, it was possible to slightly improve the situation for domestic staff.

Visions for the Trafficking Discourse

Currently, trafficking is being discussed as a high-priority topic in nearly every country of the European Union. Unfortunately, the discussion often yields the impression that it centres on issues that harm trafficked people more than helping them, since it solely focuses on the migration process. From a human rights based approach, this is unacceptable. The EU report also vehemently criticises this manner of proceeding:

> From a human rights perspective, the primary concern is to combat the exploitation of human beings under forced labour or slavery-like conditions, no matter whether such exploitation involves a trafficked person, a smuggled person, an illegal migrant or a lawful resident. In the application of the UN Trafficking Protocol, policies should therefore focus on the forced labour and slavery-like outcomes of trafficking, rather than on the process through which people arrive in such conditions. (EU Expert Group 2004: 8)

Implementing this demand would mean huge progress for trafficked people, but it would not improve the situation of undocumented migrants. They are still not granted access to fundamental human rights, and no Western European country is improving this situation. None of these countries has ratified the UN Migrant Workers' Convention. The convention emphasises that access to fundamental rights should not derive from a legal residence permit. It provides the 'right to rights' for undocumented people.

Currently, in nearly all European countries trafficked people can only obtain a temporary residence permit – and thus access minimal care – if they are willing to serve as witnesses. By doing so, the destination countries are neglecting their human rights responsibilities. Italy appears to be the sole exception since in Italy the willingness to testify is separated from granting a residence permit (see pp. 114). Hence, trafficked people have the right to assistance, support and security, which victims of other acts of violence who are legal residents are entitled to without question. Given a residence permit guarantees a minimum safety, which enables a trafficked person to start recovering and to take further informed decisions. This should serve as a good practice for other states.

Forced and Bonded Labour

Mary Cunneen

Legal Definitions of Forced and Bonded Labour

The Trafficking Protocol provides for the criminalisation of trafficking of persons for the purposes of inter alia exploitation of slavery or slavery-like practices, forced services or labour, and the exploitation of prostitution of others or other forms of sexual exploitation. While much attention under the Trafficking Protocol has focussed on the exploitation of prostitution, it is only more recently that attention is being paid to other forced labour outcomes of trafficking. Forced Labour is explicitly prohibited under the International Labour Organization (ILO) Forced Labour Convention 29 which defines forced labour as:

> [...] all work or service which is extracted from any person under the menace of any penalty for which that person has not offered himself voluntarily. (ILO 1930: art. 2 (1))

In conjunction with ILO Convention 105, these conventions apply to work or service exacted by governments and public authorities as well as private bodies and individuals. There is some lack of clarity about what precisely constitutes forced labour, but it is clear that forced labour includes slavery, bonded labour and some forms of child labour. However, not all forms of forced labour are prohibited, e.g. certain forms of forced labour extracted for public purposes, including prison labour, military service, and at times of emergencies are allowed under international law.

Although the definition under ILO Convention 29 differs from the definition of slavery under the Slavery Convention of 1926 in that it does not include per se the concept of ownership, it is clear that forced labour includes a similar degree of restriction on an individuals' freedom, often by the use of violent means, which has a similar affect as ownership on the individual.

Over the years debt bondage has been incorporated into the definition of forced labour under ILO Conventions 29 and 105. As such, the term forced labour can be taken to include bonded labour. Debt bondage, or bonded labour, is defined in the Supplementary Convention on the Abolition of Slavery 1956 as the

> [...] status or condition arising from a pledge by a debtor of his personal services or those of a person under his control as security for a debt, if the value of those services as reasonably assessed is not applied towards the liquidation of the debt or the length and nature of those services are not respectively limited and defined. (UN 1956: art. 1(a))

Debt bondage is specifically included as a worst form of child labour under ILO Convention 182 on the Worst Forms of Child Labour.

Indications for Forced and Bonded Labour

Although, clearly contrary to international law and many provisions in national laws forced and bonded labour continue in many different forms. Precisely defining whether a particular activity will fall into forced or bonded labour or merely exploitative working conditions, is a complex matter, and ultimately will depend on the aspects of individual situations. The ILO has developed several elements, which individually or in conjunction, can indicate a situation of forced labour:

- threats or actual physical harm to the worker;
- restriction of movement and confinement, to the workplace or to a limited area;
- debt bondage, where the worker works to pay off a debt or loan, and is not paid for his or her services. The employer may provide food and accommodation at such inflated prices that the worker cannot escape the debt;
- withholding of wages or excessive wage reduction, that violate previously made agreements;
- retention of passports and identity documents, so that the worker cannot leave, or prove his/her identity and status;
- threat of denunciation to the authorities, where the worker is in an irregular immigration status.

While not all cases of forced or bonded labour will also involve trafficking of persons, it is clear that many of the newer forms of forced labour do relate to trafficking offences. Migrant workers in particular are at risk, as their increasing movement often into informal or unregulated sectors will increase their vulnerability to forced labour. Recently the ILO Global Report on Forced Labour estimated that 12.3 million people globally are in forced labour, with 20% of these being so as a result of trafficking (ILO Geneva 2005: 14). The majority of forced labour occurs through economic exploitation.

Forms of Forced and Bonded Labour

Forced labour occurs in the formal, informal, and sectors not traditionally considered as employment sectors. Bonded labour in rural areas, in particular in agriculture, has in the past reflected traditional, sometimes feudal relationships, particularly affecting lower caste communities, such as the Dalit in India or Kamiaya in Nepal. However, many forced labourers in different countries are increasingly facing newer forms of forced labour relationships, where the traditional relationship between the agricultural worker and landlord is breaking down and being replaced by seasonal migration forms of working. In this context, debt bondage occurs through loans taken out, for example, in advance of the season's work, for subsistence when there is no work, for transportation to work sites, or subsistence and living at the worksite. Such forms mainly affect migrant workers and will often also come under the heading of trafficking.

Many previously formal sectors, such as construction are becoming increasingly informal with the use of contractors, intermediaries and others to hire workers, often for short terms, even only hour or day employment periods. Such sectors see increasing vulnerability to forced and bonded labour. Workers may have incurred debts to migrate to places where there is work; and rates for employment will be insufficient for subsistence without incursion of further debts. In other cases, workers will be forced to remain at work through coercion such as the removal of documents, threat of denunciation to the authorities or other forms of force.

A recent study in the United Kingdom looked at forced labour in four sectors – care, construction, agriculture and contract cleaning:

> Two Polish construction workers described how they were brought by agents to the UK. They were told that they would be provided with housing and employment, and that they could pay the agent later. On arrival in the UK they were moved around, put to work for long hours, closely monitored and paid no money. They attempted to run away, and were badly beaten in the fight that resulted, but they did manage to escape. (Anderson/ Rogaly 2005: 36)

Although this sector is highly regulated, and the treatment of these workers contravened criminal law, and civil laws and regulations, the workers were reported as being terrified of being found once they had escaped. Organisations working on behalf of migrant workers have commented on their reluctance to make complaints, even when lawfully working in the country.

Workers in the informal sector are even more vulnerable to forced labour. Domestic workers working in the sphere of private households and away from public scrutiny or contact experience a degree of vulnerability that is unparallel to that of other workers. Domestic work, although considered as the informal sector, is often not recognised either by government or employers as form of work.

Finally, forced labour occurs in sectors, which may not traditionally be classified as work sectors. Trafficking into forced prostitution or forced sexual exploitation is well documented. However, the human rights violations that occur, for example in early and forced marriage, can also be described as forced labour.

Groups Vulnerable for Forced and Bonded Labour

It is in the informal economy, or those areas that may not even by many be viewed as work, but as occurring in the private sphere, that women in particular are vulnerable to forced labour. Thus for migrant domestic workers, where the work occurs in private houses, away from public sphere and scrutiny, and typically excluded from labour rights, standards and inspections serious abuses are catalogued. In many Middle Eastern countries, for example, migrant domestic workers are required to remain with one employer through the conditions of their work permit, may have been required to attend training camps prior to be allowed to migrate for work, and have contracts that penalise with them up to three years pay should they fail to fulfil the terms of the contract or leave. Such conditions, coupled with a lack of regulation or access to labour standards and rights, leave migrant domestic workers vulnerable to forced labour and other abuses.

Child domestic workers are particularly vulnerable. Trafficking of child domestic workers occurs in West Africa as well as in other regions. Women are also more vulnerable to forced labour exploitation for a number of reasons. Firstly, the sectors in which women are more likely to work, for example prostitution or domestic work are more likely to be informal, unregulated, or even not regarded as work. Secondly, female migrants are less likely to have information about migration opportunities or access to established migration routes and networks. However, it is clear that trafficking into forced labour affects women, men and children, into diverse sectors, and all over the world. Much of the attention of those working on trafficking has concentrated on trafficking of women into forced prostitution, and as such less information is available on forced labour into sectors other than prostitution, both of women and children, and trafficking and forced labour of men.

Forced and Bonded Labour and Trafficking

As can be seen, there are clear links between the more modern patterns of forced labour and trafficking. For many implementation of the UN Trafficking Protocol has been problematic. The Protocol assumes an easy difference between smuggling on the one hand and trafficking on the other. The element of movement in the protocol has led states to equate counter trafficking policies with immigration policies. Yet as the European Commission Experts Group of Trafficking has stated:

> [...] the key element to the Trafficking Protocol is the forced labour outcomes, encompassing forced labour and services, exploitation of the prostitution of others and other forms of sexual exploitation, slavery, slavery-like practices and servitude. It is these human rights violations against the individual that the Trafficking Protocol seeks to redress. While in some cases it can be difficult to determine whether conditions are merely illegal and extremely exploitative, rather than forced labour or services, slavery, slavery-like practices or servitude, there is a wealth of history of international law, standards and interpretation of these concepts to rely on, which can provide sufficient certainty for criminal law and sanctions [...]. From a human rights perspective, there is no reason to distinguish between forced labour involving 'illegal migrants', 'smuggled persons' or 'victims of trafficking'. Thus to effectively counter trafficking, policy interventions should focus on the forced labour and services, exploitation of the prostitution of others and other forms of sexual exploitation, slavery and slavery-like outcomes of trafficking – no matter how people arrive in these conditions –, rather than on the mechanisms of trafficking [i.e. how the trafficking occurs] itself. States should criminalise any exploitation of human beings under forced labour, slavery or slavery-like conditions, in line with the major human rights treaties that prohibit the use of forced labour, slavery, servitude, etc. (European Commission 2004: 52)

Such analysis, that policies should concentrate on the forced labour outcomes, both of trafficking and others in forced labour situations, is also supported by the ILO in their 2005 report on forced labour. If such recommendations were followed, many of the current confusions of the trafficking definition – whether a case was smuggling or trafficking, whether a case was trafficking or forced labour, whether the victims had seemed to consent to elements of the forced labour or whether a victim was perceived as 'innocent' or 'guilty' – would become redundant. By concentrating primarily on the forced labour outcome the Trafficking Protocol policy makers could overcome its current definitional and practical operational difficulties and use it as a tool to more effectively tackle the human rights violation of trafficking in human beings.

Recommendations

Currently, many counter-trafficking initiatives tend to be based in law enforcement, immigration control and transnational crime, as trafficking comes under the transnational crime treaty, or within issues concerned with women or child rights, based largely on concern regarding trafficking into forced prostitution. In focussing on forced labour outcomes, rather than trafficking per se, various key actors, who in the past may not have been so central to counter-trafficking strategies, can be brought into the field. It is only comparatively recently that other actors from the labour rights field have become involved, most notably the ILO through its Special Action Programme on Forced Labour. Yet if trafficking is considered under the forced labour dimension, the roles of labour standards and their implementation must be considered. In this respect, the ILO core labour standards – forced labour, child labour, freedom from discrimination and freedom of association – are crucial. Realisation of these and associated working standards involves working inter alia with employers and supply chains, through inspections and the use of sanctions, civil and criminal laws and the roles of trade unions and other forms of organisation of workers in claiming these rights.

With the increasing movement of workers and the vulnerability of migrant workers to forced labour outcomes (and trafficking), rights of migrant workers need to be addressed. The UN Migrant Workers' Convention provides a framework for the protection of all migrant workers, whether regular or irregular. Organisations of migrant workers and organisations working on behalf of migrants need to be involved, both in countries of origin and destination.

It is clear, that using the forced labour focus to tackle trafficking, can overcome many of the difficulties with current counter-trafficking initiatives and provide additional tools in the fight against trafficking. Many involved have been concerned with the effect of dealing with trafficking as an element of immigration control:

> The protection of workers rights should not be seen as an instrument for enforcing immigration controls, since this would undermine the confidence of workers that the legislation is capable of providing the protection they need. (Statement Joint Council for the Welfare of Immigrants 2004)

To be effective enforcement of immigration control, on the one hand, and of criminal and employment law, on the other, must be separately pursued. Only if this is done will workers in forced labour situations be willing to come forward, report abuses, and assist police in their investigations and authorities in tier inspections. Concentration on the forced labour outcomes allows this to occur and to bring in actors experienced and mandated in these areas. (Anderson/ Rogaly 2005: 58)

Practical Difficulties with an Approach Focusing on Migrant Workers' Rights

Yet there are also obstacles to an approach focusing on migrant workers rights. Organising and enforcing rights for migrant workers is more difficult than in traditional, formal sectors of indigenous workers. For many migrant workers labour standards are unenforceable, and unclaimable by themselves. States have limited their commitment to granting rights to migrant workers working in the formal sector. For those in informal sectors or sectors that might not currently be recognised as work, the situation is even harder. By their nature these sectors are irregular, and not subject to formalisation, standards or enforcement of rights. The particular vulnerability of women in these sectors

> [...] raises the question as to the extent that the largely unrecognised informal sector work or services (such as domestic work, au pair or similar arrangements and the sex sector) should be regulated within migration or employment policies. (Experts Group on Trafficking in Human Beings 2004: 67)

Focussing on the forced labour outcomes of trafficking has the advantage of concentrating on the human rights abuses that trafficked people have faced, rather than the mechanisms of trafficking. It also has advantages of bringing in non-traditional actors and responses to counter-trafficking strategies. Such an approach has the potential to overcome many perceived current shortcomings of counter trafficking strategies. However, in the context of a growing informal and globalised economy, it remains to be seen whether states, employers and others can commit to such an approach and in practical terms provide rights and standards that tackle forced labour and put mechanisms in place that enable all workers, but in particular migrant workers in informal and non-work sectors, to claim these rights.

Trafficking in Children

Mike Dottridge

Characteristics of Trafficking in Children

Child trafficking involves taking control of other people's children and making money out of them. In some cases trafficking takes place across borders, in others within a single country. Like trafficking in adults, child trafficking generally involves moving children away from a familiar environment and exploiting them. However, a significant difference between trafficking in adults (men or women) and trafficking in children concerns the ways in which children are exploited. They are more diverse than the forms of exploitation to which trafficked adults are subjected. Besides commercial sexual exploitation, they include a range of other moneymaking activities involving children from five to seventeen. In addition, babies and very young children are also trafficked for adoption; in their case, it is not their subsequent activities which make money for an employer, but the illicit supply of children, usually for inter-country adoption, which itself generates an income for traffickers and other intermediaries.

Another difference between child trafficking and trafficking in adults is specified in the UN Trafficking Protocol. The Protocol differentiates between children and adults by specifying that trafficking in adults involves some element of coercion, abduction, deception or taking advantage of a person's vulnerability in the course of recruiting or procuring him or her, while these means do not necessarily have to be involved in the case of someone under 18 years of age. Recruiting a child or adolescent under 18 in order to subject him or her to any of the forms of exploitation listed in the Trafficking Protocol is viewed as trafficking; likewise any intermediary involved, however benign, can be regarded as a trafficker. This distinction in international law means that the criteria and process for identifying trafficked children and adolescents under 18 years of age should be different to the identification of adults being trafficked. However, when in the light of the definitions agreed in the Trafficking Protocol national laws on trafficking in persons have been amended over the past five years, few have incorporated this wide scope. Most laws continue to mention coercion or duress in the process of procuring children and adolescents as a defining characteristic of trafficking.

The Trafficking Protocol makes an absolute distinction between children and adults, but no distinction between older adolescents and young children. However, the nature of the coercion used by traffickers to make children do what they are told is determined greatly by a child's age.

The Specific Vulnerability of Young Children

Overall, children are vulnerable to traffickers in a range of ways that are different to adults:

- they obey adults very easily (both their own parents and others);
- they have less capacity to assess risks and to articulate their worries;
- they are sometimes easier to deceive than adults;
- their lack of education is exploited;
- young children (below the age of ten) are dependent on adults or older children for their basic needs, such as food, shelter and sentimental attachment: this dependency can be manipulated;
- an unfamiliar environment makes them especially dependent;
- young children (seven and below) can be trained to forget their original identity;
- a child can be presented convincingly as the offspring of an adult who is not its parent. Sometimes children do not require a passport of their own to cross a border, but can do so if named on the passport of a supposed parent or guardian (at times without a photograph).

Vulnerability and dependence of children, the two factors exploited by traffickers, vary a great deal with the age and maturity of children and consequently are difficult to define in law in a simple way. Children below the age of ten are generally completely dependent on someone older and routinely form a sentimental attachment with the person, who caters for their basic needs.

Teenagers, however, do not usually show the same degree of dependency as young children (although if they are in an unfamiliar environment they are more likely to be dependent on someone else than if living at or near home). If a trafficker wants to make a 16-year-old obey his instructions, the types of coercion used are usually much the same as those used on an 18-year-old or older adult.

The issues of age and maturity affect children in other ways relevant to trafficking. Older teenagers are entitled to enter the world of work everywhere in the world, and many consequently migrate to earn money away from their parental home. Some fall into the hands of traffickers, but by itself this does not seem to be sufficient justification for discouraging everyone under 18 years of age from leaving home and seeking a better life elsewhere.

Children are unfortunately particularly appealing to traffickers, both because they are easier to boss around than adults and because, since the onset of HIV/AIDS, there has been a belief among men paying for sex in many parts of the world that teenage girls are less likely to be infected or can even cure them of HIV/AIDS.

Protection of Children

Trafficked children have many practical needs, which are different to those of adults; this goes in particular for young children who are unable to assess for themselves what is in their best interests. The international legal regime obliges governments and those working for law enforcement and statutory agencies, as well as public or private social welfare institutions, courts of law, administrative authorities and legislative bodies, to make the child's best interests a primary consideration in all actions and decisions. For children trafficked out of their own countries, this implies that, as soon as a child is identified as a possible victim of trafficking, it is essential for the authorities to appoint a guardian to represent the child's best interests.

The specific forms of protection to which children are entitled have been listed by UNICEF in the Guidelines for Protection of the Rights of Children Victims of Trafficking. These cover several issues, starting with the process of identifying children who have been trafficked and ending with measures to protect them in legal proceedings. Many of the measures for children are the same as those to which adults are entitled as listed in UNHCHR's Recommended Principles on Human Rights and Human Trafficking. The options for trafficked children are essentially the same as for adults (local integration, return to country of origin or resettlement in a third country). However, the legal requirement that the child's best interests be a 'primary consideration' means that the authorities in a country to which a child has been trafficked have a legal obligation to carry out a security and risk assessment before that child can be returned to her or his country of origin. The fact that this requirement is rarely met means that at present most countries involved are in breach of their obligations under the UN Child Rights Convention.

Providing protection to trafficked children brings its share of challenges, starting with the difficulties in identifying them. It is not easy to clearly distinguish children trafficked to make money in criminal activities from other young criminals. The human rights principle concerning the protection of trafficked children (and adults) is clear – that they should not be prosecuted, detained or punished for the illegality of their entrance into a country or residence there, or for any activities they have been involved in as a direct consequence of their situation as a victim of trafficking (UNHCHR Recommended Principles and Guidelines 2002: Principle 7). However, distinguishing crimes committed by children as 'a direct consequence' of their situation as a victim of trafficking from crimes committed in other circumstances is inevitably difficult.

Trafficked children and their close relatives, like trafficked adults, face a potential threat from traffickers who suspect a child of providing information to the police. While testifying against traffickers places adults and children alike at risk, both the child's temporary guardian and the prosecuting authorities are required to consider whether doing so is in a child's best interest. If they think it is, children usually require procedures to allow them to give evidence in ways that differ from adult victims or witnesses.

Implications of a Child Rights Approach to Trafficking

Counter-trafficking initiatives based on a 'child rights approach' aim to defend and enhance the human rights of the children involved. They give explicit attention to ways of both upholding the children's best interests and enabling the views of these children to be taken into account in actions affecting them. Nevertheless, all sorts of organisations involved in promoting children's welfare claim to be practising a child rights approach, making a genuine approach difficult to identify.

Adopting a rights-based approach means listening to children about their experiences, both positive and negative. In particular, it means finding out about the effects of anti-trafficking initiatives on children and about the ways the children have found for themselves of minimising abuse. This usually means collecting information from a wider pool of child migrants, rather than focussing exclusively on trafficked children.

A rights-based approach also means upholding the best interests of children and avoiding inflicting any harm. This implies that it is obligatory to plan all interventions carefully, ensuring they are not likely to have harmful side effects, to monitor their impact and to provide adequate levels of protection to trafficked children once they have been rescued or turn to others for assistance.

The challenge involved in taking a child rights approach is that it means putting children's rights into the balance – rather than adopting blanket measures which do not allow the specific circumstances of individual children to be taken into account. There is consequently a danger that the criteria proposed by child rights advocates for determining whether it is reasonable for individual children or groups of children to migrate are too complex or nuanced to be the basis of government policy.

For example, a blanket ban on children leaving their villages (as tested in parts of West Africa and Southeast Asia), on the grounds that some or many children are subsequently trafficked is almost certainly incompatible with a child rights approach (Castle and Diarra 2003: 4). Holding up a STOP sign and telling young people that they may not leave home until they are 18 is incompatible with their right to survive and with older children's right to work and earn a living. At the same time, initiatives to prevent children from being trafficked are clearly necessary. A child rights approach involves empowering older children to make informed decisions for themselves and helping them to protect themselves against abuse when they travel, as well as creating a protective environment in which abuse is less likely to occur.

This approach also implies that when children are trafficked from one country to another, the only acceptable arrangement for their return to their own country is voluntary, assisted return. Any decision that the most appropriate durable solution for a child involves returning to her or his country of origin should make the child's best interests a primary consideration and be preceded by a security and risk assessment. Compulsory repatriation seems unlikely to be in a child's best interests. If children do not want to return home, they may well seek out new opportunities to leave their country, exposing them again to the risk of being trafficked and abused.

Problems Caused by the Common Association of 'Women and Children' as a Single Category in Anti-Trafficking Discourse

At both national and international level, the trafficking of girls and boys has been treated as if it was the same as the trafficking of adult women, as if all experienced the same sort of abuse and required the same types of protection. This approach demeans adult women, implying that they are just as dependent and vulnerable as children. It has tended to result in the focus being on the form of exploitation, which members of both categories experience in common – commercial sexual exploitation – rather than other forms of exploitation, which require different strategies to stop. It also means that needs that are specific to children are not being addressed. Critics of the practice of putting women and children into the same category point out that adult women have 'agency' in ways which children do not. While valid in asserting that women have the right to make decisions for themselves, it should be considered that older teenagers who are 'almost adults' have almost as much agency as adults.

The terminology 'especially women and children', routinely used in recent years, implies that children are being habitually considered as 'add-on' to the topic of trafficking in women. The main focus of discussions leading up to the adoption of the Trafficking Protocol was trafficking in adult women; the legal measures adopted at international, national and regional level consequently tend to be those which governments think appropriate for responding to trafficking in women, with scant regard to the reality experienced by either teenagers or younger children. One result of this is that international law adopted over the past ten years has been inconsistent.

Differences between Child Trafficking and 'Worst Forms of Child Labour'

Although the ILO Worst Forms of Child Labour Convention declares that the trafficking of girls and boys under 18 years of age is a practice similar to slavery and, as such, a worst form of child labour, the ILO itself clarified a few years later that trafficking is not a form of work, but rather a means of procuring children (ILO 2002: 18). The Convention itself makes a distinction between hazardous 'worst forms of child labour', threatening the health or even the lives of child workers, which are supposed to be identified and banned at national level, and other forms, such as forced and bonded labour, forced recruitment into armed conflict, prostitution and pornography and other illicit activities, which are prohibited unconditionally. On the basis of information collected in 2000, the ILO Global Report estimated that 8.4 million children were involved in 'unconditional worst forms of labour', of whom 1.2 million had been trafficked, while a much larger number, 170 million, were believed to be engaged in work that was hazardous.

The ILO Worst Forms of Child Labour Convention as well as the UN Trafficking Protocol are consistent in reiterating a message from the international community that certain forms of child exploitation, such as bonded labour and prostitution, should never be tolerated. However, these international standards fail to address the predicament of millions of children working away from their own family's home in circumstances which no-one knew whether to categorise as 'servitude' or not, particularly children employed as live-in domestic servants. Some of these children undoubtedly are victims of forced labour, while others, particularly older teenagers, have acceptable conditions of employment and do not want to be branded as victims of trafficking. In Europe the main purposes for which children are trafficked are commercial sexual exploitation and begging, along with some other illicit and criminal ways of earning money. This means that traffickers use two distinct groups of children: teenage girls, who are virtually young adults, trafficked for commercial sex, and pre-puberty children, trafficked for begging and crime. In Africa and Asia, there are far more ways of putting school age children to work to earn money, as poor families routinely take children out of school after only one or two years. 'Trafficked' children and other children working away from home are consequently difficult or impossible to distinguish: the Trafficking Protocol implies that the difference is exclusively in the nature of the child's occupation (commercial sexual exploitation) or contractual arrangements (debt bondage, forced labour, servitude, etc.), rather than in the recruitment process, implying that the two categories of children are indistinguishable when immigration officials or others intercept them while they are travelling to wherever they are scheduled to work or earn money.

International Instruments and their Translation into National Legislation

The inconsistencies and lack of clarity in international instruments concerned with child trafficking are undoubtedly one reason why national laws adopted or amended over the past five years have equally lacked clear definitions of what exactly is being prohibited and have thus not provided law enforcement agencies with clear indications of what evidence they should be looking for.

Numerous countries have adopted new legislation on child trafficking. Some new laws seem so convoluted that they are unlikely to be used to prosecute anyone for trafficking or abusing children. Others reflect the terms used in international instruments accurately, but still seem unhelpful in giving clear signals to law enforcement officers about signs of child trafficking or the evidence they should be collecting. In a few instances the provisions of what constitutes an offence are clear, but provisions for the protection of the children concerned undermine the law's effectiveness. In Italy, for example, the law was already used more systematically to punish criminals for exploiting trafficked children before the Trafficking Protocol was adopted, and the law was amended in 2003 to use terminology taken from the Trafficking Protocol (even though Italy had not ratified it). However, a 'catch 22' was introduced into Italian law in 1998 affecting teenagers who are trafficked into Italy. Both younger children and adults are entitled to remain in Italy indefinitely if they take part in a social programme organised by a non-governmental organisation. Even if they are not taking part in such a protection programme for trafficking victims, children are allowed to remain in the country until they are 18 years and hold a residence permit for minors. However, unless they have been participating in a social programme for three years by the time they reach 18, the law requires them to be expelled from Italy on reaching adulthood.

In the Republic of Benin, the National Assembly was considering a bill on child trafficking in 2004. Its provisions seemed clear, based on definitions from the Trafficking Protocol and the ILO's Worst Forms of Child Labour Convention. The bill seemed better than the laws of many other states, for it clearly prohibited contractual arrangements which deprive a child of freedom and regarded coercion or deception at the stage of procuring a child as an aggravating circumstance. The bill nevertheless appeared to take no account of the specific forms of exploitation common in Benin, particularly the entrenched tradition of employing other people's young children as domestic servants. It proposed to make it obligatory for any child not living with her or his natural parents to have a special certificate authorised by a Mayor. While this sounded good in theory, a similar provision had already proven nearly disastrous in another West African country (Mali), where it was onerous or impossible for children to obtain the authorisation required, thus making it impossible for children to leave their natural parents (e.g. for schooling).

Comprehensive Prevention, Counselling, Protection and Rehabilitation

Although efforts throughout the world to stop child trafficking have been largely flawed in both law and practice, the characteristics of good systems to stop child trafficking and to protect the children involved seem relatively straightforward.

As far as preventing child trafficking is concerned, efforts should focus variously on the immediate causes of individual children being trafficked, the underlying causes (such as popular acceptance of certain forms of exploitation or abuse of children) and the root causes (such as discrimination between boys and girls in terms of access to income generating opportunities). At the individual level, social work has proven effective in identifying families whose children are particularly vulnerable and providing income supplements to the families concerned, or other incentives similar to those offered to families whose children are at high risk of dropping out of school and starting work before completing their basic education.

Information can also be a powerful tool to prevent trafficking. However, this does not just mean disseminating harrowing stories about the abuse suffered by children who have been trafficked to deter parents from allowing their children to leave home or discourage teenagers from migrating. Information should also empower children who opt to migrate to protect themselves and show them how to reduce risks. It is much less common to find this sort of practical advice included in anti-trafficking programmes than simplistic messages, which suggest that children should not leave home and migrate in the first place.

Efforts to protect children who have been trafficked should be based as much as possible on assessments which children themselves make about what has been helpful and what has not, rather than simply on the strategies which adult experts consider appropriate. These efforts require effective coordination between a range of agencies or organisations, often situated in several countries. Efforts to provide good coordination are at present undermined by the very fact that there is a plethora of intergovernmental organisations backing anti-trafficking initiatives, each supporting different ministries and often proposing different priorities and strategies.

Virtually no useful assistance or protection can be offered to trafficked children unless a meaningful system for identifying them is put into place. Consequently laws are needed which prohibit the forms of child trafficking known to occur in the country concerned, which penalise the specific criminal acts contributing to the trafficking process, particularly all the different forms of abuse to which children are subjected, and which give a clear signal to immigration and law enforcement officials about what evidence they should be looking for. Experience from various parts of the world suggests that children who have been trafficked recover best in a shelter or residential centre which is designed especially for trafficked children, rather than one which includes children who have been subjected to other forms of abuse or which houses other unaccompanied children. Whatever the system for assessing the immediate and the long-term needs of a trafficked child, someone should have explicit responsibility for ensuring that decisions and actions affecting the child are in her or his best interests. In a few countries this is already achieved by appointing a temporary guardian. However, in developing countries where this looks impractical, a variety of arrangements could be found to involve a non-governmental organisation or lawyer and make them responsible for upholding the child's best interests from the moment that a trafficked child is first identified. It is equally important that countries where trafficked children are found should have clear criteria for agreeing a durable solution for every trafficked child; criteria, which spell out that the child's best interest must always be a primary consideration.

At the moment, getting all these elements into place, along the lines suggested in UNICEF's Guidelines for Protection of the Rights of Children Victims of Trafficking in South Eastern Europe, appears well-nigh impossible. However, the principles involved are much the same as those involved in other forms of child protection. The chief obstacle seems to be a lack of the political will to insist that these principles are respected.

Organ Trafficking – Challenges and Perspectives

Elaine Pearson

Definition of Organ Trafficking

Organ trafficking is the stuff of urban legend that never fails to send the media into a frenzy. The story of a naive young man being drugged and waking up in a bathtub full of ice minus his kidney is familiar to most of us. Then there is the story of a desperate third-world grandmother selling her own grandchild for a tidy profit so his organs can be transplanted into the bodies of unknown first-world children. Yet beyond the gruesome tales of media sensationalism, is organ trafficking something that is really going on, and that we, as anti-trafficking advocates, should be concerned about? If so, what does organ trafficking look like and what kind of response is needed?

Drafters of the UN Trafficking Protocol were concerned enough about trafficking in organs to include 'removal of organs' in the definition of trafficking, alongside forced labour and sexual exploitation. Therefore if we follow the Protocol's definition, trafficking for organs occurs where a third party recruits, transports, transfers, harbours or receives a person, using threats (or use) of force, coercion, abduction, fraud, deception, or abuse of authority or a position of vulnerability for the purpose of removing that person's organ(s). The fact that a person initially consented to having that organ removed is irrelevant, where some deception or coercion takes place. Bearing in mind the additional vulnerabilities of children, the simple facilitation of movement (the recruitment, transfer, etc.) plus removal is sufficient to constitute organ trafficking in children (without the need for the various means of force, deception, etc.). Organ trafficking constitutes mainly trafficking of kidneys because removal of virtually all other organs (except for parts of the liver that can also be transplanted now) requires the 'donor' to be killed, which is very rare to happen.

The global market in selling human kidneys is booming; yet whilst illegal, it rarely involves trafficking of children or completely unsuspecting victims. Extremely isolated cases of murdered children have been proven, but most reports of this kind are fed from rumour and are often unsubstantiated allegations. As medical anthropologist and Director of Organs Watch, Dr. Nancy Scheper-Hughes states:

> […] the body and organ stealing rumours of the 1980s and 1990s were at the very least, metaphorically true… speaking to the ontological insecurity of poor people to whom almost anything could be done. (Scheper-Hughes 2000: 203)

Scheper-Hughes argues rumours of organ theft continue in Latin America (and indeed elsewhere), because they serve to reinforce the fears of the poor about the power, practices and lack of accountability of the State.

More commonly, the real trade in selling organs involves desperate young people from impoverished nations voluntarily selling their kidneys out of economic need to aging rich Western buyers via an underground and often illegal system of organ brokers. That organ brokers exploit this system and cheat the kidney 'donors' (sellers) is common knowledge, yet the exploitation only becomes trafficking in cases where sellers are actually deceived or coerced into the sale, which is certainly not true in all cases. Trafficking exists when people who are promised payment, receive none or receive only a part of the amount promised. Or in cases where the kidney seller loses the ability to say 'no' to the organ removal, for example, cases where Moldavian sellers who initially voluntarily travelled and agreed to sell their kidney have then been heavily coerced (e.g. at gunpoint) to do so for a much lower price. In other trafficking cases, brokers and surgeons deceive victims about the impact of the procedures and the consequences of kidney removal, i.e. saying that the operation is minor and will not affect their ability to return to work immediately.

Global Routes for Organ Trafficking

Routes for organ trafficking criss-cross the globe, though the flow of organs is generally from poor, developing countries to rich ones with higher standards of health care. The actual operations often take place in third 'middle' countries, with the right mixture of corruption and weak medical laws to enable the activity to go on undetected or at least uninterrupted. Sellers and recipients will usually travel to these third countries for the actual operation. Victim sellers often come from countries such as Brazil, Philippines, Romania and Russia and former CIS States, especially Moldova. They travel to countries such as South Africa and Turkey for the procedures and recipients come from Western Europe, North America, Israel and the Middle East. Traffickers may come from any of these countries involved. There is a high level of involvement in organised crime in the form of the brokers involved.

India has its own thriving organ market, and organ trafficking implicating corrupt high-level medical and law enforcement officials has recently been highlighted in Punjab. Most commonly, those who willingly sell their kidneys have not received the amounts of money promised to them. If they try to file complaints against those involved, the victims themselves either face intimidation or are prosecuted and imprisoned for taking part in illegal activities. The real traffickers, the brokers and corrupt medical officials that profit from such exploitation, have so far evaded conviction (Swami 2003).

The ease with which the traffickers can change international routes to escape detection is quite astounding. For instance, the attention to organ trafficking in Moldova and Turkey as a result of the Council of Europe's Recommendation 1611 (2003) has meant that more brokers turned to South Africa as a place to conduct business, flying in Moldavians to South Africa, or accessing sellers from other markets such as Brazil.

Unlike other forms of trafficking, the gender dimension is less pronounced amongst organ trafficking victims. Indeed, we have little information on the victims per se, and more information on who are the donors (sellers). The situation varies much from country to country. In Moldova and Brazil, for example, kidney sellers tend to be young males from 18 to 30 years of age (Vermot-Mangold 2003). In India, however, a study amongst 305 sellers found 71% were women, of these two admitted they had been forced by their husbands to sell their kidneys (Goyal 2002). Scheper-Hughes has stated that the majority of kidney sellers worldwide are non-white and female. There is a lack of evidence that children are being trafficked for their organs, as stated earlier; this seems to be largely rumour and conjecture.

Organ Trafficking in the Anti-Trafficking Framework

Despite the inclusion of removal of organs under the Trafficking Protocol, organ trafficking has been largely ignored in the anti-trafficking efforts of states, international organisations and NGOs. Whilst it may be mentioned as one of a number of 'causes for concern' in anti-trafficking rhetoric, in terms of actual programmes, no anti-trafficking programmes of government, intergovernmental organisations or NGOs seem to be specifically addressing this issue.

One exception is the Council of Europe recently issuing a recommendation on trafficking in organs in Europe. This recommendation encourages member states to sign and ratify the Trafficking Protocol as well as the Council of Europe's Convention on Human Rights and Biomedicine, and its Additional Protocol on Transplantation of Organs and Tissues of Human Origin. The Council of Europe recommends a strong crime control approach to the issue, by revising the criminal laws of member states to ensure laws specifically cover the crime of organ trafficking as well as to strengthen the regional law enforcement response.

Yet governments have been slow to address removal of organs as trafficking. In enacting criminal legislation under the Protocol, many governments, including the European Union, have considered only trafficking for labour and sexual exploitation, thus excluding removal of organs as a human trafficking offence. One reason for this could be that in many countries there are already existing laws in place regarding illegal sale of organs, thus there is less need for a trafficking law to cover removal of organs. However, the Council of Europe states that such laws are inadequate since they rarely specify criminal responsibility and therefore are not useful in practice to prosecute organ traffickers.

The exclusion of removal of organs from general trafficking policies also has implications for those victims of organ trafficking who are unable to access victim protection measures that are afforded to victims of sexual and labour trafficking only. For example, laws that ensure migrant victims of trafficking are housed in shelters rather than in immigration detention facilities would in many countries not apply to victims of organ trafficking.

Anti-trafficking activists have rarely focused on the need to draw more attention to the rights of victims of organ trafficking. In fact 'organs' remain an invisible sector for existing anti-trafficking initiatives. Perhaps it is because the aspects of slavery that are so clearly manifested in other forms of trafficking are not present with organ trafficking. Thus the 'victim' of organ trafficking is rarely seen as a victim, but more as a complicit party in an illegal activity who has been cheated in the deal, but now has to bear the consequences. Indeed, the kinds of support which victims of organ trafficking need are somewhat different to what other victims of trafficking require, due to the different nature of the violation. Whilst both require some legal and social support, the health needs of organ sellers are far more extensive, whilst they have less need for psychosocial support and reintegration assistance.

Practical Responses to Fight Organ Trafficking

Thus far, the crime control approach has been used with some success to fight illegal sale of organs. There is still a need for legal reform in many countries to ensure all parties, including those medical personnel knowingly participating in illegal transplantation, are prosecuted effectively.

A State Investigative Commission in Pernambuco, Brazil, in 2003 uncovered a sophisticated organ selling ring in which at least 60 Brazilian men travelled to South Africa and sold their kidneys to recipients mainly from Israel (Rohter 2004). It is not clear how many of that number were trafficked. Some did receive all the money promised to them (ranging from $ US 3,000 to $ US 10,000), whilst others only received a fraction of what they were promised. Two brokers from Israel and six from Brazil were arrested, including former police officers. Yet the kidney sellers themselves were also arrested, since selling organs is also a crime in Brazil. Perhaps lessons in victim protection might be learned from elsewhere in the human trafficking paradigm, so for example not to criminalise those victims who are not involved in the trafficking of others.

Beyond law enforcement, there is a pressing need to assist those selling organs and protect their basic rights to health. Organ trafficking requires as much response from departments of health as from those of justice. Whilst the strong criminal response is necessary and successful, equally potential sellers of organs need more specific health information on the consequences of selling kidneys, and better access to health care in the long-term. As one kidney seller in India stated:

> They told me I didn't need my other kidney, it was a spare and I believed them. But now I can't do the work I used to, so it is worse, now I'm poor and sick and I can't work at all.

Organ trafficking may be a small problem in comparison to trafficking for other forms. Yet the rising global inequality combined with the rapid advancements in medical technology means that all stakeholders should be aware of the issue and act to prevent it before it becomes a significant problem. Prevention means both informing people about the risks of organ selling as well as taking criminal action against those who traffic others, rather than against the sellers themselves. This has been the approach in Pernambuco, Brazil, where organisations such as the Latin American Institute of Human Rights (ILADH) have been raising awareness about the risks of organ trafficking amongst poor communities.

Recommendations

There are various steps governments should take to prevent organ trafficking. At a minimum, states that have not yet done so should sign and ratify the Trafficking Protocol. Trafficking laws should include removal of organs so that victims of organ trafficking have equal access to protection measures (such as social and legal assistance) as other trafficking victims. European states should also ratify the Council of Europe's Convention on Human Rights and Biomedicine and its Additional Protocol on Transplantation of Organs and Tissues of Human Origin. Those who donate or sell organs should not be held criminally responsible unless they are also directly implicated in trafficking of organs of others. Medical staff treating recipients of trafficked organs after transplantation should not be penalised provided they behave consistently with medical ethics.

Governments should further review and monitor current kidney transplantation procedures involving live unrelated donations of kidneys with a view to tightening procedures to prevent illegal organ sales. In addition to this, governments should look at alternative measures such as increasing ethical live donations and the supply of cadaver donations.

Non-governmental and international organisations should collect more substantive data on the extent of organ trafficking and its specific characteristics (i.e. the extent of deception and coercion in obtaining of organs, failure of kidney donors to receive the payments or other rewards promised). Prevention campaigns will only be effective if based on the specific circumstances of the local context, therefore accurate information is needed on the profiles of organ donors (sellers) and those at risk of organ trafficking.

Where significant numbers exist, NGOs working on health issues as well as government agencies should extend their services to those at risk of organ trafficking and to those who have had organs removed. Such organisations can provide counselling and information to potential kidney donors as well as medical assistance to those who have sold kidneys. Frontline NGOs working on trafficking should likewise reach out to victims of organ trafficking in need of legal and social assistance. Finally, civil society has an important role to play in ensuring media reports on organ trafficking reflect the reality, rather than sensationalism. Organ trafficking should not simply become part of the anti-trafficking bandwagon without clear information on how many people are actually being trafficked for organs.

Linkages between Trafficking and HIV/AIDS

Jane Gronow & Deborah McWhinney

Linkages between HIV/AIDS and Trafficking

Trafficking and HIV/AIDS are human rights issues, interlinked through a range of socio-economic and developmental factors leading to social and individual vulnerability. Social inequality and exclusion, gender discrimination and gender-based violence, social stigma and restrictive migration policies are all factors that expose specific population groups to exploitation and to trafficking.

Those who are especially vulnerable to HIV/AIDS transmission include commercial sex workers, injecting drug users, and socially excluded populations (including ethnic minorities and children deprived of parental care). They are already highly stigmatised and isolated within their societies, rarely access the formal health care or education systems, have limited access to information and often lack the skills necessary to protect themselves. All of these factors make them equally vulnerable to being trafficked. Contexts of vulnerability are heightened by risk behaviours, such as unsafe sex and injecting drug use, which create a nexus of risk around which trafficking and HIV/AIDS are interwoven. Many of those who are at risk of being trafficked are similarly at risk of contracting HIV.

Gender-Specific Aspects

Neither trafficking nor HIV/AIDS is gender neutral. While both men and women have their own specific vulnerabilities and risks to contracting HIV and to being trafficked, women and children are much more vulnerable to sexual abuse and exploitation. Women and children living in abusive situations and/or searching for better economic opportunities as a result of living in poverty are more prone to be caught up in the trafficking cycle.

In many societies the social construction of gender and acceptance of male sexual needs and behaviour makes the abuse and use of trafficked women and girls easy to rationalise. The spread of HIV/AIDS in the context of trafficking is compounded by the huge gender inequalities that exist regarding sexuality and power relations:

> The lucrative entertainment and sex industry is predicated upon male-centred assumptions; that sex is a male right and commodity; that commercial providers of sex are largely women, that women in prostitution exist as sexualised and commoditised bodies functional to the male right. (D'Cunha 2002: 17)

If this paradigm is to be challenged, attention must be focused not only on the women who are caught up in the trafficking cycle, but upon the men who provide the demand for the commercial sex services. It is important to recognise that it is not solely women that are at risk of HIV in this relationship, but both men and women are rendered more vulnerable to HIV/AIDS:

> HIV/AIDS is not only driven by gender inequality – it entrenches gender inequality, putting women, men and children further at risk. (Tallis 2002: 5)

Sex Work and Health

There is no inevitable correlation between trafficking and sex work or trafficking and HIV/AIDS. Not all trafficked women and girls end up in the sex industry and not all those engaged in sex work are trafficked women or contract HIV. However, there is no doubt the sexual violence, abuse and exploitation which are common themes for women and girls trafficked for the purposes of sexual exploitation, heightens their risk of HIV transmission, sexually transmitted infections (STIs) and other serious health issues. Therefore, girls and women certainly have a need for a range of differentiated health services during the various stages of the trafficking process (Zimmerman et al. 2003: 24).

Girls and women working in the sex industry are already vulnerable to negative health consequences, unless they are working legally in a country where sex work is regulated and access to appropriate health care services is common. There are many factors that make it difficult to negotiate 'safe sex' with clients, including its illegal nature, general powerlessness, inability to negotiate condom use, refusal of clients to use a condom and the risk of violence for non-compliance with a client's wishes.

> Among female sex workers, those who have been trafficked have the lowest ranking and have less, if any, power in negotiating the conditions of sex. Thus, they are the ones that must endure unsafe and violent sex practices, which increase the risk of contracting STIs and HIV. (Wennerholm 2000: 7)

Without the basic knowledge of how to protect themselves and removed of the ability to control what happens to their body, trafficked women and children are more prone to contracting HIV. Women and adolescents interviewed in a European study on the health risks and consequences of trafficking had

> [...] limited information and many misconceptions about key aspects of their own health – for example, only one of 23 trafficked women interviewed during the study felt well-informed about sexually transmitted infections or HIV before leaving home. (Zimmerman et al. 2003: 3)

The trafficking of children and adolescents for sexual exploitation in many countries is largely driven by perceptions that virgins are safer or that children are less likely to be infected. Ironically, newly trafficked children and young women have the greatest vulnerability to becoming infected quickly and thus being highly infectious during their first months as a sex worker. UNICEF's former Executive Director, Carol Bellamy, stated:

Whether it is myths about the curative powers of sex with young girls or macho attitudes that sanction violent sexual behaviour towards women and girls, the links between the sexual abuse of children and the spread of HIV/AIDS are clear.

Migration-Related Aspects

Trafficking is clearly a part of the migration paradigm and needs to be seen in the context of increasing migration flows around the world. The push factors for migration are many and complex. The goal of a better life elsewhere, economic hardship and prevailing gender stereotypes are among the key factors that motivate a woman to migrate.

However, not all migration is trafficking, as trafficking involves some form of deception for the purposes of exploitation. Unfortunately, trafficking in women and girls for the sex industry is a significant part of trafficking in human beings and HIV/AIDS has inevitably become a part of the migration paradigm. This becomes especially apparent if one considers that HIV/AIDS prevalence in many parts of the world is extremely high on migration routes.

As has been previously stated, women working in the sex industry illegally are at high risk of contracting STIs, including HIV. When coupled with the fact that women who work in their home country as sex workers are much more vulnerable to being trafficked (Limanowska 2003: 8), the link between trafficking and HIV/AIDS becomes obvious.

Children trafficked for labour exploitation are frequently victims of sexual abuse. According to UNICEF, domestic workers in many countries are particularly vulnerable to abuse due to their seclusion in and dependence upon a particular household. There may be an unspoken assumption that sexual availability is part of the terms of employment, as well as physical and psychological abuse occurring regularly (UNICEF 2003: 1). Children trafficked into these situations are not only at high risk of infection; they often have no access to health or other forms of care.

Discourse on HIV/AIDS and Trafficking

There is no shortage of dialogue on the links between migration and HIV/AIDS, and whilst this has translated into a rich discussion of HIV/AIDS in anti-trafficking discourses in Asia and Africa, this is not yet the case in Europe. Similarly, the issue of trafficking emerges in analyses of vulnerability to and prevention of HIV/AIDS only in those countries with a publicly acknowledged trafficking issue.

In the first UNICEF report on Trafficking in South Eastern Europe (SEE), an absence of awareness and action on trafficking and vulnerability to HIV/AIDS across the region was reported (Gronow 2000: 5). Since 2001, the South East

European Regional Initiative aGainst Human Trafficking (SEE RIGHTs) research project has examined the trends and responses to trafficking in human beings in SEE. It has included the linkages between HIV/AIDS and trafficking as a category of analysis in each of the three SEE RIGHTs reports. Whereas the 2002 report noted that there was very little awareness of the links between trafficking and HIV/AIDS in SEE, by 2004 there were examples of more comprehensive prevention work being carried out in some countries in the region. Trafficking survivors that were identified and provided with assistance had relatively limited access to health care in 2002, but testing for STIs, including HIV, became a more regular component of victim assistance programmes by 2004.

While reproductive health and HIV/AIDS-related services are provided to trafficking victims receiving assistance in shelters by the International Organization for Migration (IOM) or local NGOs, women are often repatriated before their results are made known to them. The experience of a local NGO in Bosnia and Herzegovina revealed that if women or girls received a positive result before returning to their country of origin, no counselling or treatment was offered to them. Hence, they faced acute stigmatisation as a result of multiple discriminations (Emir Nurkic, International Forum for Solidarity, Tuzla, BiH, Interview, May 15, 2005). In some countries of SEE, girls and women were advised not to be tested for HIV as the confidentiality of the results could not be ensured. STI test results, which were more often positive than those for HIV, were also usually not followed up with adequate treatment (Gronow 2002: 3).

Health-related outreach to sex workers, injecting drug users, refugee and asylum seekers or migrant populations in European countries has resulted in information on the prevention of HIV/AIDS being provided to trafficked girls and women. Agencies working in these fields have not always been able to distinguish between sex workers, migrant sex workers and trafficked women, but this is changing as the trafficking phenomenon has become more publicised. Outreach and hotline work has increased in an effort to provide services in a manner that reaches trafficked girls and women as experience has shown that they will rarely be able to access primary health care services directly. Further, access to trafficked women is often very limited as they are kept under tight control and in private locations. Additionally, the lack of financial resources, language obstacles or their illegal migrant status often keep trafficked women from addressing health care services.

Service providers also have practical, policy, and resource limitations that often impede them from accessing and meeting the needs of these hard-to-reach women (Zimmerman et al. 2003: 3). An Italian health worker stated:

> The most significant source of contact with trafficking is through the telephone line linked to the detention centres. Direct use of the ambulatory [clinic] is extremely low. (Zimmerman et. al 2003: 84)

Harmonisation of Policies

As was documented in the 2005 SEE RIGHTs report, very few National Plans of Action against Trafficking in Human Beings contain analyses of or responses to the health needs of potential or actual trafficked victims. Similarly, it is rare that National Plans of Action on HIV/AIDS or other national developmental plans include references to the common vulnerabilities of individuals to contract HIV and to be trafficked. For instance, the issue of trafficking remains largely ignored in the Poverty Reduction Strategies developed in South Eastern Europe. Further action plans on gender equality, child rights, social support or HIV/AIDS rarely mention trafficking and do not integrate actions against trafficking into their programmes. While addressing employment, discrimination and the prevention of violence, large development organisations, such as the World Bank and UNDP, do not perceive the vulnerability to trafficking as a special issue and have not included anti-trafficking prevention into their development programmes in systematic ways (Limanowska 2005: 93).

This latest SEE RIGHTs report also concluded that little has changed with regard to the understanding of the root causes of trafficking and HIV/AIDS, and that the provision of HIV-related services to survivors of trafficking had not improved since the first report was published in 2000:

> While potential victims of trafficking are seen as a high-risk group for HIV transmission, there are still only a few programmes that offer these groups information on the prevention of HIV and no related information has been included in the National Plans of Action. (Limanowska 2005: 28)

The UNOHCHR's Recommended Principles refer to the need to ensure access to primary health care and counselling for trafficked persons, but warns that this assistance should be voluntary:

> Trafficked persons should not be required to accept any such support and assistance and they should not be subject to mandatory testing for diseases, including HIV/AIDS. (UNOHCHR 2002: 11)

Also, Article 6 of the UN Trafficking Protocol suggests the necessity for comprehensive victim support measures including medical assistance. Even though victims rightfully deserve this assistance, there are effectively no guarantees that victims will receive any of the suggested assistance since the language is non-binding.

In 2002, IOM documented the linkages between HIV/AIDS and migration and since then is working collaboratively with other UN agencies (such as UNAIDS), INGOs and NGOs to provide a variety of HIV-related services and information to migrants during the different stages of mobility. While their analysis lacks a gender dimension, it does highlight some of the common root causes:

> Many of the factors sustaining mobility, such as an unbalanced distribution of resources, unemployment, socio-economic instability and political unrest, are also determinants of the increased risk of migrants and their families to HIV infection. (IOM 2002: 1)

Addressing Double Discrimination

For many trafficking survivors, return to their country of origin is considered a failure. Many left their home country with hopes and dreams, but returned home with feelings of shame and fearing rejection from family and friends. Unfortunately, the reality is that return to one's country of origin often means having to face unemployment, poverty and gender-based violence – in short, all of the conditions that existed prior to being trafficked, and that led to their initial vulnerability. However, in addition to these 'root causes' not having been addressed, survivors of trafficking must face the stigma of having been trafficked. They are seen as 'prostitutes' who are undoubtedly 'infected' – 'vectors of disease' – who have brought shame on their families. As a way of preventing this reaction, NGOs in Ukraine and Albania often contact family members of the trafficking survivor before her return to explain that she is not to blame for what happened to her and to emphasise her status as a victim (Zimmerman et al. 2003: 98).

Many women hide the fact that they were trafficked for the purposes of sexual exploitation to their husbands or boyfriends. In the case that a girl or woman is HIV-positive, the situation is more complicated. She will face enhanced stigma from service providers and any community that she may join and cannot simply keep the information on her status from intimate partners. Often, the only place to find refuge and others to share the experience with are similarly marginalised populations.

Practical Approaches

An emphasis must be placed on the prevention of trafficking and on the prevention of HIV/AIDS. Use of a human rights framework is essential if we are to reach the most vulnerable. It is also the only way to challenge the social constructs that continue to perpetrate trafficking and the spread of HIV/AIDS. Putting adequate measures in place to address the root causes of both HIV/AIDS and trafficking should be a priority response. This means strengthening the understanding of the links between HIV/AIDS, trafficking and poverty reduction, enhancing economic empowerment for women and increasing access to information on safe migration and legal employment abroad.

To achieve this, a human rights approach is needed, as well as effective coordination between police, judiciary, health professionals, peer educators and governmental and non-governmental agencies working with victims. National Plans of Action for both, trafficking and HIV/AIDS, need to recognise and to respond to the nexus of risk around which both are interwoven.

Conclusion

Trafficking for the purposes of sexual exploitation is still widely misunderstood and linked to cultural and gender stereotypes and prejudices. Trafficking for the purposes of sexual exploitation remains one of the most insidious and widespread examples of human rights violations and is easily justified through the social construct of male sexual behaviour in most societies.

Unfortunately women and children are much more vulnerable to sexual abuse and exploitation and, therefore, to HIV, STI or other serious health concerns. As sexual violence is pervasive for many victims of trafficking, their risk of transmission is significant. Regrettably, it is difficult to provide access to health care, reproductive health services, health education and psychosocial support to women and children caught up in trafficking.

As a result, it is crucial that creative and practical solutions are found to ensure that the needs of trafficking survivors are met and that they are not subjected to further victimisation, stigma or discrimination. Ultimately, however, it is activities that prevent trafficking and the spread of HIV/AIDS that should be prioritised.

Trafficking in Armed and Post-Conflict Situations

Martina E. Vandenberg

Introduction

Trafficking has always accompanied the ravages of war. What has changed over time is the legal anti-trafficking framework. Article 7 of the Rome Statute of the International Criminal Court explicitly lists trafficking in humans as a form of enslavement, punishable as a crime against humanity. Similarly, the Rome Statute identifies sexual slavery and forced prostitution committed in the context of armed conflict as war crimes.

Conflict creates vulnerability to trafficking, while exacerbating pre-existing risk factors. Wartime destruction of homes and families, dislocation of civilian populations, disruption of economies, and collapse of the rule of law combine to produce an environment ripe for trafficking. Pre-war factors such as poverty, discrimination against women, racial discrimination, and corruption only increase the likelihood of widespread trafficking in persons during and after conflict. Like trafficking in arms and weapons, trafficking in humans generates enormous profits while also serving other non-pecuniary, political war aims. Indeed, trafficking for forced labour, forced prostitution, and sexual slavery all dehumanise the victims, and can thus serve as weapons of war.

In the aftermath of conflict, trafficking in humans simply moves into alternative forms. Post-conflict trafficking, like its wartime twin, enriches perpetrators and corrupt officials alike. The strategies designed to counter conflict-related trafficking in the modern era have failed to curtail these serious crimes.

An Overview of Trafficking in Armed Conflict

Trafficking in armed conflict takes several forms. Most common are trafficking of children for forced military service, trafficking of women and girls for forced prostitution or sexual slavery, and trafficking for forced labour.

Child Soldiers

Human rights organisations estimate that as many as 300,000 children are serving as soldiers in armed conflicts around the world. Kidnapped, recruited by force, or lured with false promises of safety and shelter, these children face horrific abuse. Girls and boys serve as combatants, spies, couriers, human mine detectors, and porters in conflicts around the world. Unaccompanied minors, orphaned or displaced by conflict, become prime targets for armed groups seeking child soldiers. In other cases, children are wrenched from their families and forced to commit or witness atrocities. Girls trapped in military service face the additional risk of sexual assault, leading to infection with sexually transmitted diseases and unwanted pregnancies. Human rights organisations have documented numerous cases of adult soldiers and commanders who force girls to become 'wives', locking the children into sexual and domestic servitude. Citing the example of the Lord's Resistance Army in Uganda, the UN Special Rapporteur on Systematic Rape, Sexual Slavery, and Slavery-like Practices during Armed Conflict concluded:

> The repeated rape and sexual abuse of women and girls under the guise of 'marriage' constitutes slavery […]. (Coomaraswamy 2000: para. 13)

Although forbidden by international law, the recruitment and use of child soldiers persists in Colombia, Sierra Leone, Liberia, Uganda, Angola, and dozens of other countries. The violence inflicted upon child soldiers, combined with the atrocities they witness, frequently cause significant psychological trauma. This trauma impedes reintegration of child soldiers into society after a conflict, and may leave children vulnerable to additional exploitation.

Trafficking for Forced Prostitution and Sexual Slavery

The trafficking of 200,000 women and girls into sexual slavery by the Japanese Imperial Army during World War II marks perhaps the most systematic trafficking campaign ever documented. According to allegations lodged in lawsuits brought against Japan by former 'comfort women', the Japanese Imperial Army, aided by private entrepreneurs, transported thousands of women and girls from the Philippines, China, Taiwan, Guam, Indonesia, and Korea to so-called 'comfort stations' created for Japanese soldiers throughout Asia. There, the women and girls found themselves forced into prostitution and sexual slavery.

Impunity for trafficking in wartime has diminished only marginally in the intervening decades. Trafficking for forced prostitution and sexual slavery continue to flourish in contemporary conflicts. In Bosnia and Herzegovina, women and girls gave detailed and chilling accounts of detention in rape camps. In just one example, Bosnian Serb forces in the village of Foca sexually enslaved women, holding them for months and subjecting them to multiple gang rapes. After some of the women courageously agreed to testify against the perpetrators, the International Criminal Tribunal for the Former Yugoslavia (ICTY) convicted three defendants for sexual slavery as a crime against humanity, finding that they had enslaved and sexually abused six women (ICTY 2001).

Similarly, during the 1994 genocide, women and girls in Rwanda spoke of being held in sexual slavery and forced 'marriages' by militias. Sexual mutilation and killings often followed the sexual violence and slavery perpetrated by the Interahamwe, by other civilians, and by soldiers of the Rwandan Armed Forces (Human Rights Watch 1996). Sexual slavery in armed conflict has continued to plague women, many targeted for their membership in a particular ethnic group. In Sierra Leone, a teenage girl interviewed by United Nations officials reported that rebel soldiers abducted her, holding her captive for three months and subjecting her to repeated rape and sexual abuse (Special Rapporteur 2000: para. 16). Most recently, human rights organisations have documented cases of sexual slavery in the conflict raging in Darfur, Sudan. There, government-backed Janjaweed militias and government forces have abducted women, sometimes holding them for days and subjecting them to multiple gang rapes (Médecins sans Frontières 2005).

Reports of trafficking of refugee and internally displaced women and girls for forced prostitution abroad during time of conflict in their countries of origin also abound. Credible reports of trafficking of thousands of war-displaced women and girls from Colombia to Venezuela, Ecuador, Spain, the United States, and Japan have emerged in recent years. Similarly, experts have documented the sale abroad of women abducted in Sierra Leone and Afghanistan (GTZ 2004: 21). Non-governmental organisations in the Balkans, however, caution that reports of trafficking of women and girls abroad during conflicts in that region were somewhat exaggerated. Through the entire Bosnian conflict, local NGOs documented only one case of a Bosnian woman trafficked abroad. And despite panic generated by rumours of trafficking of women and girls from refugee camps in Albania during the Kosovo conflict in 1999, evidence of this phenomenon was elusive.

Trafficking for Forced Labour

The most frequently cited examples of trafficking for forced labour during wartime relate to crimes committed during the Second World War. Forced labour, defined by the ILO as "all work or service which is exacted from any person under the menace of any penalty and for which the said person has not offered himself voluntarily", thrives during times of armed conflict. The internment of hundreds of thousands of male and female civilians for use as forced labourers in munitions plants and other factories during World War II constituted systematic acts of trafficking, though not conceived as such at the time. Trafficking of humans for forced labour continues in contemporary conflicts. Militaries and irregular forces often abduct children and adults for forced, non-combat labour during wartime. During the conflict in Kosovo, Serb paramilitaries and soldiers abducted some women for domestic servitude, including cleaning and serving coffee. Sexual abuse and assault frequently accompanied this forced labour, although many women were reluctant to admit that they had suffered such abuse.

Trafficking in Post-Conflict Environments

Trafficking flourishes in the post-conflict environment, as criminal entrepreneurs and ex-combatants switch from wartime to a post-war economy. Pernicious factors frequently present at the cessation of a conflict — social disruption, economic collapse, corruption and complete absence of the rule of law — provide ideal conditions for traffickers to launch operations. In addition, the influx of thousands of peacekeepers and support staff provides a ready market for forced prostitution and domestic servitude. Post-conflict zones quickly evolve from combat zones into countries of origin, transit, and destination for victims of trafficking. Porous borders, combined with the absence of law enforcement, make trafficking a profitable and nearly risk-free enterprise.

Post-Conflict Areas as Countries of Origin and Transit

Local populations traumatised and displaced by war may fall victim to traffickers promising lucrative jobs abroad. This is particularly true for women and girls held in sexual slavery or subjected to rape during the conflict, as some may fear rejection by their communities and seek alternatives to returning home. Moreover, decimated economies offer few opportunities for employment, particularly for women experiencing the all-too-common resurgence of gender discrimination after conflict.

For traffickers, profit opportunities beckon at home and abroad. Post-conflict trafficking need not involve crossing borders. Non-governmental organisations in Kosovo documented the trafficking of Serbian women and girls into Kosovo for forced prostitution after the Serbian forces' withdrawal. Albanian and Serbian criminal groups have cooperated in the post-conflict period to traffic humans within and through the Federal Republic of Yugoslavia (FRY). This internal trafficking highlights another phenomenon typical in post-conflict environments, the porous nature of internal and external borders.

Traffickers exploit unguarded borders to transport local trafficking victims out of the country, to move foreign victims through the country and to traffic foreign victims into the country. Empty border posts allow traffickers to avoid border guards who might otherwise demand bribes or disrupt transportation of victims.

Links to Peace Support Operations in Post-Conflict Zones

Often littered with landmines and wracked by poverty, a post-conflict zone might seem an improbable destination for trafficking victims. But the influx of aid workers, civilian contractors, military personnel, international police, and employees of international organisation provides a significant market for forced prostitution and domestic labour. Money also floods the post-conflict zone, as the members of the international community hire local staff, rent apartments, and establish offices.

Trafficked women report that the vast majority – perhaps up to 80 percent – of their clients are local. Nevertheless, local and international non-governmental organisations have long pointed to the links between trafficking for forced prostitution and peace support operations. The obvious connection, of course, is on the demand side, as internationals knowingly or unknowingly create a market for trafficked persons. Local citizens constitute the majority of the clientele, but often pay lower prices than international customers.

But links also exist on the supply side. In several cases documented in the Balkans, peacekeepers and international police officers faced allegations that they had engaged in human trafficking. In one case, a U.S. police officer serving with the United Nations Mission in Kosovo (UNMIK) allegedly trafficked Serbian girls to Kosovo, accepting girls as 'gifts' in exchange from a brothel owner. In another case, victims reported that a Russian peacekeeper trafficked them to Bosnia and Herzegovina, selling them to a brothel owner who forced the women into prostitution. In still another case, Pakistani International Police Task Force (IPTF) officers serving with the UN Mission in Bosnia and Herzegovina allegedly transported trafficked women across the country, delivering them to colleagues for sexual services (Human Rights Watch 2002: 52–63). Critics have assailed the United Nations Department of Peacekeeping Operations (UNDPKO) for its failure to thoroughly investigate cases of international staff members alleged to have engaged in trafficking. Typically, UNDPKO, like many other international organisations, has responded that member states and accused staff members' countries of origin must discipline their own nationals.

More often than not, however, international personnel who engage in trafficking do so with complete impunity. These cases fall into a legal lacuna. Status of forces agreements generally bar prosecution of international personnel in the courts of the post-conflict country. Judicial and legal systems devastated by conflict rarely have the capacity to conduct such prosecutions, even if the international organisation or national government employing the suspect were to waive immunity. And due to evidentiary difficulties and gaps in jurisdiction, foreign nationals alleged to have engaged in trafficking while serving in a post-conflict zone rarely, if ever, face prosecution in their countries of origin.

This impunity for international staff and peacekeepers has serious repercussions. First, the perception that international personnel operate above the law undermines rule of law and shatters the local population's trust in the international community. Second, individual international staff members' and peacekeepers' involvement in corrupt activities, including human trafficking, presents a security threat to the peace operation more broadly. Partnerships between local criminal figures and members of the international community create opportunities for infiltration of peacekeeping operations, intelligence gathering, and sabotage of peace support operations. At a minimum, the erosion of trust caused by participation – or even perceived participation – in illegal activities undermines the mission's credibility (Mendelson 2005: 17–18).

Trafficking victims find the post-conflict environment a terrifying one. Pervasive violence, plentiful supplies of weapons and widespread corruption make these regions particularly hazardous for trafficking victims. And when the trafficking victims count local and international police officers, international officials, and peacekeepers among their clients for forced prostitution services, their willingness to come forward to request assistance shrinks. Traffickers threaten, blackmail and often physically abuse their victims. Traffickers also use relationships with corrupt police officers and officials to convince trafficking victims that it would be hopeless to attempt escape.

Strategies for Combating Trafficking

The establishment of the International Criminal Tribunals for Rwanda (ICTR) and the Former Yugoslavia (ICTY), as well as the International Criminal Court, marked the dawn of accountability for trafficking conducted during conflict. A handful of defendants have faced charges for trafficking-related offences before the ICTY and ICTR. These prosecutions have highlighted the need to protect the human rights of trafficking victims. Victim and witness protection must be key elements in any strategy to combat trafficking. Prosecutions cannot proceed without such protections in place.

The post-conflict environments around the globe reflect a continuing climate of impunity. Several institutions involved in peace support operations such as NATO, the United Nations, and some national militaries have all adopted 'zero tolerance' policies on human trafficking. But implementation and enforcement of these policies have been spotty, at best. International organisations have sought to develop training programmes for staff members serving abroad, to introduce disciplinary guidelines for staff members found to be engaged in trafficking, and to increase transparency on the issue. The results of these efforts remain to be seen. Benchmarks to measure the success of these new programmes include more robust and transparent investigations of trafficking allegations, increased prosecutions of local and international traffickers, and increased attention to the human rights of victims.

Lisa Kurbiel, the UNDPKO focal point on trafficking, has stated repeatedly that the anti-trafficking strategies used in each environment must be tailored to fit the situation and must take into account the human rights of trafficking victims. Critics have argued that ill-conceived anti-trafficking strategies in Bosnia and Herzegovina and Liberia may have exacerbated the abuses against trafficking victims. Aggressive raids, critics noted, drove trafficking underground, out of public nightclubs and into private apartments, making it more difficult to locate and care for victims. International organisations can, at this juncture, boast of very few 'best practices'. But non-governmental organisations in post-conflict regions stress the importance of permitting trafficking victims to remain in safe shelters, as well as to receive witness protection and comprehensive victim services.

United Nations Secretary-General Kofi Annan has called for the creation of a monitoring and reporting mechanism to track recruiting of child soldiers and for enforcement of the International Protocol to the Convention on the Rights of the Child on the Involvement of Children in Armed Conflict, which entered into force in February 2002.

Conclusion

Trafficking in conflict and post-conflict environments constitutes a grave violation of human rights, and, in some cases, a violation of international humanitarian law. As the UN High Commissioner for Human Rights has recommended, the human rights of trafficked persons should be "at the centre of all efforts to prevent and combat trafficking and to protect, assist and provide redress to victims." (UNHCHR 2002: Recommended Principles and Guidelines on Human Rights and Human Trafficking.)

Practical Approaches

Approaches to Prevention

The question as how to best tackle trafficking in human beings is most often met with reactive measures such as victim assistance and protection as well as legislative and law enforcement responses. Each one of these approaches is crucial. However, preventing trafficking addresses the root causes of the problem and has far-reaching impacts in the long term. A comprehensive, forward-looking and sustainable anti-trafficking response requires effective preventive strategy.

Root Causes on Each End of the Trafficking Process

Rising global economic disparity, its impact on vulnerable groups and individuals as well as major social changes in countries of transition are amongst the most prevalent root causes for trafficking in human beings. Furthermore dysfunctional families and neglect or violence at home lead to special vulnerability. Poor or no school education, gender inequality and high unemployment rates mean there are only few opportunities to earn sustainable livelihoods in most traditional countries of origin.
People seek to migrate, but restrictive migration policies mean they lack opportunity to do so independently or through legal and safe channels. 'Tricked' into exploitative and abusive situations they find themselves in an unfamiliar environment totally dependent on their perpetrators, who are able to transfer and exploit persons with few risks, also due to corruption of public officials (such as border guards or police) in many countries.

Preventive measures should not only search for solutions to economic hardship, human rights abuses, social disparity and democratic destabilisation in countries of origin. At the other end of the trafficking chain, there is demand for informal, cheap and unprotected labour in countries of destination. There is little awareness in destination areas about the cruelty, diversity and impact on individual victims of trafficking in human beings as well as on the society as a whole and little interest in the working conditions of migrants. Begging children in the streets, domestic servants in the house of acquaintances, prostitutes or foreign agricultural workers do not necessarily draw attention of the greater public. Still, they could be victims of trafficking. It is crucial to reach out not only to the victims of this serious crime, but also to raise the awareness of consumers of services provided by migrants who could be trafficked, such as clients of sex workers or employers of domestic workers.

Prevention activities go hand in hand with the re-/integration of trafficked persons once they have returned to their home country. Trafficked persons who do not receive adequate support and assistance upon their return run high risk of being 're-trafficked' especially if the social environment that they left in the first place remains unchanged. Thus long-term economic and social changes are required in countries of origin for successful prevention and reintegration of victims.

Breaking the Cycle of Trafficking

Legislative and policy documents most often fall short in elaborating exactly how to prevent trafficking in human beings. Frequently, vague references are made to general initiatives such as research, information, awareness raising, education, training programmes and socio-economic development based on human rights. But how does a comprehensive strategy look like and what are the necessary elements that need to be included?

Research, Information and Awareness Raising

Research is an important tool for successful outreach, advocacy and lobbying. Standardised qualitative and quantitative research enables relevant stakeholders at national and international levels to more effectively target their prevention activities to the needs of vulnerable groups and society at large. Naturally, any research should be conducted in a sensible fashion avoiding the re-victimisation of trafficked persons. For instance, more in-depth, outcome-oriented and local research on the root causes of trafficking and their interrelatedness ensures that subsequent awareness-raising activities can be specific and therefore more effective, especially considering that root causes can vary tremendously between countries and even places in one country. Some of the root causes that require close examination are domestic violence, racism, discrimination against ethnic minorities and corruption. Many victims come from difficult social and economic backgrounds. Racism and discrimination make ethnic minorities particularly vulnerable to fall prey to traffickers. Trafficking is facilitated by organised crime and corruption. Moreover, factors relating to the demand for services of trafficked persons such as commercial sexual services or domestic work need to be researched in more depth.

Accurate information for 'at-risk' communities is vital to prevent and combat trafficking in human beings. Information about safe migration and work opportunities assists potential migrants to be aware of the risks around the migration process and know how to migrate safely. This involves giving information about contracts, work conditions, labour laws and migrant support networks in destination countries so they can make a more informed decision. Hotlines are another useful means for promoting safe migration. They are often the first contact point for persons who find themselves in a trafficking situation. In many countries, non-governmental organisations run such services in coordination with governmental institutions.

Accurate research is important to feed into effective awareness-raising and information campaigns. When tailored well to the needs of the target audience, awareness-raising campaigns are an invaluable tool for reaching out to groups at risk of trafficking. Clear, simple and age-appropriate messages should inspire their audiences to find alternatives to their stagnant situation besides putting themselves at risk of trafficking. Statements that simply discourage migration in countries of origin will have little impact on those who need to migrate due to desperation. Messages should focus on ways to migrate safely and empower recipients to take action.

During any stage of the trafficking cycle (be it well before the exploitation takes place, during the process of exploitation or after a trafficked person has returned to the country of origin) potential and actual victims of trafficking suffer from discrimination and misperception by others, both by others in the destination country and (often for women trafficked into prostitution) by their communities when they return. Awareness-raising campaigns need to make all layers of society aware of the human rights violations at all stages of the trafficking process and seek to change attitudes towards migrant workers and trafficked persons.

Addressing the Demand Side

Not only in countries of origin, but also in countries of destination there is a need for awareness raising on several levels. Firstly to lobby for legislative change, secondly to provoke change of attitudes and perceptions in order to reduce demand for informal and unprotected labour. Addressing trafficking without taking into consideration the demand side generated in the shadow economies of countries of destination would deny the holistic approach that is needed in anti-trafficking work. Addressees should not only be clients of prostitutes but also the private sector that constitutes the demand side of cheap and unprotected labour. Also, for the dimension of organ trafficking a wider public needs to be sensitised.

Education and Empowerment

The most sustainable way of preventing trafficking in human beings in the long term is to invest in the education sector. Reducing dropout rates and equipping children and youth with knowledge and life skills for success in the local labour market are basic but necessary ways to ensure their lives become independent and self-sustainable. This requires trained teachers, revised school curricula and commitment to education at all political levels. Education should also comprise impartation of life skills. Besides skills learned should not only match the short-term demands of the labour market, but also ensure that children are empowered to expand their careers in the long term. Comprehensive training for all professional groups active in the fight against trafficking in human beings will lead to improved working standards. A smoothly operating protection and prosecution system is an excellent means to deter perpetrators from committing a crime. Additionally, well-trained skills and a sensible approach will initiate being more sensitive to factors that could be defined as 'early-warning'.

Initiatives at the Grassroots Level

Community-based initiatives have proven to be successful by addressing issues and building capacity from within. Thus local communities develop ownership in dealing with difficult topics such as trafficking in human beings. Grass-roots initiatives reach out more easily to people directly at risk and returning trafficked persons that seek new opportunities in their home countries. Prevention and reintegration in countries of origin go hand in hand when it comes to empowering vulnerable groups.

Ensuring Safe Migration

Some trafficking prevention strategies have focused more on preventing migration than preventing trafficking (the exploitation associated with migration) with harmful impacts for migrants generally. Women and girls in particular have repeatedly been stopped while crossing borders of some countries, even with valid travel documents. In some cases, under the guise of 'preventing trafficking' corrupt border officials have sought additional money from women and girls to secure entry. Intercepting and denying entry to travellers perceived as potential victims or who simply fit a profile of a victim cannot be seen as a sincere initiative to prevent trafficking. Stopping them from entering a country does not stop trafficking. It denies those who are not victims from exercising their freedom of movement, and as far as potential victims are concerned they will simply find other ways to migrate or travel which may be more dangerous. At the border, most victims do not realise yet that they are being trafficked and are therefore unlikely to respond well to being intercepted. Such examples show that the approach of tightening borders to prevent trafficking in human beings is seriously questionable. More sensitisation, training and creativity are needed in order to support at-risk groups appropriately at borders. For instance, slipping brochures or pocket diaries with hotline numbers into the passports of the travellers is a way of empowering them to be aware of trafficking and know where to turn in case of exploitation at destination.

Revising restrictive immigration laws, increasing awareness about safe migration as well as developing comprehensive integration programmes can prevent trafficking in countries of destination. Based on comprehensive research and sensible awareness raising, changes in migration law and policy can prevent women and children from being trafficked by encouraging regular and safe migration channels for women or by ensuring that informal areas of work are protected under labour law.

Responsibility of Different Actors

Like any successful action prevention work needs to draw on a coordinated and concerted effort. Prevention activities require financial and political support at all levels. Particularly development agencies and monetary institutions should mainstream anti-trafficking into their programmes and advise states and implementing agencies to promote innovative and broad approaches addressing specific root causes in the area of prevention. Investing to improve the prevailing abusive circumstances of potential victims in countries of origin will help prevent trafficking. Countering violence and discrimination indirectly prevents trafficking and needs financial support as much as specific anti-trafficking programmes. Likewise anti-corruption initiatives require support, since trafficking cannot be seen in isolation from organised crime. Unfettered corruption including bribery or blackmailing enables traffickers to operate freely. Donors should bear in mind that effective prevention strategy must be specific, i.e. what works in one country or community may not always apply in another, based on social-cultural differences. It must also be adaptable, to take account of new forms of trafficking and changing modus operandi of traffickers. The private sector can offer job opportunities to vulnerable groups, which prevent at-risk persons from migrating and thus makes them less susceptible for false promises of traffickers.

Innovative Initiatives Related to Prevention

The following chapters highlight five distinct initiatives that work towards sustainable empowerment of vulnerable groups as well as pragmatically addressing demand factors:

- The International Business Leaders Forum promotes their Corporate Social Responsibility Programme "Youth Career Initiative". World leading private enterprises offer selected candidates from vulnerable groups the possibility to gain insights and build their skills in various business areas. Sebastian Baumeister and Susie Maley give an overview of the project.

- The Animus Association Foundation based in Bulgaria presents its programme for the empowerment of orphans. They assist children and adolescents in institutions to develop their social skills and thus empower them to make informed decisions about their lives. This prepares this at-risk group of young people for a better start into the labour market. Lora Beltcheva, Maria Petrova and Maria Tchomarova portray this approach.
- Lilijana Vasić from the Christian Children's Fund Office in Serbia introduces the concept of community-based intervention to multi-ethnic areas in rural Southern Serbia and Moldova. Joint projects designed by youth for youth stimulate awareness of and discussion on sensitive issues including trafficking in the selected communities.
- La Strada Ukraine successfully runs a nation-wide toll-free hotline, which provides useful information on safe migration as well as it offers counselling to trafficked persons and their families. An insider's view is presented by Kateryna Cherepakha and Olga Kalashnyk.
- Christiane Howe, a German anti-trafficking expert, analyses how to reach out to and raise awareness of clients of sex workers who may be trafficked.

The Role of the Private Sector in Developing Youth Careers

Sebastian Baumeister & Susie Maley

The Problem

Lack of economic opportunities, unemployment and loss of social cohesion are among the main factors that contribute to women's and girls' but also men's and boys' vulnerability to trafficking. In this context, economic empowerment through internships, vocational training and life skills education in cooperation with the private sector is a crucial component in mitigating the factors that fuel the supply side of trafficking.

OSCE participating States have recognised both the need for better addressing the economic root causes of demand and supply of trafficking as well as the necessity to give a more prominent role to the private sector in the fight against trafficking. In this regard, the OSCE Action Plan to Combat Trafficking in Human Beings, assigned the Office of the Co-ordinator of OSCE Economic and Environmental Activities (OCEEA) the task to

> [...] mobilise and strengthen the private sector's efforts to combat trafficking in human beings by raising awareness, and by identifying and disseminating best practices, such as self-regulation, policy guidelines and codes of conduct [...and...] facilitate contacts between public and private actors with a view to encouraging the business community to offer job opportunities to victims of trafficking [...]. (OSCE 2003: 12 and 16)

In this regard, the OCEEA has identified the International Business Leaders Forum's (IBLF) Youth Career Initiative (YCI) as a best practice in instigating a private sector programme that contributes to the prevention of trafficking through economic empowerment and supported its extension to South Eastern Europe, starting with Romania. By promoting a best practice Corporate Social Responsibility (CSR) programme, the OSCE strives to set up a role model in the region and to encourage other business sectors to get engaged in the fight against trafficking by supporting economic empowerment activities.

The Youth Career Initiative (YCI) is a programme for International Hotels to provide a six months life skills education programme, a combination of theory and practical instruction conducted by the hotel management team. The programme is designed to empower young people from disadvantaged backgrounds, by providing them with the necessary life skills so that they may lead valuable and fulfilling lives. YCI gives them a chance to improve their long-term social and economic opportunity through professional training and experience in five-star hotels. Through the YCI young people can enhance their earning potential, gain self-esteem and develop their ability to make informed decisions about their lives.

The Youth Career Initiative

The YCI has grown to become a unique global partnership of hotels, government, international and non-governmental organisations. Through the utilisation of the global resources of the hotel industry and allied partners, a worldwide hotel-based education development programme has been established. This provides a focus for the development of business social responsibility and a partnership model within the hospitality sector.

The programme began in Bangkok in 1995 as the Youth Career Development Programme (YCDP), with one hotel, nine high school graduates and two visionary leaders from UNICEF and the Pan Pacific Hotel Group. By October 2004 twenty-six hotels had joined the scheme in Bangkok and Manila and 900 graduates had gone on to careers in the hotel industry, banks and hospitals or were continuing their education (an evaluation shows that 56% have gone on to careers in hospitality, 20% into other sectors with scholarships offered every year from the nursing school and 20% into further education at the Open University whilst continuing to work to send money home). In Northern Thailand the programme has significantly reduced the number of young girls at risk of exploitation. The initiative was cited by UNAIDS as a best practice for the prevention of HIV/AIDS. The underlying rationale of the YCI methodology aims to foster sustainability of the programme and local ownership of all measures taken to the benefit of both the school graduates and the hotels.

Programme Design

Candidates are chosen whilst in their last year of secondary education, based on their desire to succeed and their lack of other opportunities. Invitations to apply for the programme are sent to pre-determined schools that have potential participants, and human resource personnel from participating hotels visit the schools to interview candidates. Local NGOs advise in-country as to the specific needs which must be tackled and where participants who are most deserving can be recruited from.

In terms of addressing 'real needs', the six-month life skills education provides participants with transferable life skills, transferable business skills as well as increased confidence through exposure to a business and customer-orientated environment. Participants are instructed in theory and receive hands-on training in technical areas such as housekeeping, laundry, engineering, kitchens, and food and beverage service. They are also taught Basic English. The training resources of participating hotels are shared, and the trainees meet regularly for joint 'life skills' sessions.

The original design of the programme takes into consideration the normal workings of a full service hotel and as such it is a transferable model that can be used to address the specific needs of a country or region. It uses the existing training programmes and standard operating procedures of the hotel as the basis for curriculum development.

The other key aspect of the programme is that it is designed for young people who have completed their school education. As the hotels must be able to incorporate the programme into their normal schedule, the participants must be educated to a certain level. The hotels are asked to deliver a life skills education programme that is within their capabilities; they are not trained in rehabilitation thus they cannot provide this service to young people they take on. The long-term impact of the fact that the participants are required to complete school is the incentive to stay at school and not drop out prematurely. This 'ripple' effect is much bigger than 'only' changing the lives of the participants on the programme, as other children in the villages also stay at school in anticipation of being able to apply to such a programme. Thus, the YCI not only increases the choices of the participants but also motivates potential candidates to continue education.

The participation in the programme further increases the trainees' credibility as a potential employee, and improves their marketability. In this regard, the final certificates and graduation ceremony are of extraordinary importance. The graduation ceremony is hosted by one of the hotels, with trainees providing all of the catering. Graduates are awarded an official certificate with the logos of all participating hotels. The example of Thailand highlighted the fact that the certificate is highly valued and has helped to motivate other children in participating schools to complete their education.

YCI also offers the tourism sector and host hotels an opportunity to contribute to the future careers of young people. Since the curriculum is delivered by the managers in the hotel, this programme in turn serves as a management development programme for the hotel staff who can teach subjects outside their day-to-day job and who can also mentor the participants. Most importantly, YCI provides a tangible process through which hotel companies and the tourism industry can deliver a quality corporate social responsibility programme at minimum cost through maximisation of resources.

When implementing the YCI in a given country, the initial process aims at securing the commitment of the management of Five Star/full service hotels to participate in the project. Thereafter an introduction by the hotel General Manager to his Human Resource team – the department managers and trainers – starts the process of developing the training programme. The IBLF has developed a YCI Implementation Guide for the hotels to facilitate this process. The hotels will then inform the YCI team how many participants they are able to accept as part of their programme.

Subsequently, an in-country coordinator is recruited from a local NGO. The in-country coordinator disseminates information about the YCI and details of the application process and works with local schools or other NGOs to identify the target audience (disadvantaged school leavers). This cooperation with appropriate organisations, including NGOs and neutral entities ensures transparency and avoids corruption. The hotel human resource team and in-country coordinator interview potential candidates who have satisfied screening criteria (i.e. must be 18 at start of programme).

Simultaneously, the human resource team of the participating hotels develop their training programme curriculum utilising the IBLF-YCI guide and their standard operating procedures. Thereafter, the actual training programme is implemented.

The Example of Romania

In Romania, the preparatory work on launching the YCI began in June 2004. Having secured the support of the JW Marriott Hotel in Bucharest an in-country coordinator was employed by the NGO Leaders-Foundation Romania. Subsequently, the participants were recruited with the help of local school heads and UNICEF.

On 30th March 2005, the pilot phase came to an end and six participants graduated, as a result of the JW Marriott providing a six-month life skills education programme to the selected participants. They have learned how to work as a team, how to interact with staff and guests in a retail environment, and the importance of being presentable and reliable in any job. The graduates have been awarded a certificate that demonstrates their successful completion of the YCI programme. Four of the participants have been hired by the JW Marriott Hotel.

Following this pilot phase, IBLF is now extending the programme to the Hilton hotel in Bucharest and twenty participants will be invited to participate in 2005. The specific project in Bucharest is funded by the German Federal Ministry for Development and Cooperation (BMZ) through the Sector Project of GTZ. Furthermore, due to the positive experience of the JW Marriott hotel in Bucharest in implementing the YCI, IBLF has also recently reached an agreement with Marriott to extend this initiative to other Marriott hotels worldwide.

Lessons Learned

Since the project was initiated in Thailand the modifications to it have been minimal as the programme was developed by a hotelier for hotels, hence the possibilities have been understood from the beginning. The most important lesson, which has been learned in terms of the implementation of the project around the world, is that the YCI needs to be understood and endorsed at the corporate level so that the corporate management can facilitate the introduction of the YCI to a given hotel at the level of the General Manager in a new country. This approach speeds up the process of gaining the local endorsement of a hotel and its commitment to implementing YCI according to international standards.

Transferability to Other Contexts

The success of the YCI raises the important question of its transferability to companies operating in other sectors. In this regard, 'capacity' and 'sustainability' are the two basic criteria, which would have to be met by a company wishing to participate in such an education programme. It is crucial to ensure that a company has the capacity to implement such empowerment training by having not only a dedicated training manager and enough staff at management level who can donate their time to provide the classroom training but also standard procedures that can become the basis for a training curriculum. In addition, with regard to ensuring the sustainability of such an approach, the training should be carried out as part of their day-to-day operations in order to make use of the existing resources so it can be part of the running of a successful business, rather than a philanthropic donation. Enhancing young people's lives can create a win-win situation with the development of the students and development of the management team as teachers.

The views expressed in this article are made in personal capacity and do not necessarily reflect the views of the OCEEA or the OSCE.

Empowerment of Orphans

Lora Beltcheva, Maria Petrova & Maria Tchomarova

Background

Even though Bulgaria adopted new anti-trafficking legislation and a National Action Plan against the Commercial Sexual Exploitation of Children in 2003 human trafficking remains to affect children and adolescents severely. One factor is the high unemployment rate, which makes it extremely difficult for young people to enter the labour market, especially for those coming from a difficult family background or lacking education. Hence a high-risk group are children brought up in orphanages. Presently no official data is available on the number of children becoming victims of trafficking after leaving the orphanages or the number of children involved in prostitution while living at the orphanages.

The Approach of Animus Association Foundation

Animus Association Foundation (AAF) is a non-governmental organisation, which develops care programmes for victims of violence, mainly women, adolescents and children. Their activities against trafficking focus on the following three main areas:

Rehabilitation Centre for Victims of Violence

The rehabilitation centre provides direct support to survivors of trafficking. It is a safe place where survivors of violence receive assistance from specially trained psychotherapists and social workers in an environment of understanding, confidentiality and tolerance.

Community Work

The community work of AAF includes lobby and prevention activities. Experiences of the work with victims of trafficking show that a long-term effect is only possible if psychotherapeutic work is combined with work in the community targeting the improvement of the environment in which victims will integrate. This community work is carried out on different levels: from multidisciplinary work and advocacy on concrete cases to training of professional groups and public awareness raising.

Training Centre

AAF established a training centre, which allows the organisation to transfer its experience and model of work to other organisations and institutions, thus contributing significantly to a change of social attitudes.

New Chances for Vulnerable Groups

In 2002 Animus Association started developing a new approach regarding prevention of trafficking in persons: empowerment for professional realisation. The essence of this new approach is creating access to information and resources for women and adolescents from vulnerable groups. The opportunities offered to risk groups can on the one hand facilitate their professional training and realisation and on the other hand decrease the risk of getting involved in trafficking through informed choice.

This approach focuses mainly on adolescents from orphanages who are one of the most vulnerable groups to trafficking. The reasons for this can be found in the specific social environment of institutions: the psychological atmosphere within orphanages, the conditions for growing up and socialising, the relationships between the adolescents and their supervisors and other personnel in the homes, the perspectives for the development of the adolescents and further aspects. At the moment orphanages and schools do neither offer programmes for personal nor for professional development of orphans. Many orphans are practically illiterate, socially incompetent and can hardly deal with social situations by the time they leave the institution. Therefore they can become easy victims of abuse. Frequently their threshold for seeking help is high, as they do not expect to receive much support anyway; they often deny their problems and are unaware of the potential assistance, which could be provided by the community. Hence AAF concentrates on girls and boys aged between 13 and 21 from four homes in Sofia and five in the countryside. The specialised staff working with the orphans (directors, psychologists, social workers) also benefit from this support as they receive training in the framework of the empowerment project and thus improve their own professional work.

The following stages are included into the approach: realising the present situation, outlining potential opportunities, planning the desired change, fulfilling and achieving set goals. With this initiative AAF addresses two important elements of life skill development: on the one hand presenting the necessary conditions for successful development and on the other hand raising awareness about the circumstances that may lead to failure and falling into a situation of abuse.

The following concept was tested in the framework of a project funded by BMZ through the Sector Project of GTZ. It was developed particularly for young people raised in institutions and consists of four main pillars:

- Training
  The training is organised as a form of group work for adolescents who are about to leave the orphanage. It offers the opportunity to learn about trafficking in human beings and how young people can avoid becoming victims of such a crime. It consists of five modules using interactive techniques that facilitate the process of empowerment by setting goals and working towards their realisation. Empowerment is presented as a process through which people can learn to discover and use their inner potentials. Important issues discussed during the trainings are: views and attitudes of participants concerning their job perspectives; setting of short-term and long-term goals; goal realisation; necessary skills for finding employment; risk of abuse and possible types of abuse in the process of job seeking; the issue of trafficking and how it can be avoided.

- Individual Consultations
  The consultations are aimed at encouraging adolescents to generate ideas and plan their job perspectives. The adolescents are assisted in setting realistic goals and working towards achieving them. Moreover, adolescents receive advice on how to find job vacancies, how to best apply for jobs, and how to achieve higher (or different) professional qualification.

- Correspondence Programme
  The correspondence programme, based on the exchange of letters and e-mails, gives the adolescents the opportunity to keep in contact with the social workers and consultants after the finalisation of the trainings. Advantages are the easy accessibility, the chance for anonymity (if preferred) and the possibility of exchanging information. Until now, the problems most frequently reported within received correspondence were experience of violence (or the risk of violence), conflicts or barriers in intimate relationships or friendships and the risk of trafficking.

- Sensitisation of Specialised Staff in Orphanages
  To achieve a sustainable empowerment of orphans AAF trains the specialised staff working in orphanages. AAF aims to enhance the staff's skills around preventing violence and to sensitise them for trafficking in human beings. Furthermore they learn how to support the empowerment process of the orphans. This is achieved by work contacts, work meetings, trainings and methodological support in applying prevention practices.

The trainings and individual consultations are designed and conducted by specialists in the area of prevention of trafficking and support of victims. AAF sets great store by well-trained experts who have psychological and training competence. Two main indicators help measuring the impact of the new approach: One is the number of adolescents who have taken part in the trainings, in the individual consultations and in the correspondence programme. Another quantitative indicator is the number of specialised staff who now have the knowledge and the will to reproduce this model.

Success and Challenges

Following the trainings AAF considers its main success to be a change of the orphans' attitudes towards victims of trafficking as well as an increased level of self-reflection. From a disregard for victims and the denial of a risk for themselves, the majority of trained children were now able to identify risk situations. These changes of attitude were observed within group sessions, through evaluation questionnaires and dialogue with the supervisors. Further positive results that could be asserted through the final evaluation were an improved practical knowledge on how to seek help in dangerous situations as well as enhanced job-seeking skills.

Through the work on self-image, self-representation and goal setting and through the rehearsal of different roles it became clear that these children have great difficulties in defining themselves and their ideas of autonomy. Regarding their professional orientation and realisation it became obvious that much time as well as individual work needs to be invested to compensate their deficits. Hence it is necessary that empowerment work has to be carried out on a long-term basis. Special attention should be paid on topics such as identity, self-esteem, goals and development of social skills. To reduce the risk of orphans being trafficked the involvement of personnel in orphanages is fundamental.

Lessons Learned

Measures of preventing trafficking in human beings among orphans are not limited to awareness raising about the topic as such, but have to be directed towards the holistic empowerment of their social skills, including training in positive strategies for finding jobs and achieving financial independence.

Effective prevention, based on empowerment for professional realisation requires new methods of training, designed specifically to meet the needs of young people raised in institutions. Their partially marginalised social position calls for the combination of individual and group training techniques and approaches that will enhance their social skills through group work and at the same time make them feel secure and protected by the safe group setting when difficult topics and questions arise. Furthermore, integration of specialised staff has proven essential for a successful implementation of the empowerment of orphans.

Potentials of Community-Based Approaches

Lilijana Vasić

Background

Serbia is primarily a country of destination for particularly women and girls being trafficked from Moldova. However, the number of trafficked persons originating from Serbia is rising as well. Both countries, Serbia and Moldova, lack a comprehensive integrated prevention programme that would address trafficking in human beings on the community level. The Christian Children's Fund (CCF) started to bridge this gap by raising awareness in local communities and by strengthening their skills to discuss trafficking and related issues in the open.

Christian Children's Fund's Anti-Trafficking Approach

Within Christian Children's Fund's child and youth anti-trafficking programmes, the primary objectives are:

- to work in participation with children and young people in order to ensure the protection of their rights, to listen to their opinions and to facilitate a balanced decision-making process on overall welfare and protection;
- to develop an effective network of stakeholders in the community as well as on the national and regional level. Stakeholders include children, parents, families, central and local governments, INGOs, local NGOs, the judiciary and professionals who are responsible for education, health, social welfare and the care of any child;
- to actively influence the development and implementation of policies, procedures and legislation in the field of children's rights and child trafficking;
- to educate those responsible for the welfare of children in protecting the rights of the child;
- to build on and expand CCF's current capacity with regard to the target groups as well as on the national, regional and global levels.

Community-Based Intervention

CCF concentrates on prevention-related projects. In Serbia, as well as in Moldova, there is no comprehensive system to prevent trafficking of children and women. Within the field of prevention CCF concentrates its efforts on young people and gears its activities towards youth living outside bigger towns. The reasons for choosing to work with young people living in semi-rural areas are simple: the majority of anti-trafficking programmes are aimed at protection, assistance, repatriation and to some degree reintegration of victims, while very few programmes concentrate on the prevention of child trafficking. Most prevention projects are performed in big cities and regional centres and focus on general awareness-raising campaigns. Community-based youth anti-trafficking projects need to involve the beneficiaries, who develop their own ideas about what can be effectively done in relation to what is needed most in their own communities. Since community-based projects have proven successful all around the world CCF chose this approach for its youth anti-trafficking projects.

The population in Southern Serbia is divided into three almost equally large ethnic groups: Albanians, Serbians and Roma. The distinct separateness of the closed ethnic groups affects the successful development of the area in a negative way. However, the traditional patriarchal and closed family structure found in this region is well suited for community-based and peer-to-peer approaches. The project was seen as an opportunity to initiate a joint community-based response to an existing problem as well as to train local youth on how to put their ideas into action. Based on the fact that people in general feel a stronger motivation and higher responsibility for action when implementing their own ideas than when an 'outsider' tells them what to do CCF inspired youth to develop and implement their own projects.

In patriarchal societies, young people often feel particularly helpless and find it difficult to approach their elders with questions about sensitive issues. Hence, CCF decided to provide relevant up-to-date information on frequently asked questions for trained young peer educators. This enabled a smooth dialogue and the certainty that suggested topics and activities were linked to the interest of the target group. CCF counted on the enthusiasm, willingness and energy of young people to bring changes to the current situation, also emphasising the fact that uninformed young people are the most vulnerable and prone to manipulation from traffickers.

The positive response triggered a replication of the same approach in Moldova, the country of origin for most of the foreign trafficked victims in Serbia. At the same time the programme aimed at initiating links and cooperation between the youth from Moldova and Serbia, two countries that stand at the opposite ends of the trafficking route. The activities of the programme in both countries were funded by the BMZ through the Sector Project implemented by GTZ.

Training and Implementation of Community-Based Projects

In Serbia as well as in Moldova, CCF worked with individual young activists, youth associations and representatives from various institutions working with children, schools and volunteers. Project partners included the Child Rights Centre and its young lawyers that are trained educators on legal, social theoretical and practical aspects of child trafficking, as well as Beosupport, a youth NGO specialising in peer education and OFER, a Roma youth NGO specialising in Roma education and youth mobilisation. CCF and its partners facilitated an initial training for young people focusing on enabling youth activists to autonomously write, budget, implement and evaluate anti-trafficking projects in cooperation with the local youth in the target communities.

In Southern Serbia youth activists from all three ethnic groups (Albanian, Serbian, Roma) participated in the initial training. Participants in Moldova came also mainly from rural areas. In both countries children and youth at risk, their parents and the wider population benefited indirectly from the measure through the higher level of information. One of the outcomes was an awareness-raising campaign for the prevention of trafficking in children organised by local youth. This initiative also celebrated the Week of Children's Rights featuring a free theatre show in each municipality of the target areas, drawing sessions on themes related to children's rights and numerous other workshops and conferences. A major achievement was the initiation of a series of round-table discussions on child trafficking with representatives from local authorities including the police. These sessions were broadcast at the most popular local radio-stations.

Additionally CCF's project promoted partnerships and direct links between the target communities and raised their interest in further joint prevention of child trafficking projects. Following this, CCF Moldova is extending the project "Peer Education in Preventing Child Trafficking" in another district of Moldova. This follow-up project receives funding from the BMZ through the GTZ implemented programme to improve the socio-economic conditions of women in the Region of Cotesti.

Empowerment Through Engagement

The expected impact of the joint project in Southern Serbia and Moldova included raising awareness about issues related to child trafficking. All youth activists have become disseminators of real facts and information and are keen to do more to inform their local communities about the problem and its consequences. As one participant of the initial training in South Serbia stated:

> My eyes are now opened. I know what my rights are and I can fight for them, but I will teach my friends who do not know that they have the same rights like any other man.

Some unexpected positive outcomes include the interest of the local media for all project activities as well as the willingness of local and border police representatives to participate in the local round-table discussions organised by young people. Youth activists also succeeded in awaking public opinion on trafficking in human beings, especially children and youth. Furthermore, the eagerness of local youth, both in

Southern Serbia and in Moldova, to start other joint projects within their communities and jointly in both countries has to be noted and commended.

Highly unexpected was the number of girls that participated especially in Southern Serbia; half of the participants and consequently local project implementers were girls. Traditionally, in these municipalities, girls are not allowed to socialise in public, let alone to travel from one municipality to another for training or project implementation. Sensitive and vigilant lobbying efforts and discussions with their parents and elder members of the families led to initial agreements for girls to participate in the project.

Due to public awareness raising it became obvious how vulnerable communities are to techniques used by child traffickers. This new perspective on trafficking is reflected in the following evaluation after the initial training in Moldova:

> I knew approximately what 'the business' meant, but I have found out very concretely during these few days that everyone is at risk.

For decades, the general climate in both countries has been characterised by a strict obedience to the authorities and little or no self-initiative. Even the youth, although growing up in a somewhat different context have not yet developed their self-initiative or self-determination, but rather wait for someone else to make decisions for them. When tackling community problems, the usual pattern is for an outsider to come in, to lecture and to determine what will be done, with the youth as inactive listeners. This CCF project has now encouraged young people to think about what *they* can do themselves. First results have encouraged them and have given them inspiration to do more and to engage more actively in community development.

Representatives from the local authorities in the three Southern Serbian municipalities participated in the project and have expressed their readiness to take part in future activities. Other NGOs and international organisations (especially in Moldova) have shown interest in either joint projects with CCF or in attracting youth activists from the aforementioned local organisations for their own future projects.

Lessons Learned

- The added value to any proposed action is immeasurable when the local communities formulate their own ideas for the project and then are authorised to implement it. The responsibility for the success of one's project produces more commitment, a higher level of responsibility and better local supervision of the activities in the field.
- Even though there is a certain level of local awareness about child trafficking, the fear about the possible consequences of breaking taboos and openly discussing this topic prevails in all areas. Therefore the initial catalyst needs to be an external facilitator who opens the discussions and presents the facts.

- The selection of participants from rural areas of Southern Serbia and Moldova was strategically well placed; it achieved a higher impact since victims usually come from the rural areas where there is an obvious lack of information and NGO activity. Due to the dire economic situation rural areas lean themselves to being more 'favourable' for 'recruitment' of victims.
- A direct personal approach to parents and families made it possible to increase the number of girls participating in community projects, especially in Serbia.
- Finally, local community projects attract a high level of interest from the local media.

In Moldova, this was the very first attempt to organise youth NGOs and activists from geographically different places to work together within one project. Initially staff members of CCF were sceptical that it would be possible to get people from geographically diverse areas to work together, but the success of this project has inspired them to try other similar youth and community-based projects.

The ultimate impact of this project has been the enthusiasm and motivation of young people from Moldova and Serbia to work effectively together in order to prevent more children being trafficked from their local communities. However, further training, access to information as well as financial support is required.

Hotlines – An Effective Tool for Outreach Work

Kateryna Cherepakha & Olga Kalashnyk

Background

Hotline services have proven to be an effective tool for establishing initial contact and offering rapid support without a lot of bureaucracy, whilst guaranteeing the anonymity of the caller. In recent years, they have been used increasingly for victims of human trafficking in both the victims' countries of origin and in destination countries. Victims of human trafficking have little trust in public institutions. Hence, an NGO-run hotline can build the much-needed link between the victim and all available support services in order for victims to make an informed decision about their next steps.

La Strada's hotline was established in the framework of the Ukrainian Comprehensive National Programme and aims to provide informational and consultative assistance to Ukrainians, who are going abroad, as well as social assistance to trafficked persons and their families.

La Strada's Hotline Approach

In its capacity as the national centre for preventing trafficking in persons La Strada Ukraine opened its first hotline in November 1997. The hotline service is conducted in close cooperation with specialists from various governmental institutions, which provide competent advice in finding best ways to assist Ukrainian citizens. It was created to disseminate information about possibilities, conditions, regulations and potential dangers of employment for Ukrainians abroad as well as to provide counselling to trafficked persons and their family members. At the beginning, the hotline had only limited resources at its disposal and therefore operated only once a week, which naturally reduced its effectiveness and capacity to quickly intervene and assist. Consequently, more fundraising allowed for more consultants so that the hotline could operate daily. From the beginning of its work until April 2005 more than 25,000 consultations were carried out via the hotline, with 7,000 consultations provided only in 2004.

La Strada's hotline was the first hotline on the problem of trafficking in human beings established on the territory of the Former Soviet Union. It offers an emergency service providing anonymous informational and social assistance by phone. The hotline's accessibility plays a crucial role. This could be observed by the tremendous increase of calls especially from the regions after the nation-wide free phone hotline was introduced in 2002. Both, men and women, make use of the hotline services. In addition La Strada provides online consultations via the Internet, through the organisation's website.

Standards for Hotline Consultants

The number of persons, who require consultations on leaving for abroad and the number of trafficked persons in need for counselling, demonstrate the importance of hotline services. Apart from offering preventive consultations hotlines also receive requests on missing people abroad. About 62% of the incoming calls are about working, studying or vacations abroad, which can also be seen as prevention of trafficking. Counselling of family members of missing persons constitute around 5% of the calls received by the hotline team. Victim assistance as well as assistance to family members of returned victims make up about 1% of the calls. Another field of advice is consultation about judicial procedures in trafficking cases; 52 calls altogether referring to this topic have been responded to so far.

After having received a request and collecting all necessary information to adequately respond to it, a consultant creates a file and engages the relevant bodies. In case of an inquiry of a victim of trafficking the hotline consultant takes the necessary steps to provide further social assistance. La Strada's consultants work with the principles of anonymity, individuality and confidentiality, which help to create a trustful atmosphere while in contact with a client. The hotline consultants are skilled in advising customers in different situations, also in areas outside the usual hotline topics. Any caller receives a positive response and can call as many times as she/he needs to. When comparing telephone consultations to other forms of communication the following advantages can be established:

- a client requesting general information calls from a rather comfortable outset;
- after dialling a number she/he can immediately talk to a consultant;
- nobody is able to see the caller, which gives her/him much wanted anonymity;
- one can finish a conversation at any moment.

Staff members of hotline services must be prepared for the fact that the women and girls calling them for immediate help can be in various dangerous situations. Callers may still be held against their will, they may have been caught in a police raid or are unprotected on the streets. Staff must respond appropriately, depending on the situation that the woman finds herself in, and determine what advice to give based on as sound an assessment as possible of the situation.

A hotline can be described as a 'big ear' since the main work of a hotline consultant is 'hearing' beyond the spoken word. Such work needs maximum concentration and builds on perception and empathy. There is a big difference between 'hearing' and 'listening', which is crucial to know for qualified hotline consultants, who may run the risk of becoming easily 'burned out' when confronting themselves with cases in a too emotional and sensitive manner. To avoid burnout effects and to improve their professional level the hotline consultants participate in trainings and receive supervision on a regular basis.

Information as Key to Making Informed Decisions

A certain percentage of hotline calls require substantial follow-up through counselling and practical assistance. For this reason one telephone consultation is divided into several stages, including queries to other specialised institutions and continuous monitoring. However, the majority of phone calls require only single consultations on practical issues such as:

- visa regulations for Ukrainian citizens who want to go abroad;
- possible consequences of illegal employment abroad;
- information about legal ways for employment of Ukrainian nationals abroad;
- contact details of non-governmental organisations abroad that offer information and assistance;
- information about foreign legislation on the status of foreigners, migrants and trafficked persons;
- contact details of Ukrainian government agencies that carry out anti-trafficking prevention work;

- contact details of Ukrainian Embassies and Consulates abroad;
- contact details of foreign diplomatic representations in Ukraine.

Besides this information hotline consultants give advice on how to migrate for work or studies abroad. This approach is based on previous experience from partner organisations, La Strada in Poland and in the Czech Republic, and has proven to be practical, useful and essential.

All hotline calls are registered in a special record with information being added to an electronic database in order to facilitate easy access. With the approval of the caller the following specifics are registered: her/his age, education, place of living (city or village without home address), source of information, query and brief outline of answer. Complicated cases and repeated calls are marked specifically.

Special attention is being paid to the regions where recruitment of women for work abroad is a prevalent problem. In 2000, with the support of the OSCE, La Strada Ukraine launched a new project to enhance regional hotlines of partner organisations that seek to:

- strengthen the network of local women NGOs in Ukraine working on anti-trafficking prevention;
- create an effective system of consulting Ukrainian citizens on anti-trafficking issues tailored to the needs of the specific region.

Many of the local NGOs that are involved in regional hotlines are also very engaged in furthering policies and strategies within their regions. Their representatives are often members of multidisciplinary regional commissions that coordinate anti-trafficking initiatives locally.

Results

Specialists from La Strada analyse the queries from callers and determine new strategies for preventive work. In this way hotlines also help in revising and defining target groups for further preventive and educational activities eventually leading to the development of recommendations for Ukrainian labour migrants in cooperation with the Ukrainian State Employment Agency.

In short, hotlines prove to be effective when the operating organisations use a comprehensive and solution-oriented approach to anti-trafficking prevention. Hotline work needs to be connected to information campaigns in order to distribute the number and nature of the hotline services. Only active cooperation between governmental agencies and non-governmental organisations will help to solve complicated cases. It is also crucial to set-up a solid network of NGOs, religious organisations and Centres of Social Services for Youth in order to render adequate direct assistance to trafficked persons.

Lessons Learned

Only targeted information campaigns can ensure that a hotline becomes sufficiently well known among the relevant target groups. An exchange of experience with specialist counselling units can be helpful for the development of creative information and education campaigns. Since hotlines work as a sort of information turntable, it is essential to network and cooperate closely with relevant organisations and experts in other branches. These include local specialist counselling units to which callers can be referred as well as human rights organisations, embassies of countries of origin of trafficked women, the police and judiciary, social offices, aliens offices, etc.

The experience of La Strada Ukraine shows that a free phone number should be offered for the hotline, since this further reduces resistance on the part of potential callers. The basic financing of the hotline should take the form of state, local authority or municipal funding, in order to guarantee a sustainable, long-term service. There are, however, ways of involving additional partners. Within the framework of media cooperation, public private partnerships or social sponsoring, for instance, the hotline can work with telecommunications businesses, PR and advertising agencies and the press in a variety of ways to keep costs down.

As the demands on the hotline staff members are complex, they must be well educated on the topic of human trafficking and trained in psychosocial skills. Furthermore they should have trainings in crisis intervention, and an in-depth knowledge of police activities, civil and criminal law options, and additional counselling and support available.

Non-Discriminatory Approaches to Address Clients in Prostitution

Christiane Howe

Background

The living and working conditions of foreign prostitutes in Germany are generally harsh. Many prostitutes live on the legal borderline; hence, they can be exploited and subjected to violent abuse, including forms of trafficking. Consequently, many measures against trafficking in women for sexual exploitation focus on victim protection and criminal prosecution, they concentrate mainly on the women affected, care of victims prepared to testify as witnesses, assistance in repatriation and income-generating measures.

So far the demand side has been neglected in anti-trafficking approaches. Little information is available on clients of prostitutes and possibilities of outreach to clients. Most of the existing international approaches tackle the problem from an abolitionist perspective. Approaches which address clients in a setting where prostitution is regularised (like in Switzerland and most European countries) or accepted (like in Germany and the Netherlands) can be found in the context of health prevention. Until now few measures have been implemented to directly sensitise clients for trafficking issues.

To assess possible approaches nine campaigns in Germany and Switzerland have been analysed for results, lessons learned and emerging opportunities to approach clients (e.g. through the Internet). The evaluation has been commissioned by the Sector Project of GTZ. Funds were made available by BMZ and the Federal Ministry of Family and Women's Affairs (BMFSFJ). Out of the campaigns analysed, only one explicitly addressed prostitute clients as a target group in connection with trafficking in women: the Terre des Femmes campaign. Others tackled clients as a target group for AIDS prevention. To illustrate the examples, two approaches, one in Germany, the Terre des Femmes campaign, and one in Switzerland in the context of HIV/ AIDS prevention will be briefly described, lessons learned and open questions will be presented.

Approaching Clients of Prostitutes through Campaigns

To adequately and successfully address clients it is important to take their motives, situation and questions into account and to demonstrate acceptance of their actions, i.e. to give them a sense of being 'allowed' to be a client. Campaigns also have to consider the difference between the client target group and the general male population. On the one hand, clients are afraid of disapproval and forfeiting anonymity; on the other hand, they do not necessarily define themselves as clients. Men are only clients for a limited time, hence, clients are difficult to demarcate as a target group.

Research suggests that access and contact to clients can be established through an affirmative and tolerant approach. This also implies the opportunity of providing clients with information on sex work, health and sex education. Involving clients of prostitutes and cooperating with them is a prerequisite for successful campaigns. It is conceivable to use their specialised knowledge of the setting of prostitution. It is also essential to address and examine the prostitute-client relationship. This is defined by the place and conditions of the relationship, the public perception and norms of sexual relationships (what is generally accepted and what is permitted) as well as the gender identity.

There are different means of approaching clients: Street-work, telephone hotlines, poster and postcard campaigns as well as using the Internet. They all imply advantages and disadvantages. A hotline for example is a low-threshold way for clients of prostitutes and men in general seeking information. Having both men and women answering the hotline has proven to be an appropriate approach. Another tool to reach clients of prostitutes is the Internet, which promises a high level of anonymity and can provide a broad outreach. In Germany, clients already discuss the issues and problems connected to trafficking in specific Internet fora. Public awareness-raising campaigns specifically addressing clients are also promising.

Don Juan Project

The Swiss project "Don Juan" is an HIV/AIDS prevention project implemented by Swiss AIDS Control. Since September 1999, the project addresses clients directly about twice a year and aims to inform them about HIV/AIDS and other sexually transmitted diseases (STDs), thus raising their awareness for prevention. Direct face-to-face client outreach in the milieu and education is part of the project conducted by appropriately trained men and women, called 'educators'. The aim of the project is to influence client behaviour by raising awareness of infection by STDs. The activities are temporary interventions.

The prostitutes in the area are involved in the project planning and informed before the measures start. The venue for client education is a tent set up at a central location and fitted out with erotic pictures. Information material as a means of starting a conversation includes matches, printed beer mats and moist tissues for the prostitutes.

In the choice of qualified educators experience in discussing gender roles, the ability to be impartial in dealing with clients and skills in approaching strangers in a communicative way play a crucial role. The results of the project evaluation show that a major success criterion for educators is their prior experience in working with prostitutes. Men who have themselves been clients make more successful educators, because this fosters empathy with and a basic tolerance of the clients approached.

From September to November 1999, the educators spoke to over 800 clients. With almost half of them in-depth discussions were held on HIV/AIDS risks, methods of condom use, other sexually transmitted diseases and everyday sexual conduct. The experience shows that an average of about four to five out of ten clients can be expected to talk. Communication with the educators encourages clients who already apply safer sex rules to continue. Of the clients who do not use condoms regularly in contacts with prostitutes, about two-thirds were induced to consider changes in their behaviour. Preventive work proved particularly efficient by addressing risks of infection with STD in non-vaginal intercourse. Many 'risk clients' know surprisingly little about this. This kind of preventive work meets a real need in the target group.

Terre des Femmes Campaign

In November/December 1999 for a total of three weeks, Terre des Femmes (TDF), a German women's NGO, launched the awareness-raising campaign "Men Show the Way". The campaign, which included posters for advertising hoardings, flyers as well as a booklet to provide men with background information and addresses of advisory centres, was directed explicitly at men. Furthermore the campaign set up a temporary telephone hotline for male counselling.

The primary aim of the campaign was to convey that trafficking in women is a human rights violation, which imposes coercive conditions of work and life and exploits the labour power and sexuality of women. It sought to make men in general and the clients of prostitutes in particular aware of the issue and discuss their role and co-responsibility as customers of the sex industry. Even though contempt for and hatred of women may be inherent to some clients' relationship to prostitutes, this is not generally the case. TDF assumed that most customers reject violence and when appropriately informed and motivated may reappraise and change their behaviour as consumers. The campaign was based on the assumption that many clients are not aware of the situation of foreign prostitutes (no residence permit, no right to work, no entitlement to insurance). It was presupposed that customers are prepared to help women in enforced prostitution, if they are informed about the practical steps they can take.

The campaign was not directed against prostitution in general or foreign prostitutes in particular, the slogans were not supposed to pass moral judgement on the clients of prostitutes or stigmatise them as criminals. Quite the contrary, the intended message was that men should only go to women who choose to be prostitutes. It was important to convey to the target group that women were not the only ones to benefit from action taken, the line of argument being that clients themselves would also gain because only a fair business relationship can provide the basis for a more agreeable service.

Lessons Learned

The evaluation has shown that clients of prostitutes can be reached through campaigns if the campaigns are tailored to their interests and questions. Even the critical topic of trafficking in women for forced prostitution captures the interest of clients and is connected with concrete questions they have. In addition, female sex workers felt supported in their efforts to comply with safer sex rules and were in favour of broader and more frequent client education. Hence, it is worth following the approaches already implemented.

Little criticism and few misgivings were voiced towards the evaluated campaigns. Most of the concerns that were brought up before starting the campaigns had to do with the supposed disruption of the prostitute's business transaction. In some of the campaigns, particular criticism was levelled at the objectives and methods: moralising undertone and the issue of arousing fears of infection. These concerns need to be taken into consideration when planning campaigns that address clients. The following points highlight the major lessons learned when addressing clients in prostitution:

- An attitude of acceptance is important, as it is to highlight that the men should gain something from the measure. A pleasing approach that captures the attention and facilitates contact should be chosen.
- Cooperation, networking and exchange of experience with existing and allied institutions and actors are indispensable. Close cooperation in planning and implementation with prostitutes, social counsellors of prostitutes' organisations, prostitute clients and brothel operators has an extremely positive effect on the projects, as does cooperation with male counsellors.
- The discussions about prostitution should be framed as a social discussion looking at gender patterns and male and female sexuality. There is a need for practical frank sex education. The approach should have the general aim of empowering both sexes to articulate themselves and enable them to engage in open dialogue.
- Public relations via various media (reports in newspapers, radio, TV) are useful flanking measures as the experience shows that people respond to this.
- Information materials and gadgets have proven to be very effective if their contents are well prepared and produced.
- Foreign clients such as visitors to large trade fairs should be addressed according to their cultural background and in their corresponding language. Hence, information materials should also be available in the respective languages.
- Localities and conditions are major contributing factors for the success of such projects. For example, client outreach on the street appears to be promising where there is a district they visit as they can be anonymously approached with little disruption in the 'second row'. Greater restraint and discretion is needed in clubs, saunas and bars. Here activities can only be carried out in close cooperation with owners and staff.
- Especially in face-to-face client education, continuity has proven an asset as the educators benefited from the recognition effect.

Specific recommendations can be drawn on how to address the problem of trafficking: Many clients are rather uncertain about the issue of trafficking in women and are concerned what they can do to help practically. Others would like to have 'clear' indicators for recognising whether a woman has been forced into prostitution. As such indicators are difficult to develop clients should be provided with contact information of counselling centres and be sensitised for the different dimensions of trafficking.

These questions need to be taken into account in any outreach activity or campaign. This may also mean establishing appropriate information and advisory services:

- Instead of directly trying to help, campaigns should encourage clients to provide presumed trafficked women with contacts of advisory centres. Some trafficked women can be difficult to reach through street social work and direct contact; pointers from clients could be helpful.
- An important but nevertheless difficult and ambivalent point for appealing to men generally is their 'helpful' side. Helping women can seem to be a viable quality of what men think of as manliness. However, the situation of the women is not easy for the clients to assess. What appears to the clients as coercion may be seen quite differently by the prostitutes. Campaigns should therefore consider what effectively helps presumed trafficked women rather than further stigmatising prostitutes.
- The Internet is a suitable medium to approach clients as the issue of trafficking is already discussed by clients in the Internet; it is comparatively inexpensive and has a low threshold. As evaluations of the German Internet sex market have shown, it is important to integrate webmasters, clients and sex workers in the conceptualisation of such Internet approaches. Furthermore, the measures need to be adapted according to local needs (Langanke 2004).
- A discussion about the development of quality standards for places where sexual services are provided and a related quality certification constitutes a next possible step. Standards could enhance access to the different stakeholders, particularly the clients, and would also foster a general impartial discussion within prostitution. This would help to ensure humane working conditions that meet statutory labour standards and guarantee the transparency of these establishments. It would also help clients to choose legal establishments. These requirements cannot be inferred from existing legal provisions. Furthermore, brothel operators and owners profit from such standards as they can disassociate themselves from illegal practices. The respectable providers will then acquire more legal certainty.

Under the new prostitution legislation in Germany where prostitution is recognised, the public can be informed better and more extensively. This could help reduce the discrimination and stigmatisation of the persons involved.

Approaches to Victim Support

Trafficked persons may cross our paths in every day life without us even knowing that they are victims of a serious crime. Trafficked persons are exploited in a variety of labour sectors, from construction, agriculture, and domestic work to the sex industry or as providers of human organs. Furthermore, children are also forced to beg and steal. Victims of trafficking are subjected to a multitude of physical, psychological and sexual abuses at all stages of the trafficking cycle. Traffickers manipulate trafficked victims on a psychological level and often also exert physical violence. Caught between dependency and violence, victims frequently do not dare to escape or often simply cannot find their way out and away from their traffickers.

Anti-trafficking activists advocate for establishing victim support systems to make it easier for trafficked persons to escape the ordeal of continuous abuse and violence. States have a positive obligation to protect people within their jurisdiction from human rights violations committed by states or by individuals. It is the prime responsibility of a state to ensure that trafficked persons are able to access adequate support and assistance. However, trafficked persons would often rather approach non-governmental service providers as traffickers may also tell victims they will be imprisoned or punished by authorities if they escape. Furthermore, trafficked persons may mistrust officials, such as police, especially if officials were somehow involved in them being trafficked.

Victim Identification and Referral

Key to any possible, let alone successful provision of victim support is the proper identification of those likely to be trafficked. Since victims are unlikely to come forward themselves, they are most often identified in the course of investigations by police or labour inspectors, who ideally should refer presumed trafficked persons to specialised support institutions. The identification process can be complex and time-consuming. It may take weeks or even months for a trafficked person to break out of post-traumatic stress disorder, to be able to speak about the ordeal and to arrive at an informed decision regarding next steps. Victims should be duly informed about their rights and obligations including the possibility of initiating judicial proceedings against traffickers. They must furthermore be entitled to an appropriate reflection period, which is long enough to enable them to recover and make an informed decision about these alternatives. The reflection period, however, should not be conditional upon the victim's willingness to cooperate with investigative or prosecution authorities.

Some countries have already adopted sophisticated means of identifying and supporting victims, basing identification on a joint assessment of state authorities and non-governmental organisations. Both the Italian and the Belgian system are models for identifying presumed trafficked persons and referring them to high quality service centres, most often run by non-governmental organisations.

Temporary Stay in Country of Destination

What happens to a victim of trafficking after having been identified and granted a reflection period? While the UN Trafficking Protocol gives minimum standards for the protection of victims of trafficking, the recently adopted Council of Europe Trafficking Convention develops more explicit measures to protect and promote the rights of trafficked victims. Under the Convention, during the reflection period trafficked persons must have access to appropriate and free housing, legal, psychological and material assistance and emergency medical treatment. However, safe and appropriate housing should not bear comparison with jails or other detention facilities as trafficked persons need to be treated as victims of crime and should not be locked up even if it was claimed that it was 'for their own safety'.

So far, with a few country exceptions, temporary residence permits are granted to trafficked persons who agree to cooperate with police. This generally entails that a trafficked person is allowed to stay in the country of destination until the testimony is heard. Residence permits should be renewable and made on the basis of harm suffered and risk of harm upon return rather than only in connection with the victim's willingness to testify against traffickers.

Immediately returning a victim to the country of origin will not solve the causes that led the person to be trafficked in the first place. It may put them again in danger from traffickers. It has further unrecognised and detrimental repercussions in that trafficked persons who return against their will are unlikely to speak out about their experiences and exploitation and thus will not prevent others from similar traps. State authorities also do have a vested interest in allowing trafficked persons to stay in countries of destination since criminal investigations still heavily rely on victim-witness' testimonies. Deporting trafficked persons closes potential victim cooperation with authorities from the very outset. The better the victim support structures function and the better coordinated they are, the more likely it is that trafficked persons signal their willingness to cooperate and serve as reliable witnesses. Victim advocates warn against rushing victim-witnesses through repeated interviews and call for protection measures so that evidence can be given safely; this avoids "re-victimisation" in the course of the criminal proceedings.

Those trafficked persons who do seek justice and signal willingness to cooperate with law enforcement require adequate victim-witness protection measures. Individual victims may have very different needs with regard to the level of protection required whereas privacy must be respected. This is essential not only for the victim's physical safety, but also to improve their chances for social integration. Media stories or research disclosing the victim's identity lead to further stigmatisation and expose trafficked persons and their loved ones to additional risks.

While residing lawfully in the country of destination, trafficked persons should be granted access to work, education and vocational training. More consideration should be given to ensuring their right to compensation as victims of crime under international and European standards. Article 15 of the Council of Europe Trafficking Convention explicitly establishes the victim's right to compensation and suggests that payments should be facilitated either

> [...] through the establishment of a fund for victim compensation or measures or programmes aimed at social assistance and social integration of victims, which should be funded by governments and complimentary sourced by the assets confiscated from traffickers.

Safe Return and Effective Social Inclusion

The safe return of trafficked victims to their countries of origin remains an operational challenge. Voluntary returns are frequently facilitated either through informal NGO networks or by the International Organization for Migration. In the worst-case scenario, victims will not be identified as trafficked persons and are deported as illegal migrants. In either case, returns often occur without having conducted a risk assessment prior to departure from the country of destination. Support available in countries of origin varies greatly.

In general, victim support upon return should help overcoming prevalent stigmatisation of returnees as well as it should empower victims to take control of their lives. In the European context, so far only few programmes are effective in enabling trafficked persons to reorientate themselves in their home countries. Such programmes also provide more medium and long-term assistance in (re-) integration where needed. Victims, who return must be able to break out of the trafficking cycle by addressing their social and economic needs.

Inter-Agency Cooperation to Protect the Best Interest of the Trafficked Person

As outlined above, victims need proper housing, psychological care, material and legal assistance, medical treatment and a secure environment. Various governmental and non-governmental stakeholders provide these services. Only when they coordinate their actions well will they succeed in building an impermeable anti-trafficking net that – on the one hand assists and supports all victims so that no-one falls through and – on the other hand intercepts and catches perpetrators so that they are being held responsible for their crimes. A net has at least two dimensions, namely a horizontal cutting across all thematic sectors, and a vertical, specifying all levels from the community to the international level. Therefore it is essential to pursue a cross-sector and cross-dimensional approach to support trafficked persons and prosecute traffickers. The underlying principle for any of this certainly has to be the well being of the victims including the promotion and protection of their human rights. Furthermore, cooperation is also needed internationally and across borders.

So, how does one create an effective victim support structure? Governmental bodies and non-governmental organisations meet and discuss what support they can offer to victims of trafficking. After assessing trafficked persons' needs and mapping these against existing support infrastructure, stakeholders develop a plan that enables victims to access prompt and tailor-made support and protection. The victim's perspective should be an integral part of any such assessment. Experience shows that a multidisciplinary and collaborative approach in identifying, referring and supporting victims is required. This is most successful when based on clearly defined mandates and responsibilities of all actors.

This idea has been well-captured in the concept of a National Referral Mechanism (NRM) aiming to create a cooperative framework between state authorities and civil society in order to support and protect victims of trafficking as well as to bring traffickers to justice. The concept of a NRM is also important in the broader context of a comprehensive anti-trafficking response because it assists in institution building, policy shaping and decision-making.

Information exchange and operational day-to-day concerns on individual trafficking cases can be facilitated through regular meetings of multidisciplinary round-tables on the local level. Experience tells that cooperation agreements with a clear delineation of responsibilities and tasks improve successful victim protection and prosecution of traffickers. Know-how gained from the operational level should flow into regularly updated National Plans of Action, which in return should lay out areas for legislative revision and reform. Multidisciplinary working groups can ensure that the implementation of policies and strategies is continuously monitored and discussed.

Innovative Initiatives Related to Victim Support

The following chapters discuss how to adapt victim support measures to the actual needs of trafficked persons by drawing upon initiatives taken by states and civil society:

- The OSCE's concept of National Referral Mechanisms is endorsed by all its 55 participating states and beyond. These referral mechanisms seek to facilitate the protection of victims and the prosecution of traffickers by means of cooperation and democratic institution building based on human rights standards. Liliana Sorrentino elucidates on how to translate the theoretical concept into action.

- Italy uses an innovative and cooperative approach in the field of victim support, which generally is attributed to its 'Article 18' legal provision that allows victims of trafficking temporary residence. "On the Road" is a partner organisation in the Italian victim support scheme. Isabella Orfano elaborates on strengths and weaknesses of the Italian system.
- Like Italy, Belgium, has developed a multi-dimensional victim assistance regime that allows trafficked victims the right to work, seek legal redress and compensation. Bruno Moens, who coordinated one of the country's three specialised victim support centres, provides insights into the Belgian model.
- Romania remains a significant country of origin with its citizens primarily being trafficked to Western Europe. The NGO Reaching Out Romania assists returned victims of trafficking in finding sustainable ways to integrate into Romanian society. Iana Matei describes the needs of trafficked women and girls and how to best respond to them in order to empower victims and facilitate their social inclusion.
- In Thailand a support group of formerly trafficked women established the non-governmental organisation Self-Empowerment Program for Migrant Women (SEPOM). One of SEPOM's main tasks is to help victims in overcoming their trauma and recover their self-esteem. Theera Srila and Warunee Chaiwongkam report on their experiences.

Cooperation for Protection – National Referral Mechanisms

Liliana Sorrentino

Coordinating Legal and Civil Support

All too often trafficked persons receive no assistance or protection, are criminalised, traumatised, expelled as illegal migrants and exposed to further harm and risks of reprisal. This is why National Referral Mechanisms (hereinafter NRM) are needed in countries of origin and destination to ensure that trafficked persons, who are victims of crime, are treated appropriately, assisted, protected and enabled to access justice, as it is their right. Adequate structures and efficient mechanisms should be in place in order to assist individuals who are possibly victims of trafficking.

A NRM is a cooperative framework within which participating states fulfil their obligations to protect and promote the human rights of trafficked persons in coordination and strategic partnership with civil society and other actors working in this field (OSCE/ODIHR 2004: 15). Establishing a NRM is about developing a coordinated response of relevant state agencies and NGOs to manage this process and make identification, assistance and protection of trafficked persons more effective. In 2003 the 55 participating States of the OSCE endorsed recommendations to establish NRMs for the proper identification of trafficked persons and appropriate referral to assistance and protection within the framework of the OSCE Action Plan to Combat Trafficking in Human Beings.

The Concept of National Referral Mechanisms

There are competing interpretations of what NRM consists of against the backdrop of an emerging discourse on the human rights approach to combating trafficking in persons amongst international, governmental and non-governmental agencies. Some reduce the NRM concept to a switchboard mechanism to refer trafficked persons to support services, while others refer to national structures and policies. This may be due to a lack of understanding of the concept or it may reflect the various approaches and agendas behind anti-trafficking work.

The idea behind NRMs as a concept is to contextualise the human rights based approach to combating human trafficking. It clearly points out that it is the responsibility of the State to ensure that appropriate structures and services do exist within their territory and are capable of fulfilling their duty to respect the dignity and protect the rights of trafficked persons in cooperation with NGOs. Thus the establishment of a NRM has to be seen in the context of democratic institution building. Accordingly, the system of victim identification, referral to assistance and access to justice needs to be tailored to the trafficking situation in the local context. In establishing such a system the NRM concept provides a number of relevant components, which apply to a variety of contexts. Some of the structures, standards and procedures that need to be developed are:

- An institutional anti-trafficking framework, providing a clear assignment of tasks and responsibilities of the various actors involved in victim identification, assistance and protection, and an operational mechanism to adequately and flexibly respond to the individual situation of trafficking cases in the country. This also ensures regular monitoring and evaluation of policies and practices.
- Guidance for police, immigration authorities, social workers, NGOs, etc. on identification and appropriate treatment of trafficked persons.
- Procedures to refer trafficked persons to specialised support services, which ensure quality standards of care. These should provide for independent legal advice and assistance, safe accommodation, medical and psychological counselling, access to education, vocational training, job counselling and long-term support to social inclusion, including assistance to return home if they wish so. Specific procedures should be provided for children to ensure they receive specialist care.

- Binding mechanisms defining cooperation between law enforcement and victim support services, thus harmonising victim assistance with investigative and prosecution efforts. This should detail procedures for reflection delay and regularisation of status, risk assessment and informed consent on cooperation, victim/witness support measures, compensation and data protection issues.

Establishing National Referral Mechanisms

In the last few years the OSCE, notably through ODIHR and field presences, in partnership with NGOs and international agencies, has assisted governments in designing and implementing national referral mechanisms. This has involved, for instance, assistance with designing a system on how to respond to trafficking patterns and building capacities to deliver protection and assistance, as well as capacities to investigate and prosecute the crime.

Commitment and Resources

A prerequisite for the establishment of NRMs is political will, translated into concrete policies and the allocation of resources. In the implementation of NRMs there are two main levels of work, a policy one and an operational one. The policy level relates to setting up or strengthening the institutional framework, which designs and coordinates policies, and ensures that structures and services are in place to protect trafficked persons. The operational level is geared towards building or enhancing the professional capacities of service providers in delivering support to trafficked persons, while developing cooperation mechanisms and standard operating procedures for managing the identification and referral process of individual cases.

Mapping and Assessment

Experiences in NRM implementation may vary from one country to another. However, it appears that in most cases the starting point is a good assessment of the trafficking situation and responses to it in the country. In other words it is a review at the national level of current practices in identifying trafficked persons, offering access to safe accommodation, legal counselling, medical and psychosocial care, and providing material assistance for subsistence, as well as of practices in police investigation and in prosecution. The assessment is crucial to become aware of the steps needed to put current practices in line with human rights obligations and to design flexible mechanisms of cooperation and referral to appropriate assistance that best fit the local context.

The main added value of a national assessment is in clearly outlining existing roles, responsibilities, operational modalities, strengths and constraints of the various state structures, NGOs and other actors involved in victim identification and protection, and in investigation and prosecution. The assessment is meant to help in devising tailor-made responses to trafficking patterns based on existing capacities and structures; in addition it should identify areas for training and improvement in current practices. The challenge is developing a shared understanding by stakeholders of the crime, of its impact on trafficked persons as well as of the current practices in investigation and victim protection, their successes and failures. This helps the various public institutions and NGO actors to acknowledge their different mandates and interests, clarify their working methods, understand each other's position, build trust in sharing a common goal and develop vision and agreement on how to render better support to trafficked persons, while making prosecution more effective.

In Moldova, for example, the technical assistance programme to establish a NRM started with an in-depth assessment of the existing institutional and legal framework on victim and witness protection to understand what was happening to the hundreds of trafficked persons returning home. The assessment included a careful participatory analysis of stakeholders and their common practices in victim identification and referral through the various stages from first assistance to social inclusion. Added to this is a mapping of existing services and capacities to provide direct services to vulnerable persons, including trafficked persons (e.g. health, social, psychological, legal support, etc.), which was translated into a database for practical individual case management. The idea of mapping stemmed from the challenge of looking at protection and assistance in broad terms, going beyond the focus of victims/witnesses and search for services for domestic violence and vulnerable groups. In partnership with other international organisations, the OSCE acted as catalyst and facilitator in this process that was led by national NGOs, such as La Strada Moldova, and State actors in the National Committee to combat trafficking in human beings.

Building Capacities

A core element in establishing NRM is developing responsible structures and adequate professional capacities to enable appropriate identification and treatment of trafficked persons, and linking up the various actors in a coordinated response to individual cases of trafficked children, women and men. This requires significant and long-term efforts to train and enhance existing capacities of law enforcement, prosecutors, judges, social workers, victim's support agencies, etc. The process should also be accompanied by the development of appropriate methods of working, and transparent and measurable standards of care for the support services, which are provided by public institutions, NGOs and other actors.

The challenge often is supporting this process within a context of limited resources and a very weak social security system. A strategic approach, which identifies priorities, mid- and long-term responses tailored to and sustainable in the local context, becomes crucial to progressively improve local capacities and build up more inclusive protection for trafficked persons.

Cooperation Models

Another fundamental aspect of building NRMs is defining cooperation models between state and civil actors and detailing standard procedures for processing individual cases. Forging effective cooperation, good communication and trust between NGOs and public institutions may often imply a long process of negotiation and discussion to mutually understand and respect each other's role and profession, to overcome prejudices and to find a fair balance between the interest of human rights protection and those of prosecution. This process is very important in establishing clear ground rules, translating the terms of this cooperation into memoranda of understanding or into internal directives ensuring transparency and accountability.

The process of forging this cooperation should be an inclusive one, ensuring contribution and participation of all actors that are responsible or volunteer to provide assistance with a view to enhancing support for trafficked persons. In this regard it should be pointed out that in practice the starting point is often a round-table of practitioners, dealing at the operational level with concrete individual cases of trafficking.

In some countries the adoption of standard operating procedures for direct assistance to trafficked persons has been the starting point to ensure that the process of assistance is built on respect of the rights of trafficked persons. In other cases the management of a coordinated response has become the competence of an ad hoc state agency handling the whole process of identification and referral in partnership with the various actors. NRM could also be embedded in a framework law addressing all aspects of combating human trafficking, delineating roles of the various ministries and state structures defining the status of trafficked persons and related rights.

What is important is to detail in a transparent and accountable manner the specific duties and responsibilities of each agency at each stage of the referral process, as well as devising the mechanism to render operational and effective cooperation. Thus for its functioning the role of a coordinating body/focal point becomes crucial. This role could be that of a drop-in centre, it could be within the competence of a state agency or of an NGO, or a joint competency.

In this field an interesting example comes from the experience of the Serbian State Agency for Coordinating Protection to Trafficking Victims, which operates under the Ministry of Labour. The initial establishment of the Agency was supported by the Ministry and the OSCE Mission to Serbia and Montenegro in 2004. The Agency works in strategic partnership with NGOs and local authorities; it coordinates the process from the early stage of identification and needs assessment throughout the referral process including support in dealing with authorities for issues relating to residence permit and criminal justice process. The establishment of the Agency and its daily work are an example of an ongoing process of forging cooperation and joint responsibility of state and civil actors in protection of trafficked persons.

Lessons Learned

Political will, clear objectives, priorities and adequate human and financial resources, including regular funding of NGO support services are definitely the prerequisites.

The methodology of NRM building would appear to be transferable: assessment, dedicated national structures capacity building, quality standards, and monitoring are the building blocks, which need to be adapted to fit the country situation, local capacity and legislative framework.

The NRM response should ensure clear terms of reference for specific agencies in the referral process thus providing for a system where the law and order approach does not combat criminality; NRMs and laws should work in fair balance and complement each other. This is successful when law enforcement and service providers are in a constant dialogue, when they work based on mutually agreed terms of cooperation and empower the trafficked person to make informed decisions. Such effective collaboration is often built on much more than institutional cooperation; it requires good individual personal relationships based on mutual trust and confidence.

In conclusion, it is important to emphasise that the process of establishing NRM is per se important as it helps in moving towards implementing a human rights based approach in combating human trafficking in the OSCE region. In whatever form it is put into practice, ultimately NRM must be assessed on the extent to which it does no harm and enables trafficked persons to become aware of their rights and options, make their own decisions, receive support, and have access to justice; as well as on the extent to which it provides for transparency, accountability and a clear delineation of responsibilities of those institutions and actors that are mandated to protect and assist trafficked persons.

The opinion and views expressed in this article are those of the author and do not necessarily reflect the views of the OSCE.

A Victim-Centred Approach – The Italian Model

Isabella Orfano

Human Rights in Anti-Trafficking Interventions

Trafficking in human beings is widely acknowledged as a severe crime in international and European documents as well as in many national legislations. In most cases, though, the focus of these documents and of the corresponding policies is on the fight against the criminal organisations and illegal migration. No adequate reference is made to the fact that trafficking is primarily a human rights violation. In many cases this is mentioned, the related measures promoted, however, are not in line with the international human rights standards. Indeed, too often the legislations seem to be based on the false assumption that the struggle against traffickers is incompatible with the protection of the human rights of the trafficked persons.

As a result, the main anti-trafficking strategies fail to protect the human rights of the trafficked persons, regardless of the states' obligations to do so in compliance with the international norms. Thus governments do not further the investigative activities and the prosecution of the crime, even though valuable evidence and information could be derived from trafficked persons once these are adequately protected, assisted and provided with a legal status.

In Italy, the civil society and the non-governmental organisations have always been at the forefront of action against social exclusion. This is particularly true for the laws and the strategies elaborated and implemented to support trafficked persons and combat the phenomenon as such. A long-lasting 'welfare mix' culture characterises the Italian social policies and interventions system based on a fruitful cooperation between the public and private non-profit sectors that jointly work to achieve common goals. Such collaboration is the key feature of the current scheme that provides social assistance and integration to victims of trafficking.

The Social Assistance and Integration Programme (Article 18)

Italy passed its first law to specifically punish the offence of human trafficking in 2003 (no. 228/2003: 'Measures against trafficking in persons'). This law brought about a great improvement over the previous system. In compliance with the UN Trafficking Protocol norms, it includes the specific crime of trafficking in persons in the Penal Code and, inter alia, provides a new definition that covers all forms of trafficking, slavery and servitude as well as internal and cross-border trafficking. The law also establishes the compulsory confiscation of profits deriving from trafficking and the set-up of a Fund for Anti-Trafficking Measures.

In Italy the anti-trafficking law completes the most effective tool implemented so far to support trafficked persons and fight human trafficking: Article 18 of the Legislative Decree no. 286 of 1998 (Immigration Law). The latter has proven to be an effective instrument to support trafficked persons, investigate the phenomenon and punish the traffickers. Most of all, under this article thousands of migrant people – women in particular – have been acknowledged as victims of trafficking and provided with special assistance, protection and a residence permit for humanitarian reasons. From 1998 until August 2004, 4,287 permits have been issued in accordance with Article 18.

Article 18 applies to foreign citizens in situations of abuse or severe exploitation where their safety is seen to be endangered as a consequence of attempts to escape from the conditioning of a criminal organisation or as a result of pursuing criminal action against the traffickers. A residence permit is issued for six months and can be renewed for one year. People granted this special permit have to participate in a social assistance and integration programme offered by various NGOs and local authorities. They are also afforded access to social services, educational institutions and enrolment with the State's employment bureau and are thus provided with the opportunity to find employment.

The enactment of Article 18 of the Legislative Decree no. 286/98 has represented a milestone both in the fields of assistance and social inclusion policies for victims and the fight against trafficking in human beings. Through financial support endowed by Article 18, the Italian Government set up the first structured Programme of Social Assistance and Integration aimed at trafficked persons, introduced a set of complementary actions and, concurrently, strengthened the fight against traffickers and exploiters. The Interministerial Committee for the Implementation of Article 18 is the managing body of the programme and complementary actions; it is composed of representatives of the Department for Equal Opportunities, the Ministry of Justice, the Ministry of Welfare, and the Ministry of Interior.

The Projects

Since its activation, the Programme has funded 378 projects throughout the country. In order to run a project under Article 18, NGOs, associations and local authorities (municipalities, provinces and regions) must yearly submit their project proposal to the Department for Equal Opportunities, which technically and financially runs the programme. NGOs applying for the funding must involve a local authority as project partner and must be enrolled in a special register of NGOs and bodies carrying out assistance to migrants. It is important to underscore that each grant – by law – is co-financed by the Department for Equal Opportunities (70% of the eligible costs) and by the local authority involved (30%).

Not every agency engaged in the project implementation necessarily directly provides all types of services. In several cases, in fact, the wide range of activities is assured by the projects' network. The projects function as reception centres and assistance providers that offer a so-called 'individualised programme of assistance and social integration' tailored to the needs of the person sheltered and in compliance with the law. Within each individual programme various activities and services are offered to the hosted person, such as: shelter, health care, psychological support, legal counselling and assistance, educational and language classes, orientation, vocational guidance, job insertion and, upon request, voluntary return to the home country.

It is noteworthy to mention that undocumented migrants are entitled to register in the National Health Service for essential health services. They receive the so-called 'STP' (*Straniero Temporaneamente Presente,* Temporarily Present Foreigner), which is a card with an identification code number. The STP provides access to specialist care, emergency, maternity and hospital cover. The STP holders are then entitled to basic health assistance without being referred to the police.

Residence Permits

Residence permits under Article 18 can be obtained in two ways: through the so-called 'judicial path' or through the 'social path'. The first procedure, the judicial path, requires the formal cooperation of the trafficked person with the police and the judiciary through the filing of a complaint against his/her perpetrators. The second procedure, the social path, does not entail the formal reporting to the police on the part of the trafficked person but the submission of a 'statement' (containing provable key information) by an accredited agency according to Article 18 or by the public social services of a municipality on behalf of the trafficked person, when she/he is not willing or able to directly cooperate with the competent authorities. Experiences in Italy showed that many women who first started on the social path, later on decided to officially press charges against their traffickers and/or exploiters, once they had been reassured in their legal position and gained new trust in the support of the institutions. However, it must be noted that, once the police has confirmed an offence they are legally obliged to follow it through with an accusation; in this case also a person within the social path may be asked to testify. Both within the 'judicial path' and the 'social path', a trafficked person or the prosecutor can also request a special evidence pre-trial hearing when there are specific conditions that may jeopardise the trafficked person's safety or the reliability and integrity of the evidence collected.

Both procedures lead to the conversion of the residence permit under Article 18 into a residence permit for education or for work, allowing the permit holder to stay in Italy in conformity with the regulations governing the presence of non-European Union foreigners. This is a key aspect of the system in place, which, on the one hand, promptly provides appropriate measures to escape from exploitative and coercive situations unconditionally placing the human rights of the trafficked person at the centre of the support intervention and, on the other hand, builds favourable conditions to fight the crime. As a matter of fact, granting the hosted person a wide range of services and a legal status to live and eventually work in Italy is a fundamental step to overcome his/her fear of deportation, traffickers' retaliations, mistrust towards authorities, all elements that often profoundly hinder his/her willingness to cooperate with the competent authorities and denounce his/her exploiters.

The efficacy of the Social Assistance and Integration Programme is confirmed not only by the significant number of trafficked persons who entered and successfully concluded the scheme but also by the considerable rise of arrests and sentences of traffickers and exploiters as a result of the collaboration of persons (mainly women) who benefited from the programme. Additionally, it is important to underline that no instrumental abuse of Article 18 by migrants to legalise their irregular stay on the Italian territory has been detected due to the specific structure and procedures of the system in force, as both police sources and scientific studies indisputably established.

Other Anti-Trafficking Measures

Another important tool to combat trafficking in human beings is the *Numero Verde Nazionale contro la Tratta* 800.290.290. This is a national toll-free hotline directed at trafficked persons, clients, social and law enforcement agencies and the population at large. Financed by the Interministerial Committee for the Implementation of Article 18, the *Numero Verde* is composed of a central headquarter that functions as a filter for the calls and 14 territorial branches located in 14 different regional or interregional areas throughout Italy. In most cases, the territorial branches of the *Numero Verde* are managed by the same NGOs and public institutions that are responsible for the implementation of projects funded within the Article 18 Programme. Information is provided in various languages spoken by the target groups concerned, including English, Albanian, Russian, French, Spanish, Romanian, and Bulgarian.

Other instruments funded under this Article 18 programme aim at public awareness raising, research and support for a voluntary return and integration.

Conclusions and Recommendations

A comprehensive system aimed at the protection of trafficked persons and at fighting the related crime can be set up through an integrated and holistic approach based on the following elements:

- a comprehensive anti-trafficking legislation, supporting policies and interventions that are human rights–based, gender and cultural sensitive, include a child rights approach and are not connected with the victim's direct cooperation with the law enforcement agencies;
- a coordinated multi-agency approach that implies the involvement of all actors on all levels and the establishment of a formalised national referral mechanism or of a similar scheme;
- exchange and cooperation with service providers and other relevant anti-trafficking agencies of countries of origin, transit and destination;
- employment of specifically trained professionals (outreach workers, shelter operators, psychologists, etc.), including cultural mediators from the countries of origin and legal consultants, and continuous further training courses on relevant issues;
- prompt access to safe and appropriate accommodation, free legal counselling and assistance to comprehensive health and education schemes for the victim;
- updated information and access to civil court procedures for legal compensation, also with the support of interpreters;
- quick issuance of a special renewable residence permit and of a work permit that can be converted into a permanent permit for study or work reasons, thus allowing victims to become regular migrants and fully-fledged citizens;
- protection of family members, who may run very substantial risks at home or in other countries (family reunion should be ensured regardless of income or other requirements);
- adequate and regular funding to support the long-term sustainability of the service providers engaged in the anti-trafficking field;
- monitoring and evaluation systems to assess the results both at the social and the judicial level, to identify best practices to assist trafficked persons, and to set minimum standards required for the agencies working in the field;
- multidisciplinary and multi-approach studies, with special regard to new forms of trafficking and exploitation other than sexual, and consequent development of new identification and assistance models and services.

Specialised Service Centres – The Belgian Model

Bruno Moens

Background

In Belgium trafficking in human beings was thrust into the limelight following the release of a book in 1992, "They are so sweet, Sir", which unravelled the mechanisms behind trafficking and exposed the sexual exploitation of women (De Stoop 1992). The publication of the book was the main impetus for setting up a Parliamentary Investigation Commission tasked with the elaboration of a structural response to fight trafficking in human beings and child pornography. The recommendations of the Commission's final report in 1994 marked the outset of the organic development of an integral, integrated and multi-dimensional anti-trafficking policy which is focussed on four pillars: actions and initiatives in the field of administrative law, social and labour law, criminal law and policy, and finally victim support.

The Integral Approach of Victim Assistance

Three centres act as regional focal points for the referral and support of victims: Payoke for the Flemish region, Surya for the Walloon region and Pag Asa for the Brussels region. These centres are by law recognised non-governmental organisations, specialised in assisting victims of trafficking and offering a range of support services to victims of trafficking and smuggled migrants, who cooperate with the judicial authorities (hereinafter referred to as 'victims of smuggling').

> The anti-trafficking law punishes any act of enticement into prostitution (with or without consent). Penalties are higher where this enticement includes deception, violence, threats, constraints or the abuse of a foreigner's vulnerability. (ILO 2005: Human Trafficking and Forced Labour Exploitation. Guidance for Legislation and Law Enforcement. Special Action Programme to Combat Forced Labour 2005)

As such, under Belgian law either commercial sexual exploitation or smuggling with the use of threats, violence, abuse of the vulnerable or precarious position of a foreigner are understood to be trafficking. All three centres are financed through federal and regional government funding and are coordinated by the Centre for Equal Opportunities and Combating Racism, a governmental organisation. The latter represents the three centres in the inter-ministerial working group on trafficking and serves as an interlocutor between the government and the centres.

The mission of the specialised centres is to offer judicial, administrative and psychosocial support to victims of trafficking and smuggling within a victim-centred approach (Pag Asa 2003: 2; Payoke 2005: 5; Surya 2005: 3). Furthermore their mission states that the centres conduct awareness-raising and sensitisation activities on the issue of trafficking through training and information sessions for concerned actors, community groups and service providers. In addition to this the centres file recommendations to concerned governmental actors in view of taking appropriate action to improve the protection of and support to victims.

For every new client the assistance starts with an intake procedure. Under the intake procedure victims are informed about the residence procedure, and their situation as well as their needs are assessed. On this basis and under mutual agreement an assistance plan and contract is developed which focuses on legal assistance and psychosocial support in view of integration.

Legal assistance is aimed to ensure that the victim's rights and interests are defended. The centres follow up the criminal proceedings and provide victims seeking compensation with the assistance of a lawyer. The centres assist women, men and children, victims of trafficking, both for sexual exploitation as for economical exploitation, as well as victims of smuggling, who cooperate with the competent judicial authorities. The centres do not have a mandate to offer assistance to victims who do not wish to file complaints against their perpetrators, which constitutes one of the main shortcomings of the system. In this respect, assistance to this category of victims is limited to the organisation of a voluntary return or referral to organisations dealing with undocumented migrants.

Assistance to minors is restricted to the application and follow-up of residence documents and judicial assistance. As for shelter, housing and psychosocial support, underage victims of trafficking and smuggling are being referred to and taken care of by social organisations specialised in the support and protection of children.

Psychosocial support to victims entails a wide range of services such as lodging, personal safety, physical and mental well being, educational and vocational training, employment and job placement, financial support, etc. (Dormaels et al. 2004: 88). Most of these services are offered in close collaboration with other social service providers. From the start of the assistance victims are allocated to the safe houses of the specialised centres where they are lodged for a maximum period ranging from three to six months. During their stay in the shelter they undergo a routine medical check-up, are obligatory registered for language and integration courses and are prepared for independent living.

Apart from individual referral to psychotherapists, focus discussion groups are organised for those living in the shelter (Dormaels et al. 2004: 88). Administrative support offered by the centres mainly consists of the follow-up, application and information exchange with the competent authorities within the procedure for the issuance of residence permits for victims of trafficking and smuggling.

Residence Scheme and Work Permit

Only the specialised centres are entitled to apply to the Immigration Office for the issuance of residence documents. The centralisation to only three focal points as far as the application for residence documents is concerned, facilitates a smooth handling of the procedure and an enhanced collaboration between the centres and the Immigration Office. The residence scheme consists of three phases: a reflection period of 45 days (an order to leave the country within 45 days), followed by a three months period (a declaration of arrival) during which the Immigration Office requests information from the Prosecutor's Office on the nature of the case and whether the plaintiff can be considered as a victim of trafficking or smuggling. Finally a six months document (a certificate of registration in the foreigner's register) is granted and is extended for the duration of the criminal proceedings.

A permanent residence permit for an indefinite period of time is issued to a victim when the following conditions are met: the declaration of the victim has resulted in a verdict of the correctional district court or, when the perpetrator has not been sentenced on the basis of a trafficking or smuggling offence, he has at a minimum been summoned by the prosecutor before the court on the basis of a trafficking or smuggling offence. In both situations the declaration of the victim should be considered by the prosecutor's office of indispensable importance to the proceedings of the criminal case.

In all stages of the residence procedure victims are eligible for public assistance such as health insurance, mental and physical health care, housing, subsistence allowance, etc. From the start of the assistance victims are obliged to be allocated in the shelters managed by the specialised centres, for a period ranging from three to six months. After this initial period of assistance they are allocated in transit apartments or housing is actively sought through the collaboration of housing services.

Except for the reflection delay, victims are entitled to work officially in Belgium: they receive a work permit for a period of seven months under the three months declaration of arrival and a work permit for one year under the six months certificate of registration in the foreigner's register. The work permits are not tied to a specific employer. The centres provide assistance in obtaining the work permit and in registering the victims at the local employment offices that offer vocational trainings and job placement services.

Compensation

Victims of trafficking as well as smuggling have the right to seek legal redress and compensation. As an injured party the victim can institute an action for compensation before the criminal court or, alternatively, before the civil court. In general, victims introduce civil actions before the criminal court concurrently with the criminal proceedings. A prerequisite for introducing damage claims before the criminal court is that the damage for which compensation is being sought resulted from the criminal offence. The criminal court therefore gives judgement on the damage claim together with a decision on the criminal proceedings. In general the criminal courts grant compensations to victims of trafficking averaging between 1,250 € and 17,000 €. The amount of compensation depends on the seriousness of the offence, the duration of the offences inflicted upon the victim and the financial amounts gained from the criminal activity (Moens 2002: 114).

Cases of sexual exploitation tend to result in higher compensations than those of economic exploitation or smuggling. Despite the fact that victims are generally granted compensations before the criminal courts, full payment of damage claims remains problematic as perpetrators often claim to be insolvent. Convicted perpetrators who serve a prison sentence are more inclined to pay off compensation, usually by amounts not exceeding 25 € a month, as this is a prerequisite to obtain an early release. Occasionally victims have been granted compensation directly out of confiscated proceeds of crime from trafficking offences.

In case victims have been granted compensation by court ruling but have not been compensated due to the insolvency of the offender, the victim can apply for compensation with the Fund for Victims of Violent Acts. Compensation by the Fund for victims of economic exploitation is however restricted: the acts of violence need to be specifically addressed in the judgement and be proven by way of medical certificates. The three specialised centres and the Centre for Equal Opportunities and Combating Racism are entitled to act in court as a civil party as well as to take action in court proceedings on behalf of the victim, although the latter is rather exceptional. Compensation claims filed by the specialised centres are principally symbolic in nature and amount to 1 €.

Remaining Challenges and Lessons Learned

The assistance and protection programme for victims of trafficking and smuggling has been shaped on a legal basis. Social intervention programmes for victims are relatively new: at present very few practices have been evaluated in order to show a clear track record of demonstrating their appropriateness, effectiveness or impact. Nevertheless some of the centres are planning to overall assess and evaluate their protection and support scheme to victims. From the side of the government an evaluation is planned focussing specifically on the modalities and scope of application of the residence scheme.

As to the application of quality norms, at present no overall quality monitoring mechanism has been put in place although the Centre for Equal Opportunities and Combating Racism envisages the elaboration in the near future of applicable quality standards on the assistance of victims. Some aspects of assistance could be transferable, but need to be adapted as practices vary in different countries.

Therefore transferability is highly dependent on legal parameters, availability of resources and political will and commitment in other countries.

At present some key successes can be noted. The activities of the specialised centres have led to a better understanding of the society on the issue of trafficking and of its victims in particular, an increased awareness of the media when they report on trafficking as well as an increased awareness of other service providers on the issue of trafficking and the need for victim protection. The initiatives of the centres furthermore resulted in the adoption by the government of policies towards a victim approach and the convincing of the government to have a systematic approach towards the structural funding of the specialised centres. The close collaboration with concerned governmental actors also established a partnership with the government in which the centres were able to develop a mutual trusting relationship within the issue of protection and assistance to victims.

Within their activities the centres developed partnerships with other service providers to ensure a more holistic assistance approach, with NGOs from other countries in terms of exchange of good practices and collaboration in view of a voluntary return and integration in countries of origin as well as with international institutions through international projects and participation in events, in particular on the issue of residence permits and victim's protection and assistance. A close partnership has also been developed with policy makers in terms of shaping a more victim-centred approached.

Sustainable Social and Professional Reintegration

Iana Matei

The Situation

The conspicuous absence of trafficking statistics from Romania alarmingly indicates the lack of national interest in human trafficking and the situation of trafficked Romanian citizens. Victims have been largely marginalised by all segments of society. It is only recently that mass media has begun to report their plight with a degree of compassion or outrage, finally identifying trafficking as a human rights issue. Public compassion and perception of 'victims', however, lags far behind.

The overwhelming majority of victims of trafficking are exploited youth who are often runaways or castaways from dysfunctional homes where they have already suffered physical, psychological and sexual abuse. Romania is a country whose crippled economy and weak social service structure provides virtually no social safety nets to assist them. With a scarcity of jobs in a male dominated society, young girls are particularly vulnerable to carefully crafted offers promising 'unique' opportunities that will bring good jobs and good money outside the country. Impoverished, abused, and without education or family guidance that would foster intelligent decision-making, these young women become easy prey to savvy traffickers who befriend them and tempt them with offers they can hardly refuse.

Police reports indicate that when young people finish high school in rural areas, they frequently move to urban areas. Young people search for better opportunities, more excitement and the trappings of Western culture, which they perceive to be more easily accessible in large cities. Many fall prey to trafficking syndicates and see their dreams collapse while being exploited and abused. Upon their return to Romania psychological, medical and social care provided in a specialised shelter should support these women and girls to find their way back into Romanian society.

There are thousands of victims waiting to be assisted in rescue and reintegration. Without any reintegration programme, the majority of these victims (re)turn to prostitution. They are ashamed of what has happened to them and are almost exclusively looked upon not as victims, but as active and willing participants or even criminals. Ashamed of the stigma and often sold by family and friends, they view themselves as deserving the life that was forced upon them without finding refuge and care at home. The religious culture in Romania, predominantly Orthodox, provides only little help to this problem. Trafficked persons are stigmatised as 'unforgivable' and receive no hope for redemption. So, where can they turn? Who saves these children and young women from the brutal crimes committed upon them?

The Services

Reaching Out Romania (ROR) provides shelter, counselling and support to women and girls trafficked for sexual exploitation. ROR literally travels to wherever girls and women are left by local authorities in order to pick them up and start the long process of recovery. Through extensive counselling in both, group and individual settings, foundations for renewed self-esteem and social integration are being laid. Counselling services with on-site social workers are provided around the clock.

The programme, which was supported by the German Government through the Sector Project in 2004, aims to fully integrate victims of trafficking into Romanian society by equipping women and girls with all necessary skills to lead an independent life once they leave the programme. ROR's current shelter is situated in a rural area and has twelve beds, one kitchen and two bathrooms. Besides mere accommodation ROR offers psychological, medical, educational and vocational assistance as well as life skills training. Particular emphasis is put on life skills in the 'home' environment (menu planning, shopping, budgeting, etc.) in order to facilitate a rapid and practical re-entry into society. The organisation assists trafficked persons also in finding accommodation for the time after the programme.

Access to education is a priority, also because many of the victims come from rural areas with only very limited educational opportunities. Basic to advanced skills are evaluated on an individual basis and education is provided free of charge to the victim. Even though the girls and women are expected to continue their education and to find a job, they are not required to pay for the services provided by ROR. Regular employment assists them in establishing their autonomy, in gaining their independence and ultimately in moving out on their own. When a victim decides to move out of the shelter counselling services continue to be provided as needed.

In 2003, ROR has opened a tailoring workshop that employs women from the reintegration programme. This initiative produces bed linen for local hotel businesses and is almost self-sustained. While re-orientating their lives under psychological supervision women and girls have the opportunity to develop tailoring and managerial skills. Their monthly wages are saved in personal accounts until the time they leave the programme. This activity's final goal is to enable the girls to open their own business using the skills and money they get in the programme.

Medical care in Romania is poor. Despite the Romanian Government's efforts to improve health care services, doctors and medical care personnel are poorly paid and generally have to supplement their income to survive. As a result qualified doctors look for employment in larger cities such as Bucharest, where services are generally better paid. Many doctors also try to go abroad for work in order to earn salaries consistent with their education. In the state-run system where health care is supposed to be provided at no charge, a poorly paid medical community will almost exclusively provide care only when paid for. Consequently, medical care for trafficked girls and women is restricted to available funds. For Reaching Out Romania this implies strong financial limitations.

The Individual Programme

The specific needs of each programme participant are carefully monitored and evaluated from the very beginning. Girls and women are often traumatised, ashamed and carry a societal stigma that is very difficult to break. It is vital to help victims in building basic living skills through training and education. A tailor-made programme should assist them in dealing with stress trauma as well as it should help victims to find their ways back into society. Basic skills include reading, social interaction, self-evaluation and self-esteem, selecting clothes and dressing. All stages of counselling, educational enrolment, educational progress reports and medical evaluations are retained in detailed records describing the individual progress and milestone development of the beneficiaries.

Since its foundation in 1999, Reaching out Romania has provided care and shelter to 127 victims of the sex traffic trade. Even though the organisation does not set any time limit for residence, the beneficiaries' progress is carefully managed and tracked to ensure safe and lasting inclusion into society. At present the success rate of ROR is 84% with 31% of the victims living in the shelter, 37% of girls and women being reunited with their families and 16% living independently. The remaining 16% of women and girls are back on the streets.

The Perspectives

Reintegration without lasting alternatives has little chance for success. Without a sound programme and a safe environment, women who have been rescued maintain the risk of returning to the only form of earning their living they are experienced in. Many victims of trafficking have received little education and possess only a few life skills. Hence, it is vital to provide a safe nurturing environment that starts the process of healing and education for these victims of crime as well as to lay a stepping-stone for their independence and healthy self-esteem.

As one option, Reaching out Romania sees a great potential in developing the concept of agro-tourism further: attracting tourists into the region by offering them friendly service and fresh local produce in an appealing setting. This would help to overcome the conventional 'no future' perception of agricultural occupation amongst youth on the one hand as well as foster community building between generations in rural areas. A bed-and-breakfast place in a region with enormous potential for tourism could in the long run generate funds to cover the expenses for the shelter for trafficked women and girls. Naturally grown products produced by small farms in the community will be sold to the pension in order to be used in the restaurant. With the money obtained from selling the products, local farmers will be encouraged to produce quality goods. The agro-tourism staff will facilitate meetings between producers and other potential beneficiaries. Reaching out Romania seeks to create alternatives also for producers of agricultural goods and to encourage them to open their own bed-and-breakfast hotels.

Lessons Learned

When a woman or a girl after having been trafficked is returned to Romania but not referred to an effective reintegration programme, she will go back to the same abusive and/or poor family with no job, but a strong feeling of shame and guilt and the high risk of being re-trafficked. She knows the recruiter and assumes that people in the community also know what happened to her. In order to break the cycle of abuse or re-trafficking, trafficked persons need to learn that they are not perpetrators but victims and that – with some support – they have positive long-term perspectives in their societies. However, this calls for a change of attitudes and perceptions, both in the minds of victims and the public at large. More programmes that promote a long-term and empowering approach in assisting returning victims are needed. After having consulted and supported numerous victims of trafficking Reaching Out Romania advocates for a change of anti-trafficking strategy. Emphasis has to be put on programmes promoting prevention and long-term reintegration.

Self-Empowerment of Migrant Women

Warunee Chaiwongkam & Theera Srila

Background and Methodology

The Self-Empowerment Program for Migrant Women (SEPOM) is a support group of and for formerly trafficked women from Thailand to Japan and their Thai-Japanese children. It is based in Chiang Rai, a province in the North of Thailand. SEPOM's staff consists of volunteers and formerly trafficked women.

SEPOM focuses on improving women's capabilities, raising their awareness of the danger of becoming victims of trafficking and supporting their rehabilitation into the community. Victims receive psychological, social and legal support, e.g. by giving them access to correct information on Japanese legislation, translating Japanese texts into Thai or coordinating their interactions with various organisations in Japan. SEPOM also deals with problems relating to nationality, search for the fathers of inter-ethnic children, and the assistance of victims in their divorce from Japanese husbands. Educational work is undertaken with inter-ethnic Thai-Japanese children to improve their way of life. They are integrated in activities that promote art and discipline to live in society.

SEPOM's work is based on a participatory approach. By integrating the target group in the planning of projects women learn from each other's experiences and no longer view themselves as worthless, uneducated, incapable, socially unlucky and hopeless people. After they become familiar with SEPOM such feelings fade away and their way of life changes. They learn how to jointly work on social issues and understand how to solve their own problems and those of others, which results in the women realising and accepting their own value. Women in the support group even succeed in counselling HIV/AIDS victims.

Consequently, SEPOM's work method is based on the presumption that women are capable of improving themselves and are able to solve social problems. SEPOM encourages victims to learn how to mutually solve the problems of migrant women and educates potential victims using experiences from ex-victims. Campaigns, such as using drama to reflect on the life of women who were victims of human trafficking, are organised through the media.

Women working with SEPOM also conduct research, using various methods such as data collection and analysis obtained from women's direct experiences. Thereby women are approached to participate in SEPOM's work while at the same time data on trafficking is collected. This data is very valuable since many facts are being revealed rather to formerly trafficked women, who conduct the interview, than to any 'neutral' researcher. Parts of the research have been funded by the BMZ through the Sector Project of GTZ.

SEPOM is also active in the area of advocacy by facilitating seminars with various governmental and non-governmental organisations. The government is lobbied to provide accurate and balanced information about destination countries to give potential migrant workers the opportunity to make informed decisions. Awareness raising on the community level promotes a change in the community's attitude as well as realising the impact, situation and danger of trafficking.

For prevention and reintegration, SEPOM helps to improve the financial situation of (potentially) trafficked women by organising a micro credit system and by supporting them in finding stable careers. Women in need of education are trained, thus increasing their job prospects. They are also encouraged to become community leaders. Consequently, potential female migrant workers migrate much less abroad.

SEPOM organises fora for ex-migrants, where they learn about their rights and exchange experiences in order to explore new ideas and plans as well as to strengthen their independence and equality. This approach helps them to rely on themselves in the future.

Regional Setting

SEPOM's work is concentrating on seven districts in the province of Chiang Rai. Mae Sai is the most Northern district of Thailand, bordering with Myanmar, and on a migration route to and from China through Myanmar. The area abounds in human trafficking. In the district of King Ampoe Doiluang most of the residents were farmers. However, due to economic difficulties and the fall in prices, many left their homes and families and migrated for a living. Some residents remarried and gave their children into the care of their elderly parents, who were unable to adequately look after them. In Ampoe Mae Lao jobs are scarce resulting in the emigration of workforce. Furthermore, most people in this area were farmers who cultivated only one single crop, which led to agricultural failure. Since there is no price guarantee from the government the farmers are overwhelmed by debt and migrate to neighbouring countries. The Wiang Chai District has an arid climate and is also not fully viable from agriculture alone with no alternative job opportunities. This results in even more labour migration than in the other three districts. Human traffickers are abundant in this district.

Cooperation

SEPOM collaborates with government agencies, domestic and foreign organisations, non-governmental organisations and community leaders, as well as with volunteers from Australia's Volunteer International, who participate and help building an international network.

SEPOM's work is coordinated between Thailand and Japan, e.g. by making videos about trafficking victims and displaying them in Japan. SEPOM cooperates with Japanese organisations and supports the enactment of anti-trafficking legislation in Japan. The target group used to think that jobs overseas could improve their lives and generate enough income to improve the financial status of their families. They were primarily interested in financial benefits and did not care so much about their human dignity. After working with SEPOM, these attitudes altered based on exchange with other people who had similar difficulties in life. Hence people chose not to migrate and continued their traditional way of life on sufficient economic foundation by respecting the values of life and avoiding materialism. This then prevents them from becoming the victims of traffickers.

Lessons Learned

The organisation encountered many problems in tracking down returning trafficked persons, due to the fact that the real victims could not be reached. Hence, they were unable to participate in the activities. The target group must be approached immediately after their return. Women who worked with SEPOM have changed their attitudes and have a better insight into their own problems. They are willing to transfer their experiences to the community and to people who ignorantly believe that working abroad always improves their lives.

As many self-help groups, SEPOM's work has been delayed by the limitation of funds and personnel. This left the organisation incapable of following all members of the target group and helping them in time. Some victims, who could not be reached fast enough, committed suicide. This experience taught SEPOM that quick action is needed when working with traumatised persons.

It is essential to render opportunities to the target group, the victims of human trafficking, so that they can participate in the organisations working on their behalf. They should be empowered to analyse their situation, plan projects according to their needs and be integrated in the implementation of measures.

Approaches to Capacity and Institution Building

Comprehensive victim support and successful prosecution rely greatly on existent and functioning systems of cooperation as well as on the expertise and professionalism of all cooperating partners involved. Trafficked persons need to be referred to competent entities that are able to respond to the specific needs of the victim.

Institutional Anti-Trafficking Framework

A victim support and referral system should fit into a broader anti-trafficking infrastructure that involves relevant actors from the operational to the policy level. Cooperating partners need to know what they can expect from each other in terms of qualitative action and social skills. It is vital that any such anti-trafficking framework is orchestrated by the local government and strengthened via formal or informal but transparent agreements facilitating cooperation between various levels and civil society.

In the European context the OSCE calls upon their member states to appoint national coordinators at the ministerial level and/or a multidisciplinary round-table. The task of the national coordinator is to facilitate information exchange between various departments and organisations, to coordinate anti-trafficking initiatives, to bring the outcomes of the round-table discussions to the attention of decision-makers as well as to establish ties with other coordinating bodies across borders.

Governmental and non-governmental members of the round-table should arrive at and agree to a consolidated work/action plan. Experience shows that action plans without timelines and budgets are likely to remain plans without action. All activities should forecast appropriate timeframes and estimated likely costs as well as mechanisms for evaluation. An action plan should be a dynamic tool that is regularly reviewed and amended in the course of its implementation. Round-tables are best fitted to monitor the implementation of the work/action plan and to revise it accordingly. Responsibility, transparency and accountability are frequently used buzzwords that have their particular relevance also in the institutional anti-trafficking framework.

Of course, any anti-trafficking response needs to be fine-tuned and adapted to the local situation. Frequently, sub-working groups composed of national subject-matter experts are established in order to address specific issues such as legislative reform or social protection in greater detail. Implementation of a protection mechanism based on international human rights standards should take into account the particular laws, constitutional structures, commitments and obligations of the government and infrastructure of governmental and non-governmental sectors.

Training and Networking

Basic social skills such as confidence, trust and mutual respect for each other's work are essential to overcome the different objectives of law enforcement and social service providers. These social skills should therefore be ingrained into regular and standardised work practice. Building capacity means to improve and uphold professional standards and to engage in constructive networking between various professional groups, which should be based on the proper conduct of ethical and professional standards (i.e. Codes of Conduct).

A first step in building the capacity and expertise of various professional groups is for them to understand why and how trafficking in human beings is relevant to their profession. Such groups include police, prosecutors, judges, lawyers, labour inspectors, labour unions, diplomatic staff, social workers, psychologists, medics, shelter providers and others. As well as setting the social and political context of why such trainings are needed, specialised training materials and methodologies must ensure a sustainable impact over generations of newly recruited staff. Training materials must be based on international standards and put the best interests of the victim at the core of all analysis and recommended action. Experience shows that the development of training materials benefits greatly from a multidisciplinary approach and the involvement of all stakeholders. Based on a comprehensive training needs assessment, training materials should be dynamic documents that should be constantly reviewed and revised. In order to achieve maximum outreach and coverage it is useful to institutionalise training in the curricula of relevant training centres, and to link the issue to other relevant areas such as security, health or gender-based violence.

Once qualified training has reached out to the critical mass within a professional group it is important to enhance their networking skills with others. Take the example of law enforcement: it is essential to bring police, prosecutors, judges and service providers around one table to jointly discuss concrete cases, practical approaches and interpretation of the law. Any such networking exercise is highly beneficial to combat human trafficking. Networking should certainly not stop at the national level but go beyond international borders. The essence and key messages about trafficking in human beings do not vary greatly from trainings conducted in countries of destination to countries of origin. However, training materials of course need to be adapted to the country specifics and particular needs of the respective target audiences. Effective training requires participants to open themselves and reflect on new ideas, innovative approaches and changing attitudes. This may be particularly relevant for professional groups, which are in direct contact with traumatised victims of trafficking.

Recently, important steps towards the training of professionals were taken by international agencies that run peacekeeping operations. In an effort to especially draw from lessons learned from the (post-) conflict areas of the Balkans and Africa, international organisations seek to sensitise and train their civilian and military staff on possible anti-trafficking actions and due standards of behaviour.

Innovative Initiatives Related to Capacity and Institution Building

The following chapters take a closer look at some exemplary initiatives building the capacity of various professional groups in an institutional framework:

- Stakeholders jointly developed an integrated and multidisciplinary anti-trafficking strategy in the framework of Local Security Agenda development in Pernambuco, a province in the North East of Brazil. Diana Segovia showcases the steps involved, orchestrated and coordinated by the local government.
- Bronwyn Jones introduces an innovative programme that coaches local journalists in South Eastern Europe towards a more professional and sensitive media discussion on trafficking in human beings.
- The International Labour Organization's work focuses substantially on forced labour outcomes of human trafficking. Beate Andrees presents activities in the field of standard setting and capacity building, starting with close monitoring of the recruitment process to developing tools for workers' and employer's organisations.
- Nicaragua's police force has successfully managed to incorporate a gender perspective to their work. Countries of Central America and the Caribbean gathered to learn from their experiences and discuss how to mainstream trafficking into their police work. Johanna Willems describes events that led to the adoption of a Regional Action Plan to Combat Trafficking in Human Beings.
- In 2004, the North Atlantic Treaty Organization (NATO) adopted a Policy to Combat Trafficking in Human Beings. One of the main areas of concern is providing adequate training to all civilian and military personnel taking part in NATO operations. Gabriele Reiter gives insight into the multidisciplinary development process of NATO training materials.

Local Agenda for Community Security

Diana Segovia

The Situation in North East Brazil

Brazil is a source and destination country for men, women and children trafficked for sexual and labour exploitation as well as for organ trafficking. It is estimated that as many as 150,000 Brazilians today are held in servitude, forced labour or sexual exploitative situations. The North and North East of Brazil, including Pernambuco, belong to the poorest regions of the country, and are also the most affected by trafficking with the majority of internal trafficking routes originating there. However, these regions are also a source for trafficking persons for sexual exploitation to the US and Western Europe. Recent research suggests that about 241 trafficking routes exist in 20 states of Brazil. More than half of these routes lead to international destinations (Pesquisa Pestraf-Brasil 2002*)*.

Traffickers make use of various methods to recruit from vulnerable groups, such as for example convincing parents to allow their minor girls and boys to move to bigger cities in order for them to receive proper education. Upon reaching the cities, however, contrary to the original promises, the minors are forced to work in slavery-like conditions or are being sexually exploited. Most of the victims have only poor education, and many are of African descent.

Local Strategies to Prevent Trafficking in Persons

Even though trafficking in persons is a global phenomenon, it originates and takes place in cities and local communities. Therefore, to prevent trafficking, especially in women and girls, local governments must take action to overcome the high degree of inequality, gender disparity and social exclusion existing in many of those communities. This means providing social and legal support and protection to vulnerable groups, protecting human rights as well as promoting equal opportunities.

In 2004 in Pernambuco, Brazil, the Latin American branch of Local Governments for Sustainability (ICLEI) in cooperation with the Government of Pernambuco developed the project "Local Strategies to Prevent Trafficking in Persons (LOST)" in response to the local authorities concern about trafficking in persons in their cities and communities. The aim was to support local governments to combat trafficking in an integrated, collaborative and participatory manner as well as in close cooperation with different levels of government, police and civil society. Additionally, the venture intended to promote a regional policy dialogue with other governmental institutions to replicate the initiative in other states of Brazil and the rest of Latin America. The project was implemented with the support of the German Government through the Sector Project.

Conceptual Framework of the Project

The project was integrated in ICLEI's Just, Peaceful, and Secure Communities Program, which conceptualises human rights and community security as a condition for sustainable development of countries. The Local Security Agenda is the instrument for local governments to approach insecurity, injustice and conflict using the Local Agenda 21 methodology. This includes, among others, participatory governance, stakeholder involvement and cooperation between administration and citizens. The goal is that the local government initiates and facilitates a process in which the relevant local actors, including police or other security forces, are involved. The common task is to take stock of the situation in order to define goals for improving security at the local level. Initiatives on Local Security Agendas address the causes for violence, insecurity and conflict, identified by the stakeholders, as well as appropriate measures. An additional goal is the active inclusion of security forces – also coming from the regional or national level – into local actions and into the civil society. The LOST project was inspired by the participatory local agenda methodology and aimed to create conditions that reduce trafficking by implementing the following activities: public awareness raising, information exchange and capacity building especially for at-risk groups.

ICLEI's participatory approach follows a range of key principles:

- The integration of issues and interests of a wide range of stakeholders, such as community groups, NGOs, governmental agencies, professional groups and companies to achieve multi-sector planning based on local concerns.
- Action plans formulate a shared vision and identify local priorities for measures.
- The diffusion of information in form of awareness-raising activities, monitoring and evaluation procedures, such as indicators, are major tools in the process and help to keep track of the progress.
- Measures and projects are oriented towards long-term objectives.
- The impact of local action on global issues is taken into account.

Pernambuco's Action Plan to Prevent and Combat Trafficking in Persons

In 2003, the State of Pernambuco established a programme to prevent and combat trafficking in persons through a decree-law. The multi-dimensional programme aims to develop preventive measures, to improve the prosecution of traffickers and to protect trafficked victims. The main components of the programme are:

- promotion of partnership and cooperation on different levels of government and civil society;
- enhanced participation of all stakeholders;
- promotion of integrative and integral preventive strategies;
- capacity building and education of trainers;
- prosecution and law enforcement;
- legal and social assistance to protect and support victims.

The State of Pernambuco followed a 5-step planning and implementation process in order to achieve its goals:

- Step 1: Creation of an Inter-Institutional Commission to Combat Trafficking
Before formalised as an inter-institutional commission, the expert group working on trafficking issues in Pernambuco was based on voluntary efforts that were mostly facilitated by the Latin American Institute for Human Rights (ILADH). The group advocated for a national anti-trafficking programme in Brazil. The goal was to bring together different governmental agencies, political leaders, police, international organisations, law enforcement agencies and NGOs to lobby for the inclusion of anti-trafficking measures into the Government Agenda. These efforts resulted in an integral and collaborative programme called "Pernambuco State Program to Prevent and Combat Trafficking in Persons". In July 2003, the commitment of the political body and the official support was reflected in a state law. The bill endorsed the creation of an inter-institutional commission whose work is supported by an executive board consisting of government agencies and civil society as well as a Special Secretary within the police department.

- Step 2: Generating Baseline Data through Local Assessment
Initially, the assessment of the local challenges and community concerns as well as the collection of baseline data was carried out by the expert working group. They used multiple methods such as observation, document analysis, interviews, consultation, questionnaires and focus groups in order to gain a more detailed overview of the situation and generate statistics. However, the absence of reliable indicators and registers complicated the quantification of trafficking and trafficking victims. Following this process, the stakeholders, including the commission, government agencies from the regional and federal level and NGOs, were invited to verify the joint assessment. The community assessment revealed a narrow understanding of what defines trafficking, focussing on topics such as prostitution, sex tourism or illegal migration.

Deriving from the baseline data, the commission organised an international seminar in March 2004 to discuss findings, exchange experiences, share knowledge and clarify concepts.

- Step 3: Development of a Code of Conduct
  Building on the experiences and research provided by the expert working group, ILADH and the Commission organised a planning workshop in August 2004, with more than 100 institutions and community representatives taking part.

  The outcome was the joint elaboration of a Code of Conduct (CoC) as an ethic instrument to promote human rights and the drafting of an anti-trafficking action plan. The CoC aims to inform and to raise awareness. However, the main goal is to commit different sectors such as education, arts, business, mass media, government and tourism to get involved in the activities formulated in the programme plan of action. In December 2004, the CoC was officially adopted by the Government of Pernambuco and then published and promoted through media, Internet and public presentations.

- Step 4: Formulation of a Plan of Action
  In the entire process there were no ready-made solutions as the participatory and consensus-based approach put emphasis on the joint assessment, planning and implementation of activities. They were carried out in the areas of prevention, victim support and protection, and prosecution, including e.g. information campaigns and capacity building activities; establishment of free telephone hotlines; creation of a special centre for social and health assistance; establishment of a special commission (with federal police support) to investigate cases.

- Step 5: Monitoring and Evaluation
  The commission has set up a monitoring and evaluation system to analyse the impact of the activities and to review the plan according to failures and success of the implementation. Based on the CoC an overall assessment of the activities will be undertaken and made available to the general public. The first report of the programme's performance and impact was submitted to the government of Pernambuco in March 2005.

Lessons Learned

In the case of Pernambuco, political commitment and strong participation of the most relevant actors was a prerequisite for the overall success of the programme. Participation in decision-making, planning and action were key elements for the stakeholders to identify their own needs, realise synergies and resolve conflicts. Identifying a long-term vision to approach the complex issue of trafficking in persons is essential.

The stakeholder approach including the participation of international organisations helped the actors to cooperate rather than to compete as well as to empower them to incorporate a regional and global perspective. The inclusion of vulnerable groups themselves (not just through isolated consultation) contributed to a better understanding and increased knowledge of the problem, stimulated learning and empowered the community.

Furthermore, the experience has shown that reliable data on trafficking dimensions, a clear definition of the phenomenon and the assessment of local needs are crucial for the design of a plan of action.

Improving Media Coverage through Journalist Training

Bronwyn Jones

Media Coverage on Trafficking in Persons

In many regions there is little media coverage on the issue of trafficking in human beings. If media tackles the issue, the coverage is mostly one-dimensional or biased, and victim protection (e.g. anonymity) is often neglected. In Southern and Eastern Europe, crime and social issues are not seen as important enough for the media to cover. There is a tendency to regard serious journalism and political reporting to be about covering politicians and political parties only. 'Lower' issues, like trafficking, get either merely a brief mentioning in serious local media or receive sensationalist treatment through the tabloids. Looking at criminal and social reporting as a barometer of how policies actually work and relating the way of reporting to progress in general is a new concept in the region.

Many of the best journalists and editors in the South Eastern European region regard trafficking simply as a crime story, usually involving prostitution. Other means of trafficking, like labour exploitation, organ trafficking or the exploitation of children are rarely covered.

Without a more comprehensive approach on trafficking in persons by the media there is little accountability in the institutional structures that are supposed to deal with the problem. The one-dimensionality of the media becomes replicated in society's image of trafficking too. It is simply seen as something that happens to foreign women on their territory. Trafficking is always the problem of another group of people who has come to one's country and allowed trafficking to proliferate. In other words, the problem has nothing to do with *oneself,* so why bother? Considering the other issues of life that people have to deal with, trafficking becomes a low priority.

Media and Development International (MADI)

In April 2004, the non-governmental organisation Media and Development International was founded to provide media solutions to development issues. MADI works in a variety of media on social development issues including training journalists on coverage of social topics, creating public awareness-raising campaigns, advising on media relations for NGOs, INGOs and other organisations.

Human trafficking has become a large part of MADI's portfolio, partly because its work began with trainings on the topic. One of the first major projects was a Regional Journalists Training Programme on Trafficking for South Eastern Europe, which is still in the implementation phase. This programme began with a Regional Media Decision-makers' Conference on Trafficking in October 2004 in Belgrade and has continued with the Bulgarian Reporting Training Project in March 2005.

Through the trainings, MADI seeks to show how trafficking can be covered in all of its dimensions from the root causes to the responses of the government and how this reporting affects the larger society as a whole. Before, there was no comprehensive programme on a media level dealing with trafficking in persons regionally. Previous approaches that had been incorporated were in many ways inadequate, judging by the quality of the press in the region and its coverage of trafficking in particular. Hence, MADI created a programme that addressed these issues on a regional basis.

Background of Journalist Training in Bulgaria

In 2004, MADI created a programme that trained journalists how to cover trafficking in persons. The first complete training seminar lasted 10 months and was funded by BMZ through the Sector Project of GTZ. Eight journalists from various Bulgarian cities took part in this programme. The participating reporters not only learned good reporting and editing standards, but also were able to pass on what they had learned to their colleagues. Journalism is learned by doing, therefore, MADI's training projects were set up to produce stories. Those stories were distributed to the public and created an immediate standard for journalism and an immediate response from the public. Often, if a story is good enough, other journalists and media in the region will pick up on it or even copy the techniques used to create this story. Imitation is the highest form of flattery, so MADI hoped for the articles to be copied around the region in order to redevelop standards.

For the journalist training programme, MADI worked with a team of journalists from a variety of media outlets across Bulgaria and in different media. The group was facilitated like a reporting unit: journalists were recruited for the programme in cooperation with the Media Development Centre (MDC) in Sofia, which was also the base for operations. The Bulgaria project focused on reporters from outside Sofia where the need for training was the greatest. Trafficking problems occur more often in rural areas and so far had not been covered to the same extent as in the capital.

Methodology of the Training

The reporters were given a three-day workshop covering various trafficking issues, reporting techniques as well as the creation of a standard process for the entire programme. As time or financial resources often restrict journalistic work in the region, the project was kept on a tight rein: the reporters were asked to keep up a very stringent level of work in their process of outlining the areas of research, writing and careful editing. Each step was examined and discussed among the group; various techniques like when to use tapes, how to approach subjects, which story angles to choose and how to check facts were demonstrated. Examples of previous stories were used as a basis for discussion and reporters were asked to reflect on them. The participating reporters planned their stories, working individually as well as in groups with the local and international editorial trainer in order to develop their articles. The reporters were enabled to think about their stories on a holistic and deeper level, considering all of the options that were available.

The trainer team consisted of a local prominent editor and journalist and an international trainer from MADI. They visited every participating reporter in their hometown and encouraged all reporters to share information and work together as much as possible. In the middle of the month, the group had an editorial meeting bringing the journalists together to discuss their improvement. Journalists contacted MADI at least once a week with a progress report on their story. During the individual and group sessions, the reporters were questioned on their story and advance. The trainer team gave a diagnosis as to the problems they were facing, why and how to resolve the issues.

One of the issues the group consistently dealt with was the question of how well governments in this region actually protected and assisted potential victims of trafficking as well as those victims who were returned. To answer this, the group discussed questions of corruption within institutions as well as the rights of minorities, women and children. Often victim protection in the region is still inadequate and there is a lack of safety nets to protect trafficked persons. This is sometimes replicated in journalism as well. If the governments do not pay enough attention to victims' rights then that message is filtered down throughout society, including the media.

The editing process was the most difficult training module for the group. Their stories were not only fact-checked throughout the process, but also fully proofread for readability. As publications do not always reach international journalistic standards, editing became very labour-intensive.

Having the journalists work together and share information was more successful than originally imagined. The journalists called each other to talk about their meeting and to check on various facts for their story if they thought someone else was more knowledgeable (one journalist, for example, became the expert on legislation for the group). This exchange was strongly encouraged as it made the programme run much smoother.

The trainers also helped the team with contacts in the capital and abroad. The fact that none of the participating reporters had a good command of the English language cut down the depth of contacts they had abroad. Even using the Internet became a major problem. MADI therefore facilitated contacts to the embassies of the United States of America and Germany and to other State Agencies (National Security Service, Agency of Employment, Foreign Office) in Bulgaria as well as across the border in Macedonia and in the US, as two of our stories had links to those countries.

The Results of the Training Programme

In total, six stories and at least four follow-ups have come out of this programme. The trainer team spent roughly 50 hours on the support of each story. At the end of the programme, the reports will be placed on the Journalists Network on Trafficking site (www.jnet-trafficking.org), which is run by MADI and hosted by the Media Development Centre in Sofia. This regional site seeks not only to promote original reporting on trafficking but also to be a 'one-stop shop' of resources for journalists who cover trafficking as well as a place for reporters to network across borders.

The website is also used for monitoring progress as the MDC will continue to monitor the work of the journalists involved in the programme. Follow-ups or updates to the stories done will be published on the site. For the next six months, MDC will also look at the Bulgarian media as a whole and see if the stories produced have had an impact in terms of imitation, follow-ups and improvement in the overall tone of journalism regarding trafficking. In addition to this, journalists and others will be encouraged to directly respond on the website to the articles. The stories will also be published and broadcast nationally throughout Bulgaria. Furthermore the stories on the website will be translated into English as well as Albanian, Bosnian, Croatian, Serbian, Macedonian, Bulgarian and Romanian. They will be released for republishing elsewhere free of charge in exchange for a credit to the website.

Lessons Learned

These types of programmes require a great deal of intensive labour for both the participants and the trainers. Looking at the time needed for such training programmes, they should last no less than a period of two weeks. The fact that most of the journalists were working their regular jobs in addition to writing the stories made it rather difficult to fully concentrate on the programme. Making an arrangement with their home paper or station to allow them to work full-time on the project would help very much with regard to time constraints. During the training process it became obvious that the individual work with the journalist is of high importance. In addition more emphasis should be put on support of the fieldwork and the editing process with the reporters. In order to raise the professional quality of journalists' writing to a national and international level, a long-term approach is required.

Addressing Labour Market Dimensions

Beate Andrees

ILO's Capacity Building Programmes Against Trafficking in Human Beings

In the turmoil of civil war and economic transition in South Eastern Europe, trafficking in human beings was quickly associated with forced prostitution, the spread of organised crime and endemic corruption. For years, the image of young and deceived women trapped in illegal brothels in Kosovo or Bosnia-Herzegovina has influenced policy responses in Europe. Ministries of the Interior and special police units have taken the lead in fighting trafficking, cracking down on criminal networks, bars and brothels. While this has helped many women to escape their exploiters, it is now increasingly recognised that trafficking is a more complex phenomenon, which has to be tackled from a labour market perspective. It is also embedded in global labour migration flows. Women are discriminated in both, national and global labour markets, and therefore make up the majority of trafficking victims.

According to a recent International Labour Organization (ILO) estimate, at least 2.45 million women, men and children are trafficked at any given point in time, one third of which are trafficked for non-sexual purposes (ILO 2005a). Trafficking for labour exploitation occurs in various economic sectors, such as agriculture, construction, textile and garments or domestic service. Many victims of trafficking – be it for forced sexual or labour exploitation – are treated as 'illegal migrants' and deported without receiving justice for the wrong they experienced. Those who recruited and exploited them often go unpunished due to weak law enforcement and support structures for victims seeking to denounce their exploiters. Once returned to their home countries, former trafficking victims may fall back into the hands of traffickers, desperate to find employment abroad.

This reality indicates the need for better law enforcement and victim support on the one hand as well as more effective prevention on the other. While policy responses and legal reforms have become stronger in most European countries, implementation and enforcement still lag behind. Whether anti-trafficking programmes will indeed make a real dent in the future, will not only depend on sufficient resources but also on the experience of professional groups to deal with the issue. Training programmes are therefore key among the various responses against trafficking in human beings. The following chapter will present some ILO initiatives to strengthen the capacity of labour market actors in national anti-trafficking programmes. It will start with a brief introduction reflecting the assumptions underlying such capacity building and how it generates social change. This is followed by examples from Europe where the German Government through the Sector Project of GTZ supported some of the training activities.

Basic Assumptions of Anti-Trafficking Capacity Building

The contemporary view of capacity building in development cooperation is that it goes beyond knowledge transfer and face-to-face training. From a more holistic point of view, capacity building should promote policy dialogue, institutional pluralism and cooperation, information sharing and network creation. A further challenge is to sustain capacities in an environment where financial resources are scarce and where there are many competing issues that merit the attention of government and other social actors. Hence, capacity building has to be grounded in a strategy that empowers people, enables them to generate social change and to solve problems with limited resources.

Capacity building in the context of anti-trafficking programmes has to be based on solid knowledge of the forms, causes and consequences of this crime. And since trafficking very often affects at least two countries, these measures should span international borders. Before embarking on actual training programmes, the ILO conducted a range of rapid assessment studies in origin, transit and destination countries. The studies highlighted the circumstances under which children, men and women are being trafficked, the role of intermediaries, push and pull factors linked to labour markets in countries of origin and destination, forms of coercion and types of coercive employment in the destination countries. The results showed a wide spectrum of trafficking cases, ranging from young women who have been deceived and forced into prostitution to men who responded to deceptive job offers abroad and ended up in forced construction work (ILO 2005a).

Hence trafficking can take on different forms but common to all is the exploitation and violation of human rights at one stage of the trafficking cycle. Most victims leave their country voluntarily in an attempt to seek more lucrative employment abroad. It is only over time that they realise the trap of dependence and exploitation from which they find it difficult to escape. However, only a minority of victims are physically restricted from leaving their employment. Most submit to the exploitation in the hope of finding a way out and returning home with sufficient money. Based on this research, the ILO developed a range of capacity building programmes that have some features in common:

- first, they are based on human/labour rights and the empowerment of victims to claim their rights;
- second, they target mainly labour market actors while at the same time trying to build alliances between civil society groups, police and other government authorities;
- third, they focus on the long-term prevention of human trafficking by addressing labour market imbalances that stimulate supply and demand for trafficking victims.

In South Eastern Europe, much of anti-trafficking training has involved police and border guards due to the immediate need to suppress organised crime. So far, little has been done to address root causes, such as poverty and unemployment in the countries of origin, gender discrimination and the absence of sound migration policies (Limanowska 2005). The reason is not only the lack of budgetary resources or external funding, but also the lack of cooperation among various actors and the absence of long-term strategies. In 2004, the ILO organised a tripartite seminar with tripartite delegations from Albania, Romania, Moldova and Ukraine on human trafficking. This was the first time that labour market actors, such as trade unionists, employers and labour ministries from the region explored labour market based strategies against trafficking in human beings together with national anti-trafficking coordinators, representatives from international organisations, NGOs and others. Following this first ILO initiative in the region, the capacity building programme was then broken down into several components.

Capacity Building on Monitoring the Recruitment Process

In 2003, the ILO initiated a pilot project in Romania to address abusive recruitment practices that could easily degenerate into trafficking. The project involved government representatives, labour inspectors, police, trade unions and employers' organisations. A reference group of all actors validated a training manual on recruitment that was developed by the ILO with the help of independent experts (ILO 2005b). This tool has now been translated into several languages and is widely used in training activities in Europe and beyond.

The training manual is based on research that helps to understand the different modus operandi of traffickers, also using travel, model, entertainment or au pair agencies as a cover for sending people abroad. It also works on the assumption that improved monitoring of private recruitment agencies would gradually eradicate the market for criminal recruiters. In most countries, private recruitment agencies are mainly interested in the recruitment of highly skilled migrant workers, leaving the low skilled to the public employment services or informal recruiters, such as traffickers. Hence, apart from the detection of cover activities it is also important to improve standards in the recruitment business at large so that potential migrants can trust their recruiters. Monitoring recruitment is of course only one step in limiting the market for traffickers. It has to go hand in hand with the monitoring of labour markets in destination countries and other prevention measures.

The validation phase in Romania as well as subsequent training activities helped to assess the effectiveness of the training. The lessons learned mirror the merits and limits of capacity building. First, prior to actually starting the training, it is important to assess the existing legal framework on private recruitment agencies and human trafficking as well as relevant administrative regulations in the country. Often, legal frameworks are inexistent or lack clarity, so the training has to be flexible in order to account for these limitations. The actual training should also empower participants to assess current laws and policies and to propose changes if necessary.

Second, apart from government and law enforcement, business associations of private recruitment agencies and trade unions should participate from the beginning of the activity. A training programme that involves all actors concerned with their different views on the problem is more likely to reveal contentious issues and to stimulate dialogue. In this particular context, it may also promote self-regulation of the recruitment industry. Third, law-abiding recruiters will need support from employers who eventually recruit migrant workers. As long as employers knowingly recruit through informal networks or do not ask questions about their labour providers, recruiters working within the legal framework will find it difficult to stand up against illegal competitors. Hence, after a first training focusing on core actors, the programme should then be extended to other countries and sectors affected by human trafficking.

These lessons learned are reflected in the training manual. The modules of the training programme can easily be adapted to specific circumstances in each country and to the needs of different professional groups. It contains good practice examples from across the world. The core of the manual consists of a section on monitoring systems, such as licensing, registration, rating or codes of conducts. The training is structured in such a way that different professional groups can provide input through their knowledge and expertise. This is crucial to ensure interagency cooperation in the implementation phase.

Capacity Building on the Forced Labour Outcomes of Human Trafficking

Another important component of ILO's anti-trafficking programmes is the training of policy and lawmakers, enforcement and judicial authorities, social partners and NGOs on the identification of trafficked victims. While empirical evidence on trafficking for labour exploitation is growing, the number of convictions is still very low. This may be due to the fact that many victims in labour exploitation are still largely perceived as 'illegal migrants' that do not deserve the same protection as victims of sexual exploitation. Furthermore, in the absence of clear legal frameworks, perpetrators are often prosecuted under related criminal offences, such as smuggling, extortion or bodily injury. This may be problematic in at least two respects:

- first, penalties under these offences are usually significantly lower than trafficking offences, hence not acting as an efficient deterrent;
- second, victims do not receive the same protection as trafficking victims and may thus be less willing to testify in court.

Following the adoption of the Palermo Protocol, supplementing the UN Convention against Transnational Organised Crime, many governments are now revising or amending their legislation to account for the offence of trafficking for forced labour. Since forced labour is an issue the ILO has dealt with under its Forced Labour Convention No. 29 since 1930, it is in a position to provide legal advice and training on this issue. For this purpose, a legal guide was developed that is now increasingly used in training programmes (ILO 2005c). The training is based on the assumption that victim identification will require improved cooperation between law enforcement officials, trade unions, NGOs and others. Cooperation has to be fostered vertically – between international, national, community and individual levels – and horizontally – across agencies and sectors. Capacity building programmes have just started and it is yet too early to assess the outcome. In the current stage it was key to build partnerships with other intergovernmental and national organisations that have already gained knowledge on the identification of trafficking victims in the sex industry. One major outcome of this component will be the development of indicators helping law enforcement authorities and others to identify likely victims who will then benefit from special protection measures.

Conclusion and Perspectives

The examples demonstrate recent ILO training initiatives to strengthen local capacities against trafficking in human beings. They are part of a larger ILO effort to eliminate human trafficking, also focusing on the worst forms of child labour and the need for better migration management. By shifting the attention to the forced labour outcomes of human trafficking, the ILO emphasises the labour market perspective and the role of labour market actors in national anti-trafficking programmes. In today's globalised world, millions of women, men and children are still trafficked for work or services they have not chosen or cannot leave freely. Capacity building measures against trafficking have to account for these coercive practices in order to empower victims as well as other actors to break the chain of dependence and exploitation.

In addition to training programmes on the monitoring of recruitment agencies and identification of victims, the ILO is currently developing sensitisation and capacity building tools for workers' and employers' organisations. Trafficking in human beings has not been high on their agendas given that is was so closely associated with prostitution and organised crime. With the growing recognition, however, that trafficking may affect supply chains of major companies, both trade unions and employers are increasingly willing to get involved in anti-trafficking programmes. Here again, the ILO can assist in disseminating knowledge, creating networks and developing strategies for future change.

Incorporating Gender Issues into Police Reform Processes

Johanna Willems

Trafficking in Persons in Central America and the Caribbean

Trafficking in persons, especially women and children, is an everyday reality in the Central American and the Caribbean region. Poor socio-economic circumstances in this region motivate many people to search for better economic opportunities in other parts of their home countries or in foreign countries. As elsewhere, trafficking takes place mostly from poor to wealthier regions either within countries or across borders. Victims of trafficking are being exploited in the sex industry, in sweatshops, restaurants, bars and hotels, and as domestic servants. Trafficking affects each country uniquely; however, little information is available on the extent and means of trafficking in this region. Lack of a uniform definition, absence of indicators and the extremely low number of prosecutions complicate the quantification.

Government representatives recognise trafficking as a problem, often as an increasing one. Despite this, so far, with the exception of the Dominican Republic, the issue of trafficking in persons has not been incorporated into national agendas and efforts to tackle the problem often take place on an ad hoc basis. Up to now, few organisations in the region have taken up explicit anti-trafficking work.

Regional Project for the Incorporation of a Gender Approach in Police Forces

Since 1996, the Nicaraguan police are working on the implementation of a gender approach in its institution and on responding to the different needs of men and women in their services. This includes for example the establishment of special commissariats for women and children, special recruitment campaigns for female personnel and training measures for police personnel on gender issues, especially gender-based violence.

The success of the Nicaraguan police has captured the interest of other police institutions in the region and they have articulated their need for support in the area of gender and security. Consequently, in 2000, a regional project called "Incorporation of a Gender Approach in the Modernization of Police Institutions and Security" was established in Central America and the Caribbean. In the context of the project, the Nicaraguan police force in cooperation with the Project for the Promotion of Gender Policies implemented by the Deutsche Gesellschaft für Technische Zusammenarbeit (GTZ) GmbH and commissioned by the Federal Ministry for Economic Development and Cooperation (BMZ) advises other police institutions in the region on the incorporation of gender policies within the institutions as well as on gender sensitive police services for the population. A regional gender advisory committee with delegates from each institution was established to consult with the Comisión de Jefes, Jefas y Directores de Policía de Centroamérica y el Caribe (Commission of Police Directors in Central America and the Caribbean), created in 1991.

This framework laid the basis for the work in the area of trafficking in persons, considering the fact that most of the victims in the region are female and that gender discrimination can be regarded as one contributing factor to trafficking in women and girls.

The police institutions together with some non-governmental organisations are among the first institutions in the region to confront the problem. Police forces, in cooperation with organisations of the civil society, play an important role in the identification of victims without whose testimonies convictions of traffickers are almost impossible.

Train-the-Trainer-Course for Police Officials

Several training measures were implemented during the above-mentioned project. The first regional Train-the-Trainer-course took place in 2002 in Managua, Nicaragua; it lasted four weeks. 33 police officers, male and female, from seven countries and twelve institutions took part in this first training. The programme consisted of the different components:

- participatory approaches for the facilitation of trainings;
- planning and implementation of trainings;
- basic knowledge on gender inequality and approaches to incorporate gender sensitive approaches in institutional work;
- specialisation in gender issues connected to police work, such as gender violence and gender-balanced human resource work.

The participants evaluated the course as a great success; hence, another four-week-course was planned for 2003. The topic of trafficking in persons, especially women, was incorporated into the programme of this follow-up course. An anti-trafficking expert from Nicaragua facilitated the module.

This time another 31 officers from thirteen institutions in eight countries, namely Belize, Costa Rica, El Salvador, Guatemala, Honduras, Nicaragua, Panama and the Dominican Republic, participated in the training. The focus of the training module on trafficking was on:

- definition and concept of trafficking in persons;
- reasons for trafficking;
- trafficking cycle;
- possible police interventions to tackle the phenomenon of trafficking (focusing both on prevention and prosecution);
- protection of the rights of the (potential) victim.

One of the outcomes of the course for the region was that it still remains to be clarified what constitutes trafficking and how smuggling and undocumented migration can be differentiated from trafficking. However, the participants stated in their evaluations that they had gained a better understanding of the concept of trafficking and saw the issue as important for their institutions.

A great advantage of incorporating the issue of trafficking into such a comprehensive programme was that the problem did not stand isolated, but was put into the broader context of gender inequalities, the protection of victims of gender-based violence and the access to security for the whole population. Due to the course anti-trafficking activities have gained more attention and were consequently put on the priority agenda of police institutions in the region.

Regional Action Plan to Combat Trafficking in Persons

In July 2004, the regional gender advisory committee met in Tegucigalpa, Honduras, to exchange experiences on the progress made in implementing a gender approach in the different institutions. The agenda included the issue of trafficking in persons and the role that the institution (can) play in fighting the problem; a vivid discussion arose around this topic.

Consequently, in November 2004, the Comisión de Jefes, Jefas y Directores de Policía de Centroamérica y el Caribe under the presidency of the Nicaraguan Police Director Edwin Cordero Ardila adopted a "Regional Plan on Trafficking and Smuggling in Persons". The police institutions thereby recognised that trafficking in persons, especially in women and minors, is an increasing problem in the region and anti-trafficking measures need coordinated regional efforts to be effective. The plan explicitly states that cooperation is not only necessary within the various police institutions across the borders, but also with organisations of the civil society; this can be seen as a positive development. Even though the plan has a strong focus on trafficking for the purpose of sexual exploitation, it also lays ground for anti-trafficking measures in the areas of labour exploitation and organ trafficking.

Developing Training Modules for Peacekeeping Operations

Gabriele Reiter

Background

Instability, threats to security and rule of law, provide fertile ground for organised crime, including trafficking in human beings. These characteristics often prevail in conflict and post-conflict countries or regions, where the North Atlantic Treaty Organisation (NATO) makes its resources available for peacekeeping operations in order to re-establish stability and security. Hence, it is within the mandate and competence of an international military peacekeeping operation to inter alia assist the host nation in its efforts to curb down on trafficking in human beings.

Trafficking in human beings inflicts upon peacekeeping operations in various ways. As a form of organised crime closely linked to corruption and other criminal outgrowths it is considered to be a challenge to mission security and the protection of its forces, which are major concerns for any military presence. However, experience of recent years shows that personnel of peacekeeping operations are not only viewed as the guarantors of peace, security and stability but in a number of reported cases also as wrongdoers. Reports of peacekeepers involved in trafficking cases have a detrimental impact on the image and credibility of a peacekeeping operation.

In order to secure mission security and mission credibility, the two main pillars of successful mission accomplishment, civilian and military personnel employed in areas of operation as well as in the headquarters need to be aware of trafficking in human beings, its symptoms and serious human rights implications and how to deal with it. These deliberations led the North Atlantic Treaty Organisation to take action on both, the policy and the operational level.

NATO Policy to Combat Trafficking in Human Beings

In late 2003, NATO and its partners started discussing how to best counteract the crime of trafficking in human beings in the setting of international peacekeeping operations. Two delegations to NATO, respectively the US and Norwegian representations were instrumental in initiating and sustaining the debate. In March 2004, delegations of the Euro-Atlantic Partnership Council (EAPC) invited a selected group of anti-trafficking experts from international and non-governmental organisations to NATO Headquarters for an exchange. Subsequently to the internal debate, the EAPC adopted the NATO Policy to Combat Trafficking in Human Beings, which was endorsed at the Istanbul Summit in June 2004.

Building on the definition of the UN Trafficking Protocol the NATO Policy calls upon NATO member states and partners to review their anti-trafficking legislation to secure standards of behaviour, to ensure that all personnel taking part in NATO-led operations receives appropriate training as well as to support responsible authorities in the respective host country in their efforts to combat trafficking in human beings. The Policy actually goes a step further and requests that its provisions are also applicable to contractors. It furthermore gives guidance on how to implement all policy areas and calls for continuous monitoring and evaluation of the implementation of the Policy. The Policy is accompanied by an implementation plan, which details responsibilities of both, the military committee and civilian committees. Moreover, military branches are tasked to develop specific policy provisions, within existing peace support operations, for the role of NATO-led forces in supporting within their competence and mandate, the efforts of responsible authorities in the host country to combat trafficking in human beings.

Development of Training and Educational Materials

First steps towards the implementation of the NATO Policy were taken in the field of training and education. In September 2004, the Geneva Centre for Security Policy (GCSP) organised a workshop on "Curriculum Development on Combating Trafficking in Human Beings" in support of the NATO Policy. As a member of the Partnership for Peace Consortium, GCSP provided a platform for exchange for more than 80 participants from over 30 countries, from NATO institutions, national training institutions as well as subject-matter experts from international and non-governmental organisations. Workshop participants compared ongoing training initiatives as well as they assessed experiences and lessons learned from previous peacekeeping operations for their application in new areas of NATO operations. Extensive discussions about approaches towards training strategies and NATO's implementation thereof resulted in the constitution of a multidisciplinary Core Working Group that would coordinate the development of training and educational materials. In addition, a Reference Group was established as an open advisory forum that could be consulted throughout the drafting process.

The NATO Policy gives explicit guidance for the development of training and educational programmes. Training and creating awareness are key elements to ensure the successful implementation of this policy. It anticipates that training will provide information required to identify trafficking and will put military and civilian personnel on notice of consequences for engaging in trafficking (NATO 2004: 6). The Policy requests that three training modules are elaborated: a General Module for Civilian and Military personnel to be employed in a NATO operation, a Module for Military Commanders and Civilian Leaders as well as a Module for Military Law Enforcement. In order to ensure the greatest effectiveness, training modules should:

- be provided to all levels of military and civilian personnel;
- include information tailored to the specific situation/requirement of the target audience;
- be developed with input from anti-trafficking experts of international and non-governmental organisations with experience in combating trafficking;
- where feasible focus on 'Train-the-Trainers' events to ensure the dissemination of appropriate information on all levels;
- include case studies and interactive methods of training;
- make use of distance and computer-based training. (NATO 2004: 7)

The implementation plan tasks NATO's Allied Command Transformation based in Norfolk as well as NATO educational institutions, the NATO School in Oberammergau and the NATO Defense College in Rome, with the development of training and educational materials, which draws extensive subject-matter expertise from GCSP, the Sector Project of GTZ as well as from the International Organization for Migration.

Core Working Group and Drafting Teams

The NATO School agreed to chair the Core Working Group and offered to host its first meeting in November 2004, where its 15 members discussed and agreed upon the detailed framework, structure and outline of various learning packages for use in NATO training institutions. Additionally, small multidisciplinary drafting teams were identified to create the respective modules and collect case studies within a time period of three months. Built on the constructive dialogue between security and human rights experts as well as professional trainers the drafting teams managed to fulfil their tasking in the narrowly pitched timeframe. They presented prototypes of the three modules accompanied by case studies and other relevant resource materials to the Core Working Group and the Reference Group in February 2005, where the materials were revised and adopted.

The modules are designed to discuss the NATO Policy and its relevance for NATO-led operations, to introduce trafficking in human beings in the broader framework of organised crime and to give guidance and inspiration in implementing all areas of the NATO Policy. On the basis of this work an Advanced Distributed Learning Module was developed and presented to the public in June 2005.

The training modules were immediately piloted at NATO School and NATO Defense College. The Core Working Group recommends that trainings be conducted by a team of trainers, one uniformed and one civilian. The training materials are made available to EAPC member states through NATO Headquarters in Brussels. It is hoped that all member states adapt the materials according to their country specifics (including legislation and Codes of Conduct) and carry out anti-trafficking training for all staff prior to their deployment in NATO-led operations.

Lessons Learned and Recommendations

The quality of the training materials benefited greatly from the multidisciplinary and participatory approach that NATO initiated with talks prior to the adoption of its policy, continuing throughout the development process. Moreover, the extensive exchange and the close cooperation between military structures and experts from international and non-governmental organisations helped to overcome common misunderstandings and stereotypical perceptions of each other. All cooperating partners stated that they had benefited from this process. Various areas of the NATO Policy still need to be taken further such as the review of reporting procedures, of staff guidelines or of relevant doctrines governing NATO's action in specific fields like Civil-Military Cooperation (CIMIC). The training materials have to be seen as 'work in progress', which needs to be regularly reviewed and revised. Training for civilian and military personnel must inform especially on standards of behaviour and the consequences of misconduct. This includes adequate information about reporting lines and internal procedures. And all staff should be trained on their specific roles and responsibilities when encountering trafficking cases in order to respond accurately and efficiently within their competence and mandate. Commanders play a crucial role in that they are the living example for their troops. Any policy and implementation thereof needs to be supported by senior ranks of the organisation.

It is hoped that the successful implementation of the NATO Policy and its comprehensive training programmes will enhance the responsibility, credibility and accountability of military and civilian personnel serving in NATO-led operations. With this, NATO and its partners can make a significant contribution to combating trafficking in human beings as well as to safeguarding peace, security and stability.

Approaches to Advocacy Work

Advocacy entails raising awareness of people on a particular issue in order to bring about change. It may include lobbying for change and bringing practical findings to the policy and legislative levels of a country or an association of countries. It may also include awareness raising amongst a particular target audience, be it vulnerable populations or the community at large to generate action on behalf of trafficked persons. Lobby efforts will only be taken seriously when based on accurate research and reliable data. This approach allows to adequately address the nature and extent of any problem area as well as to develop tailored strategies and targeted trainings.

Governments seek public support for many legislative changes in areas closely related to trafficking in human beings. Advocacy must therefore also target the broader public in order to provoke change of attitudes and perceptions. In countries of destination this relates foremost to the public stance towards foreigners and migrant labour force. In countries of origin advocacy needs to change the attitude towards victims and their perception in society. This idea could also be perceived the other way around: If a broad public calls for a change in policy or legislation, decision-makers are more likely to tackle these demands on the national and international level.

The anti-trafficking discourse developed in such a way that different stakeholders have actually been advocating for various agendas in parallel to each other. Different perspectives such as human rights, law enforcement, gender-equality or migration should be mainstreamed into one comprehensive anti-trafficking response promoting the best interest of the victims and protecting their rights. However, often enough advocacy debates tend to be hijacked as a playground for moralistic debates about issues such as the legalisation of prostitution. Whereas governments certainly need to address such questions, by confusing trafficking with prostitution they have deflected some attention from responding to the immediate needs of trafficked persons.

International and Regional Standards

NGOs undertook concerted lobbying during the negotiations of the UN Crime Commission developing the UN Trafficking Protocol. Whilst the Protocol was first and foremost being developed as a tool to aid international law enforcement cooperation and combat rising transnational organised crime, non-governmental organisations from around the globe lobbied to ensure that victim assistance provisions would be included and made mandatory upon states. In addition, some NGOs advocated for a broader definition of trafficking beyond prostitution.

Lobbyists succeeded in establishing a definition to prosecute trafficking for forced labour, slavery and servitude regardless of international border crossing. They were also successful in ensuring specific victim support measures were mentioned, even if the wording on state responsibility remained rather weak.

These advocacy efforts have proven to be beneficial in two ways: UN-accredited NGOs were able to bring the views and experiences from grassroots NGOs to the negotiation table at the United Nations. Meanwhile grassroots NGOs have been able to make use of the language lobbied for in the UN Trafficking Protocol when advocating for legislative change in their home countries.

The ratification process of the UN Trafficking Protocol is accompanied by the development of a number of high-level policy documents primarily aimed at supplementing the UN Trafficking Protocol with stronger human rights language in the areas of prevention, victim assistance and protection as well as prosecution and law enforcement:

- In 2002, the UN High Commissioner for Human Rights released Recommended Principles and Guidelines on Human Rights and Human Trafficking.
- In addition, the OSCE Permanent Council in 2003 adopted an Action Plan in order to aid governments in implementing their commitments to combat trafficking in human beings.

These documents also constitute excellent lobbying tools for advocates to press their governments for change.

- To complement the UN Convention against Transnational Organized Crime and the UN Trafficking Protocol "with a view to improving the protection which they afford and developing the standards established by them" (CoE Convention 2005: Preamble) the Council of Europe member states negotiated and drafted a Convention on Action against Trafficking in Human Beings. This Convention was adopted only in May 2005. Even though, it is creditable that the Convention foresees a monitoring mechanism, it remains to be seen how useful the incorporated monitoring mechanism will be for advocacy purposes.

National Initiatives

Advocacy efforts certainly have to be based on identified gaps and shortcomings. Often shocking news stories or case studies have triggered the development of concerted advocacy efforts, particularly on the national level.

It is crucial to build alliances between local stakeholders and agree on common goals to develop an effective advocacy strategy in the short and long term. Partnerships in advocacy with governments, especially sympathetic departments, alliances with trade unions or others are also an important way of bringing about (and sustaining) change. Effective advocacy is always based on accurate information, which is why accurate and careful research on trafficking is needed. While such national advocacy efforts may be aided by international actors, changes will be most sustainable when solutions to identified problems are found jointly and owned locally.

Involving victims in advocacy better reflects their right to self-representation. Advocates should take care to represent what victims want and need as much as what the advocates think that victims need. This will ensure that advocacy is effective. For example, advocates now recognise the importance of child participation, as they should be encouraged to speak for themselves, and recommend changes they want, whilst at the same time they should not be forced to actually 'take the stand' unless they want to.

So far, advocacy has focused a lot on changing the law and policy. However, what is equally important is changing practice. It is crucial to observe and ensure that law enforcement and social service providers actually do follow the guidelines that have been put in place.

Innovative Initiatives Related to Advocacy

The following chapters touch upon significant advocacy initiatives at national and regional levels. Examples from an international NGO based in London and an international organisation with a programme in Abuja showcase the development of lobbying efforts:

- Within the European context, Anti-Slavery International's lobby work has focused on the establishment of mechanisms to better protect the rights of trafficked persons. Mary Cunneen gives an overview over the main features of advocacy on the European and national level as well as elaborating on the need for relevant partnerships.
- The International Labour Organization's Action Programme against Human Trafficking and Forced Labour in West Africa prepares its advocacy efforts through baseline studies assessing the situation on human trafficking in Nigeria and Ghana. Victoria Nwogu describes how the findings are being used to develop a strategy and to advocate for change.

Lobbying in Europe

Mary Cunneen

Background

While international awareness of trafficking in human beings has increased in recent years, much work is still needed to effectively tackle the issue. The role of non-governmental organisations in advocacy at the national, regional and international level is important to sensitise policy makers and institutions and to ensure that a human rights perspective, based on the experience of those who have worked for many years directly with trafficked persons, is at the centre of any counter-trafficking policies. This is particularly acute at the European level, where with a mixture of countries of origin, transit and destination it requires not only consideration of prevention strategies, but also how to enable safer migration based on reliable standards, and to protect the rights of those who may be, or are, vulnerable to trafficking into forced labour situations.

Goals and Approach of Anti-Slavery International

Anti-Slavery International is committed to eliminating all forms of slavery in today's world. The organisation works towards this by exposing current cases of slavery and campaigning for their eradication, supporting the initiatives of local organisations to release people, and pressing for more effective implementation of international laws against slavery. In Anti-Slavery International's trafficking work the overall goal is the elimination of trafficking in persons as guided by relevant international laws. To achieve this goal, Anti-Slavery International contributes to existing counter-trafficking networks and mechanisms and actively seeks areas that are insufficiently covered by other organisations and agencies. Moreover Anti-Slavery International searches for fields of activity where it can 'add value', in particular in-house skills and expertise, and use its ability to influence public debate, government policies and the directions of larger organisations.

To this end, Anti-Slavery International within its anti-trafficking programme is currently working towards:

- Wider recognition that migrants are frequently exploited in conditions of forced labour and greater acceptance of the principles set out in the Migrant Workers' Convention.

- Identification of concrete measures (e.g. mechanisms to prevent the removal of documents by employers; greater opportunities for regular migration; improved protection of migrants' rights; better regulation of recruitment agents/agencies) to reduce trafficking and forced labour of migrants, particularly those working in informal labour sectors, such as domestic work.
- Progress on the establishment and implementation of regional and national mechanisms, both legislative and practical, which offer better protection of human rights and support to trafficked people and migrants in slavery-like conditions.
- Progress on the establishment and implementation of regional and national mechanisms preventing forced labour and slavery-like practices of trafficked people and migrants, such as the minimum standards of employment for domestic workers.

Lobby Work in Europe

Within the European context Anti-Slavery International's lobby work has focussed on the establishment of mechanisms to better protect the rights of trafficked people as well as instruments and policies to prevent forced labour of trafficked people and migrants. Anti-Slavery International has considered it important to lobby on these issues in Europe for two reasons. Firstly, counter-trafficking measures in Europe, in particular in destination countries, have tended to be less comprehensive and received less attention than counter-trafficking measures in countries of origin. Secondly, as an international organisation based in the UK, Anti-Slavery International has felt it important to address slavery in its own region, as well as elsewhere in the world. To this end Anti-Slavery International has worked at a number of different levels. Firstly at the UK level Anti-Slavery International has worked closely with NGOs, academics, service providers, local authorities, social services, police and government officials to press for anti-trafficking legislation in the UK, for both sexual exploitation and other forced labour outcomes, and for support measures for victims of trafficking including a project to assist and accommodate those trafficked into prostitution. Anti-Slavery International has also worked with a coalition of migrant rights organisations to highlight the need to address migrants rights to prevent trafficking, and to lobby for the ratification of the Migrant Workers' Convention.

Policy Support and Networking

On the European level Anti-Slavery International has identified opportunities to also press for these issues in various fora. The European Commission established a group of experts from a variety of academic, NGO law enforcement, government and other backgrounds to advise the Commission on trafficking in human beings. Through membership of Anti-Slavery International's Director in the European Experts Group on Trafficking in Human Beings the organisation has sought to bring these issues to the attention of the European Commission, and to facilitate other NGOs to feed their concerns and experiences into the Group. The report of the Group, which was published in December 2004, will form the basis of a communication from the Commission in 2005 on trafficking. From Anti-Slavery International's perspective the report covers the organisation's main concerns and recommendations for action on trafficking, in particular the need for a human rights based approach and for greater victim protection measures, as well as the necessity to protect the rights of migrant workers. Anti-Slavery International hopes that the report will inform EU policy, as well as be a useful lobbying tool for NGOs.

Anti-Slavery International also lobbied hard on the draft Council of Europe Convention on Action against Trafficking in Human Beings. The organisation formed a lobby coalition with Amnesty International, who was relatively new to the issue of trafficking, but had good access to the Council of Europe mechanisms as well as La Strada International and also cooperated with Terre des Hommes, who have considerable grassroots experience in trafficking. The coalition's lobbying included releasing a joint statement and recommendations of over 180 NGOs, providing detailed comments for the drafting committee, lobbying Members of Parliament and attending two meetings of the committee to make presentations and interventions.

Besides the lobbying work with the EU, Anti-Slavery International has also worked with the OSCE, both ODIHR and the Special Representative on Trafficking to bring its concerns and recommendations to OSCE policies. In addition, Anti-Slavery International is a member of the Alliance on Action Against Trafficking.

In carrying out lobbying work both in the UK and Europe, Anti-Slavery International has sought to work in coalitions, both of NGOs, but also to work with other cross-sector actors where possible. Anti-Slavery International's most effective work has been where the organisation has been able to work across a broad group of actors and sectors. One example was in the UK where Anti-Slavery International has been member of the government's counter-trafficking task force and has co-chaired the NGO sub-group on trafficking. Anti-Slavery International also found working beyond traditional trafficking organisations, for example with migrant workers' rights organisations to be effective. The use of Anti-Slavery International's specialist knowledge and its links to grassroots partners, to involve larger organisations in anti-trafficking lobbying has proven effective. Thus in the UK Anti-Slavery International has worked with UNICEF, amongst others to lobby the UK government.

Success and Challenges

Anti-Slavery International's lobbying work in conjunction with others has had quite some successes in achieving the specific goals set. In particular in the UK legislation for trafficking for all purposes has been introduced and the Poppy Project, a support project, providing accommodation and assistance measures for those trafficked into prostitution is being piloted. However, the remit and numbers of women able to access this initiative is limited. Above all government, law enforcement and others are more sensitised to trafficking, the need to protect trafficked persons' rights and the need to look at trafficking in the context of migration, and migrants' rights policies.

Similarly at the European level, within policy discussions, recommendations and some implementation, issues of protection of the rights of trafficked persons, the need to look at migration policies, and to protect migrants' rights, are at the forefront. The Council of Europe Trafficking Convention contains some provisions which the coalition, including Anti-Slavery International, lobbied for. The action plan of the OSCE, and the OSCE Special Representative on Combating Trafficking in Human Beings, have taken forward Anti-Slavery International's and other's concerns. The ILO in its Global Report on Forced Labour is proposing a similar coalition against forced labour, with many policy recommendations in line with Anti-Slavery International's goals. The report of the European Commission's Experts Group reflects Anti-Slavery International's concerns and it is hoped that the formulated recommendations will be reflected in future Commission policy.

However, Anti-Slavery International and our partners also face difficulties in advancing advocacy goals within both the UK and European context. The reality of many European governments especially in countries of destination – including the UK – has been to view trafficking within a criminal law enforcement context, with primary concern over border and migration controls. Thus, although Anti-Slavery International and others have been successful in raising the issues of the need for protection of those trafficked, and the need to consider migration policies and migrants rights, and although many involved will express similar concerns, translation into policies and in particular legislation that protects the rights of trafficked persons has been less forthcoming.

This difficulty can be seen most clearly in the recent negotiations around the Council of Europe Trafficking Convention. Although a strong NGO coalition was formed, with a mixture of both international and grassroots organisations, that supported clear recommendations for the Convention, the ability for NGOs to ultimately influence the Convention was limited, because of previous political positions taken by member states, in particular the EU. The effect of the coalition's lobbying was firstly to enable more European NGOs to have access to, and become involved in the negotiations. Secondly, by being able to present a united lobbying position, supported by a large number of NGOs throughout Europe with considerable experience on the issues, the drafters of the Convention were better informed about NGOs' concerns and recommendations, as well as better prepared to bring basic human rights standards into the discussions. Anti-Slavery International is of the view that without the input of the NGO lobby the provisions of the Convention would be weaker.

More generally, the experience of building cross-sector-wide coalitions that can agree on recommendations provides greater strength than organisations lobbying individually. The most powerful coalitions tend to be those that can work across sectors – for example in the UK the trafficking working group that comprises of NGOs, government, law enforcement, social services and others concerned with trafficking, is an effective forum for advancing concerns, policy and issues. Similarly participation in a coalition supporting migrants' rights enables alliances to be formed, and support obtained beyond usual actors. Within the Council of Europe negotiations, the ability to join both national NGOs with grassroots experience, and international organisations with experience of lobbying the Council of Europe, strengthened the effectiveness of both types of organisation.

Ultimately though, to bring about change, policy makers have to be convinced of the political desirability of following NGO recommendations. Within Europe, promoting human rights protection for trafficked persons has to be seen within the context of political concerns regarding migration, border control and immigration policies. Change of these political concerns of necessity will need to come from the bottom, country level up. While international support for recommendations of managed migration policies, protecting the rights of migrant workers, promoting core labour standards, and protecting the rights of those who have been trafficked, may have increasing support internationally, NGOs need to work at a national level to persuade their governments to follow these policies. Only by NGOs placing pressure on national governments can policies be changed to better protect the rights of trafficked persons. Strong coalitions of national organised NGOs are needed who can gain access and lobby at national government level and coordinate work across Europe.

And while governments are willing to discuss managed migration in response to demand for migrant workers in several sectors, they seem equally unwilling to provide comprehensive rights for migrant workers.

Strengthening Advocacy Through Providing Baseline Studies

Victoria Nwogu

Background

Nigeria and Ghana are both source, transit and destination countries for human trafficking. The factors which influence a high rate of migration from both countries and thereby human trafficking include aspects such as poverty, quest for better life, adventurism, high family size, gender discrimination and inequalities.

Over the past few years, many non-governmental organisations and government agencies in both countries have worked individually and collectively to develop strategies for combating the phenomenon of human trafficking and forced labour. Their efforts include information and awareness-raising campaigns targeted at prevention; enactment of new legislation; rehabilitation of trafficked persons; security surveillance; investigations and prosecution. These efforts have faced several challenges with the major problem being the lack of credible data to determine the magnitude of the trend and influence appropriate planning. Moreover, much of the existing information on human trafficking remains in the hands of different law enforcement operatives who lack adequate mechanisms for information sharing with all stakeholders. This has led to improper coordination of efforts.

Stakeholders involved in anti-trafficking work in both countries agree that advocacy efforts to get governments and other decision-makers to channel their interventions to the appropriate areas of need require action research. Only then can they properly articulate the nature and extent of the problems that have to be addressed. It is only when the facts and figures match the need or demand that the right amount of attention to the problem required to stimulate change can be generated.

Thus the need for locally driven action research on trafficking and forced labour with alternating research and action phases has been expressed very strongly in both countries. Key in this effort is the need to determine the links between areas of origin and destination, demand and supply factors.

In response to these needs the ILO Action Programme against Human Trafficking and Forced Labour in West Africa (ILO-PATWA) conducted baseline surveys to determine the nature and trends of human trafficking and forced labour in selected states and districts in Nigeria and Ghana. PATWA is designed to address the broader structural dimensions of the demand and supply aspects of forced labour and trafficking in Ghana and Nigeria as sending countries and the Netherlands as a destination country. Like all ILO projects, PATWA operates with governmental and non-governmental partners in both countries. Its ultimate beneficiaries are women and youth in various communities in selected states and districts in Nigeria and Ghana.

Methodology of the Baseline Studies

In both Nigeria and Ghana, focal areas were selected in which baseline studies were conducted by social workers and gender desk officers, labour officers and local NGOs. The methods employed in data collection for the studies in Ghana and Nigeria differed. While the research in Nigeria adopted an academic approach favouring tools such as questionnaires, in-depth interviews, expert interviews and focus groups discussions, the main approach in Ghana was the Participatory Rural Appraisal (PRA) and only to a lesser extent interviews, observation, questionnaires, community discussions and focus groups. The PRA tools involved the local people working in collaboration with the field researchers in:

- drawing maps showing who lives where and the location of important local features and resources such as water, forests, schools and other services;
- developing flow diagrams to indicate linkages, sequences, causes, effects, problems and solutions to the problems of irregular and uninformed migration leading to human trafficking and forced labour in their communities;
- creating seasonal calendars showing how food availability, workloads, family health, prices, wages and other factors vary during the year;
- organising hearing chairs to enable people air their grievances followed by collectively developing participatory action strategies.

The reasons for this difference in approach is that while the research in Nigeria was centred mostly around the city capitals and a few rural communities, in Ghana the geographic areas covered were mostly rural communities in the North.

The focus of the study was on attitudes about and perceptions of trafficking, linkages between trafficking and migration, factors that help persons to resist trafficking as well as on factors that facilitate trafficking. Prior to the studies, training workshops were conducted in Ghana and Nigeria for field researchers consisting of social workers, gender desk officers, NGOs, and labour officers. The training workshops were instrumental in clarifying concepts, exposing participants to innovative participatory rural appraisal approaches and for team building. The data collection instruments were developed at the workshops.

Preliminary Findings of the Baseline Studies

Whilst the final results of the baseline studies are yet to be completed by the researchers, the following are preliminary findings:

- There is a high incidence of migration from the rural communities to the urban city centres and beyond the shores of both countries. The internal migration far exceeds the external.

- The most vulnerable age group ranges from 15 to 25. In Ghana specifically, the survey found that young people perceive migration as part of their life cycle expectation, to start life elsewhere and only return when they have acquired all they need to fulfil the basic needs of life.
- Poverty and the quest for a better life are the major reasons for migration in both countries.
- The few migrants who returned after 'succeeding in acquiring wealth' were seen as role models and gave more impetus to others to travel.
- Many of the communities covered in both countries have little awareness of human trafficking or illegal migration. They only know of migration in general terms as involving the movement of people outside their communities and are aware of its possible negative consequences and other forced migration risks experienced by people from the communities. The study found cases of recruited migrants and indications of trafficking and forced labour across the borders.
- In Nigeria information about cultural perceptions and attitudes on forced labour and trafficking seem to be deeply rooted in the contrasting religious beliefs and values placed on children and women in the respective communities. These perceptions, attitudes and values operate within the dominant cultural system to ensure that both children and women especially conform to certain traditional dogmas. In an attempt to conform, these groups are gradually pushed into conditions of vulnerability.
- Overall, preliminary results from the study show that cultural perceptions operate to reinforce and advance existing poverty levels. Hence, to some extent, the perceptions and attitudes held by many of the respondents about government policies and governance in general have cumulative and influencing effects on individual vulnerability to the pull and push factors of trafficking.

The findings of the surveys will be used in advocating to the government grassroots targeted programmes aimed at building the capacities of vulnerable groups by empowering them economically.

The results will also form the basis for the design of local level interventions to prevent trafficking and facilitate the reintegration of returnees. The project in Nigeria has already commenced a round of mobilisation training workshops for women, youth (as vulnerable groups), hotel and transport workers unions (as facilitators or accomplices in the human trafficking process) in the four pilot states as a first step towards mobilising their various constituents to engage pro-actively in the fight of combating human trafficking and forced labour in their states. The findings of the baseline survey were presented to the various groups at these workshops to show the nature and trend of human trafficking and forced labour in these states and serve as basis for shaping action plans to raise awareness among their members. Other targets for advocacy are the traditional and religious leaders in the focal states and districts to enlighten and sensitise them about the trends and enlist their support to mobilise community vigilance against traffickers who recruit from their communities or use them as transit points.

Lessons Learned

One of the lessons learned is that there is a need to involve the relevant government agencies and to support the development of databases as well as structures to monitor the situation. A strong data base combining information from various stakeholders such as law enforcement agents, care givers, NGOs and other government actors, containing actual cases reflecting adequate geographical spread would have assisted the research process in coming out with more quantitative data.

Another fact to take into consideration is the procedural nature of trans-border human trafficking. The research was concentrated in states which in this context are largely source areas. In order to capture the various aspects of trafficking, it could be important to involve transit and destination countries to observe and document the experience of victims.

Other lessons specific to Nigeria are linked to the selection of operational areas. The vast size and diversity of Nigeria presented a major challenge in determining the states in which to commence local level interventions. The project was able to overcome this challenge by strategising with stakeholders and agreeing to ensure a wider reach by selecting states from the North and South. In the selection of the states in the two zones, current information on trafficking flows was taken into consideration so that one source and one transit/destination state were selected.

In Ghana lessons learned are that a greater involvement of the researchers in the field during the data collection stage helps to ensure a low degree of errors and internal consistency in the data collected. Also, seasonal surroundings need to be taken into account: The baseline survey was conducted during the dry season, a period where many of the people move to southern Ghana as a means of escaping the harsh weather conditions of the dry harmattan and usually return at the onset of the rains. The baseline study could be undertaken towards the end of the rainy season or within, just after the harvesting season.

Conclusions and Recommendations

International organisations, governments, and non-governmental organisations have developed a great number of recommendations to prevent and combat trafficking in human beings. This chapter aims at giving a condensed overview on conclusions and recommendations resulting from the various standards and recommendations mentioned throughout the different chapters of this publication.

Conclusions

Trafficking will continue to flourish as long as root causes on each end of the trafficking process continue to exist and are not addressed in a comprehensive fashion. Rising global economic disparity, its impact on vulnerable groups and individuals as well as major social changes in countries of transition are amongst the most prevalent root causes for trafficking in human beings. Specific causes are made up of armed and post-conflict situations and major natural disasters, which result in long-lasting social and economic destruction. In such disturbed environments trafficking occurs as a result of the massive social upheaval and lack of social order. However, just as important as addressing the root causes in countries of origin is to focus on the demand for informal, cheap and unprotected labour in countries of destination and to sensitise the private sector to take action against the exploitation of forced labour.

To effectively address the complex issues involved in trafficking in human beings, strong political will, comprehensive policies and coordinated action between all stakeholders are needed. In this context it is crucial to state that trafficking certainly is a development issue that calls upon donors to critically reflect upon their role in addressing the root causes. Thus, poverty reduction, the promotion of human rights and gender equality, economic empowerment as well as institution building, promotion of democratic processes and anti-corruption efforts are essential. The coordination of actors based on agreed referral systems is indispensable and the work of relevant professional groups needs to be founded on continuous capacity building as well as high professional standards. Reviewing and revising the professional conduct when carrying out anti-trafficking work as well as applying legislative and policy measures is thereby of utmost importance.

More than many other issues of social importance, the anti-trafficking discourse is led by underlying ideological positions, e.g. concerning prostitution or migration. The trafficking discourse must maintain the rights of the victim as a core focus, whilst taking care to ensure that certain groups, such as undocumented migrants are not penalised, stigmatised or harmed in the course of anti-trafficking activities.

Since the process of elaborating the UN Trafficking Protocol has taken its course, all relevant stakeholders came to the understanding that the best interests of the victim should be at the core of all anti-trafficking interventions. Considering the victim's perspective should be the starting point for all interventions not only to comply with the human rights standards set forth in various international documents, but also to facilitate an effective prosecution through the stabilisation and strengthening of the position of the victim. Victim support measures should be crafted according to the needs of the specific individual, bearing in mind that children need specific and specialised protection different to adults. Thus, assistance programmes must adapt to the particular needs of specific groups (e.g. children, youth, women, and ethnic minorities), within which the victim's needs may vary from person to person based on their experience. Uniform 'one-size-fits-all' services for all victims of trafficking are unlikely to be effective. To adequately shape interventions trafficked persons and at-risk groups should be involved in designing anti-trafficking programmes. To allow trafficked persons to access and exercise their full rights their identification as victims of trafficking is a key issue. Non-governmental organisations continue to report about ongoing deportations of trafficked persons to their countries of origin without having been identified as trafficking victims.

The anti-trafficking framework is frequently used to clamp down on undocumented migration. What is needed though, are more comprehensive migration policies that facilitate safe labour migration. Trafficking in human beings is not the only crime and human rights violation that occurs in the migratory process, but at one end of a scale of abuse of migrant workers.

Recommendations

Conclusions and lessons learned in the key areas of prevention, victim support, capacity and institution building, and advocacy led to the following recommendations.

Prevention

In order to achieve efficient prevention, anti-trafficking initiatives should broaden their approach beyond awareness raising and address the root causes of trafficking. In addition to projects and programmes in the countries of origin, donors should include concerted efforts to address the demand side in their own home countries.

- Governments and NGOs need to make information about safe migration available to potential migrants: this group needs to be aware of the risks around the migratory process and to know how to migrate safely if they choose to. Hotlines, for example, are a useful means to disseminate accurate information.

- Local communities and stakeholders should conduct accurate research, which feeds into effective awareness-raising and information campaigns as well as it forms a basis for developing strategies and policies. In addition, an open debate about trafficking in human beings will assist in breaking taboos and ending prevalent stigmatisation.
- It is essential to reduce school dropout rates and equip children with knowledge and life skills in order to ensure their independence and self-sustainability. Education and training departments should regularly review school and training curricula and monitor the conduct of training and educational units.
- Upon their voluntary return victims should receive immediate and adequate assistance and support in order to break the 'cycle of trafficking' and thus help them to start an independent life in their home country. Governments, IGOs and NGOs should recognise that sustainable reintegration also prevents re-trafficking and therefore need to be incorporated into a trafficking prevention strategy.

Victim Support

In order to assist and protect trafficked persons it is essential to identify them properly. The identification process can be complex and time-consuming. In any case, state authorities and non-governmental service providers should conduct a joint assessment in order to avoid exposing the victim to repetitive questioning and to ensure quality standards of interrogation procedures of presumed victims.

- Regardless of their willingness to cooperate with law enforcement, all presumed trafficked persons should be granted a reflection period, prompt access to safe and free housing, legal, psychological and material assistance, and medical treatment. Identified victims should also receive renewable residence permits that allow them to work in the destination country and to access education or vocational training. Of great importance in this context is that victims should not be held accountable for offences related to them having been trafficked.
- Support services in the country of origin should immediately reach out to victims upon return, facilitate their social integration and prevent them from becoming re-trafficked. It is of utmost importance that support services work cross-border and exchange experiences and information.
- Effective and successful victim support relies on political will, clear objectives and priorities as well as adequate human and financial resources. Regular funding should be made available by governments and other donors to support long-term rehabilitation activities as well as the long-term sustainability of service providers.
- Governments should ensure that trafficked persons are only returned to their country of origin after a sound risk assessment and where possible, on a voluntary basis.

- While states have a positive obligation to protect people within their jurisdiction from human rights violations committed by the state or individuals, many victims would rather approach non-governmental organisations for assistance. All governmental and non-governmental stakeholders, who provide services to trafficked persons, should cooperate closely within their mandates and according to clear rules maintaining minimum human rights standards.

Capacity and Institution Building

States should establish an institutional anti-trafficking framework based on human rights standards and a sound assessment of local realities and needs. Multidisciplinary working groups should develop and implement long-term work plans and strategies to prevent and combat trafficking in human beings. Such an approach will only be successful if it is participatory and inclusive involving non-governmental as well as governmental actors.

- Networking across sectors on the national level as well as across borders can achieve tangible results and helps to overcome stereotypical perceptions specific professional groups or people from different countries have of each other.
- Training materials must be based on international standards and put the best interests of the victims at the core of all analysis and recommended action. In order to achieve maximum outreach and coverage it is useful to institutionalise training in the curricula of relevant training centres. The valuable and specialised skills of those experienced in anti-trafficking should be mainstreamed into regular and standardised work practice of relevant professional groups.
- To tackle the fact that armed and post-conflict environments constitute a fertile ground for trafficking as one form of organised crime, international peacekeepers, aid workers and contractors should be trained on anti-trafficking issues. Furthermore Codes of Conduct for people within the support network need to be developed and implemented; resulting from that, misconduct will have to be disciplined and penalised.

Advocacy Work

Relevant stakeholders should ensure that awareness-raising campaigns are well tailored and deliver clear and simple messages to address particular target audiences in countries of origin and countries of destination. Ideally, trafficked persons and at-risk groups should be involved in the design and development of such advocacy measures. In addition, the general public needs to be informed about the extent and the different facets of the phenomenon in order to lobby for an improved legislation.

- Advocates should carry out research in a sensitive way in order to avoid the re-victimisation of trafficked persons. More in-depth, outcome-oriented and local research on the root causes of trafficking and their interrelatedness ensures that subsequent awareness-raising activities can be specific and more effective.
- Lobbying should go beyond advocating for policy and legislative changes and also entail monitoring the application of such laws, drawing attention to prevalent shortcomings if present. Civil society and especially rights activists can play an important 'watch-dog' role.
- Governments, international organisations and non-governmental organisations should actively engage in forming partnerships and alliances across sectors as an important way of bringing about and sustaining change.

Directory of Authors

Beate Andrees currently serves as anti-trafficking specialist of the International Labour Organisation/Special Action Programme to Combat Forced Labour with focus on research and training, as well as project management for the areas of Europe and Central Asia. Before, she worked as a consultant and lecturer for several German public institutions and published widely on migration and conflict issues.

Sebastian Baumeister is Democratization Officer with the Organization for Security and Co-operation (OSCE) in Europe Mission in Kosovo working on minority issues. Previously, he worked at the OSCE Office of the Co-ordinator of Economic and Environmental Activities in Vienna, focusing on promoting private-public partnerships with regard to preventing trafficking in human beings through economic empowerment of potential victims. Before joining the OSCE, he worked with the United Nations Industrial Development Organization.

Lora Beltcheva is Coordinator of the project "Pilot comprehensive training model on empowering minors from orphanages and prevention of trafficking" which is implemented by the non-governmental organisation Animus Association Foundation in Bulgaria.

Warunee Chaiwongkam is a former victim of trafficking. Since 2003, she is responsible for the Women's Programme of the Thai non-governmental group Self Empowerment Program for Migrant Women, which supports returning female migrant workers in Thailand. She furthermore carries out research and collects data on migrant women.

Kateryna Cherepakha is Head of the Council and Social Assistance Project Coordinator at the International Women's Rights Centre "La Strada Ukraine".

Mary Cunneen is the Director of Anti-Slavery International and a member of the European Experts Group on Trafficking in Human Beings appointed by the European Commission.

Mike Dottridge is a consultant on human rights issues. Previously, he worked at the International Secretariat of Amnesty International and was director of Anti-Slavery International. He was also a member of the team advising the UN High Commissioner on Human Rights during the preparation of the High Commissioner's Recommended Principles and Guidelines on Human Rights and Human Trafficking. His recent publications include 'Kids as commodities? Child trafficking and what to do about it' (Terre des hommes 2004).

Jane Gronow is currently Senior Programme Officer for United Nations Children's Fund in Russia and Belarus. She has worked on HIV/AIDS, sexual violence and trauma and trafficking issues in various capacities, including advocacy, counselling, service delivery, research and programme development. Most recently she authored reports on trafficking and on HIV/AIDS in South Eastern Europe and was the HIV/AIDS Sub Regional Advisor for the Balkan Regions for United Nations Children's Fund.

Christiane Howe, sociologist, has previously worked as education officer and at agisra, an intercultural women's organisation in Frankfurt, Germany. She served on the board of the German network Coordinating Group against Trafficking in Women and Violence against Women in Migration (KOK). Recently, she conducted a research project on clients of foreign prostitutes. She has co-edited and co-published books on labour migration and trafficking in women. She is working in the context network of non-governmental organisations focusing on the areas of migration and prostitution. Since June 2005 she collaborates in a research project on space and gender by exemplifying prostitution.

Bronwyn Jones is the Director and founder of Media and Development International. Before, she has worked with a variety of partners on media development issues in South Eastern Europe. She holds Master's Degrees in Media Studies and International Affairs respectively, and began her career in documentary film and television in New York City.

Olga Kalashnyk is Vice President of La Strada Ukraine and Hot Line Coordinator. She works at the International Women's Rights Centre "La Strada Ukraine".

Barbara Limanowska works as consultant on the issue of trafficking in human beings for various international agencies. In the framework of the South Eastern Europe Regional Initiative against Human Trafficking, she has written numerous reports. Currently she works for the Office of the High Commissioner for Human Rights in Sarajevo assessing the implementation of anti-trafficking measures in Bosnia and Herzegovina.

Susie Maley is Manager of the International Tourism Partnership with the Prince of Wales International Business Leaders Forum and works on the implementation of the Youth Career Initiative worldwide.

Iana Matei is the founder and President of the Romanian non-governmental organisation Reaching Out, which provides direct assistance to survivors of trafficking. As a psychologist she has worked with street children in Australia before returning to Romania to deal with the problems of street children there.

Deborah McWhinney is currently the Sub-Regional Coordinator for HIV/AIDS and Trafficking for United Nations Children's Fund in South Eastern Europe. She has been a feminist activist for more than 20 years and has worked on developmental issues in a number of countries in Africa and Eastern Europe.

Bruno Moens currently conducts a three years research into relevant socio-economic and cultural factors contributing to trafficking in human beings in Nigeria. He previously coordinated one of the specialised Belgian anti-trafficking centres (Payoke) and worked as a consultant in Belgium, Eastern Europe and Africa.

Victoria Nwogu is a lawyer and holds a Master's Degree in International Affairs and Diplomacy. She is currently the National Project Coordinator in Nigeria for the International Labour Organisation Action Programme against Forced Labour and Human Trafficking in West Africa. Prior, she worked with Global Rights; Partners for Justice as the Programme Associate on Human Trafficking advocating for legislative review and reform in Nigeria. She has conducted research on various human rights issues and contributed to various publications within the human rights community in Nigeria and abroad.

Isabella Orfano is currently the International Officer of the Associazione On the Road, one of Italian's main anti-trafficking NGOs. She collaborates as researcher and consultant with public authorities and private social agencies that carry out studies and programmes concerning prostitution and the fight against trafficking in human beings at the local, national, and international level. She is co-author of several publications on trafficking and related-issues and a member of the European Experts Group on Trafficking in Human Beings appointed by the European Commission.

Elaine Pearson has researched globally on the issue of trafficking. Currently, she works as a consultant on trafficking and migration issues. Coming from a legal background, she has conducted extensive research on victim protection and the human rights impact of anti-trafficking measures, implemented trainings and developed a handbook on trafficking and human rights. Her recent publications include "Redefining Victim Protection" (Anti-Slavery International, 2002) and "Coercion in the Kidney Trade?" (GTZ, 2004). Elaine was formerly the Trafficking Programme Officer at Anti-Slavery International and prior to that worked at the Global Alliance against Traffic in Women in Thailand.

Maria Petrova is Coordinator of the project "Public-Private Co-operation in the Prevention of Trafficking and Sexual Exploitation of Minors in Travel and Tourism Industry", which is implemented by the Animus Association Foundation in Bulgaria.

Nivedita Prasad is Project Coordinator and researcher at Ban Ying, a counselling and coordination centre against human trafficking based in Berlin, Germany. She teaches antiracist social work in various universities.

Gabriele Reiter is a consultant on anti-trafficking issues. She worked with research institutions and intergovernmental organisations on issues such as research, legislative review, advocacy, policy development and training of professionals; in addition to this she is author/editor of numerous publications on this issue. Most recently, on behalf of the Geneva Centre for Security Policy, she coordinated the work of the Core Working Group to develop training materials for civilian and military personnel of peacekeeping operations led by the North Atlantic Treaty Organisation.

Babette Rohner is sociologist and social worker assisting trafficked women at Ban Ying, a counselling and coordination centre against human trafficking based in Berlin, Germany. She teaches gender issues and child rights issues at the Free University in Berlin.

Helen Santiago Fink is Senior Economic Affairs Officer and Programme Manager for the Anti-Trafficking Programme on Public-Private Co-operation in the Prevention of Trafficking in Human Beings at the Office of the Co-ordinator of Organisation for Security and Co-operation in Europe Economic and Environmental Activities. She has significant experience working with socio-economic development issues in Southeast Europe, Commonwealth of Independent States, the United States and Caribbean Basin region.

Diana Segovia is currently the Latin American Coordinator of the Local Agenda 21 Campaign at Local Governments for Sustainability. She is a specialist in decentralised governance, local development, political reform and community participation. Previously, she had worked as a consultant for international organisations on good governance, institutional and justice reform, and poverty issues. She also has a special interest in women's development issues.

Liliana Sorrentino works as Adviser in the Anti-Trafficking Assistance Unit of the Organisation for Security Cooperation in Europe. Previously, she worked with the organisation's Mission to Moldova as an Anti-Human Trafficking Officer and managed projects in the field of legislative review, prevention of trafficking, assistance to its victims and prosecution of traffickers. She has experience in research and NGO field work on social and human rights issues, including asylum and trafficking in persons.

Theera Srila is responsible for the Children's Programme of the Thai non-govermental group Self Empowerment Program for Migrant Women, which supports returning female migrant workers in Thailand. She also conducts research on the situation of migrant women returning to Thailand.

Maria Tchomarova is Executive Director of Animus Association Foundation in Bulgaria, psychotherapist and also Social Assistance Manager of La Strada – Bulgaria.

Martina E. Vandenberg is attorney in private practice. Before joining Jenner & Block LLP, a private law firm in Washington, D.C., she served as a researcher at Human Rights Watch, where she investigated trafficking of women and girls to post-conflict environments and rape as a war crime in the Balkan Region.

Lilijana Vasić is Regional Coordinator for Child and Youth Trafficking Prevention Programmes of Christian Children's Fund and Director of Pomoc deci. As a journalist by profession she has been actively involved in humanitarian and development programmes in Serbia for the last four years. She focuses on support for most vulnerable groups such as refugees, internally displaced people, minorities, children and youth.

Johanna Willems holds Master's Degrees in Women Studies as well as European Studies. She currently works in a supra-regional anti-trafficking project for the Deutsche Gesellschaft für Technische Zusammenarbeit GmbH, which is commissioned by the Federal Ministry for Economic Development and Cooperation. She has previously worked in a gender project on Nicaragua, focusing on security sector reform in Central America and the Caribbean.

Directory of Organisations

Animus Association Foundation (AAF)
(La Strada - Bulgaria)
PO Box 97, 1408 Sofia, Bulgaria
24 hours hotline: +359 2 981 76 86
animus@animusassociation.org; www.animusassociation.org

The organisation is based in Bulgaria and is a member of La Strada, an international association to prevent trafficking in women in Central and Eastern Europe, specialised in providing psychological and social help to survivors of violence and develops a centre for the rehabilitation of women, adolescents and children survivors of violence. Animus Association Foundation works actively in the community by initiating prevention campaigns, lobby activities and providing training. The international project Regional Empowering Initiative for Women at Risk and Survivors of Trafficking as well as the Initiative and Empowerment Programme for Women's Professional Development and Autonomy are seen as one of the most effective preventive measures against trafficking.

Anti-Slavery International
Thomas Clarkson House, The Stableyard, Broomgrove Road, London SW9 9TL, United Kingdom
info@antislavery.org; www.antislavery.org

Anti-Slavery International is the world's oldest international human rights organisation. The main areas of work include forced and bonded labour, the worst forms of child labour, trafficking of human beings, and slavery based on discrimination based on descent. Anti-Slavery International works at local, national and international levels through research, awareness raising and campaigning in order to eliminate slavery.

Ban Ying
Anklamer Strasse 39, 10115 Berlin, Germany
info@Ban-Ying.de; www.ban-ying.de

Ban Ying, Thai for "House of Women", is a German non-governmental organisation founded in 1988. Besides its efforts in the fields of lobbying and outreach Ban Ying's work comprises two projects, a shelter and a coordination centre for trafficked women from all regions of the world. Ban Ying offers social and legal counselling as well as it accompanies victims through criminal proceedings.

Christian Children's Fund Inc. (CCF) – Udruzenje Gradjana Pomoc Deci
CCF in Serbia/Pomoc deci, Kolarceva 7/IV, 11 000 Belgrade, Serbia and Montenegro
ljvasic@EUnet.yu; www.christianchildrensfund.org

CCF, also registered as "Udruzenje gradjana Pomoc deci", is a non-profit organisation in Serbia and Montenegro. It is an active member of the National Team to Combat Trafficking in Serbia and its Working Group to Combat Child Trafficking. Apart from its anti-trafficking work, Pomoc deci also works on promoting the improvement of ethnic minority education and issues related to public health, especially HIV/AIDS and TBC prevention.

context e. V.
Palmengartenstr. 14, 60325 Frankfurt/Main, Germany
info@context-cps.de; www.context-cps.de

Context is a German network of non-governmental organisations working on research, training and networking in the areas of migration and prostitution. The organisation aims to integrate people working in the field of prostitution as well as to find innovative solutions to combat trafficking in women.

Geneva Centre for Security Policy (GCSP)
7 bis, Avenue de la Paix, P.O. Box 1295, 1211 Geneva 1,Switzerland
info@gcsp.ch; www.gcsp.ch

The GCSP is an international foundation established in 1995 within the framework of the Swiss participation in the Partnership for Peace. The GCSP is engaged in training diplomats, military officers and other civil servants in international security policy, research and seminars to support the training activities, conferences and outreach to promote dialogue on various security-related issues, and networking in the security field.

International Labour Organization (ILO) – Special Action Programme to Combat Forced Labour
ILO Special Action Programme to Combat Forced Labour, Route des Morillons 4, 1211 Geneva, Switzerland
andrees@ilo.org; www.ilo.org

The ILO is a specialised agency of the United Nations. Its mandate is to promote decent work through the supervision of labour standards, employment creation, social dialogue and social protection. In 2001, a Special Action Programme to Combat Forced Labour (SAP-FL) was set up in order to help eliminating forced labour by promotional means. Since its establishment, SAP-FL has spearheaded ILO's action against trafficking of women and men for forced sexual and labour exploitation. The ILO addresses trafficking through a labour market perspective, involving social partners and labour market institutions in origin as well as destination countries.

International Labour Organization (ILO) – Action Programme against Forced Labour and Human Trafficking in West Africa (PATWA)

ILO Office in Abuja, Nigeria

vickylegal@yahoo.co.uk

The ILO Action Programme against Forced Labour and Trafficking in West Africa (PATWA) is part of the Special Action Programme against Forced Labour's technical cooperation to assist member states in the implementation of ILO Forced Labour Convention No. 29. PATWA is designed to address the broader structural dimensions of demand/supply aspects of forced labour and trafficking in Ghana and Nigeria as sending countries and the Netherlands as destination country.

International Women's Rights Center "La Strada Ukraine"

P.O. Box 26, 03113 Kyiv, Ukraine

Hotline: 8-800 500 22 50 (free of charge in Ukraine); +38 044 205 37 36, 205 36 94 (for people living in Kyiv and abroad); lastrada@ukrpack.net; www.lastrada.org.ua

The International Women's Rights Centre "La Strada Ukraine" started its work as partner of the International La Strada network in 1997. The programme assists victims in contacting support networks and to inform women/girls about the possible dangers of trafficking. Its work includes raising awareness among authorities, media and the general public about the implications of this human rights violation. The main directions of La Strada Ukraine's activities are information, lobbywork, prevention, education, hotline and social assistance to victims of trafficking.

Local Governments for Sustainability (ICLEI)

Latin America and Caribbean Secretariat

Praça Pio X, no. 119, 11° andar, CEP 20040-020, Rio de Janeiro, RJ, Brazil

iclei-latam@iclei.org; www.iclei.org/lacs

ICLEI was founded in 1990 as the International Council for Local Environmental Initiatives, with the support of the International Union of Local Authorities, and the United Nations Environment Program (UNEP). ICLEI is a democratically governed membership association of cities, towns, metropolitan governments, and local government associations. Its mission is to build and serve a worldwide movement of local governments to achieve tangible improvements in global sustainability. The Latin American and Caribbean Secretariat implements pilot measures against trafficking in persons as a component of its Just, Peaceful, and Secure Communities Program.

Media and Development International (MADI)

P.O. Box # 558, Brooklyn, NY 11238, USA

bronwyn.jones@madimedia.org; www.madimedia.org

MADI is a non-profit consultancy providing professional media consultation and development programmes for international and non-governmental organisations globally. MADI works to find media-related solutions to development issues. The staff has extensive expertise in both media and international development, which provides a unique perspective in developing and creating effective and sustainable projects. MADI is based in New York City and works extensively in South East Europe as well as in other areas of the world.

Associazione On the Road (OTR)
Via delle Lancette, 27 – 27A, 64014 Martinsicuro (TE), Italy
mail@ontheroadonlus.it; www.ontheroadonlus.it

Funded in 1990, On the Road provides support and assistance to sex workers and trafficked persons through structured services (outreach units, drop-in centres, shelters, etc.) managed by trained professionals. Based on a multi-agency approach, OTR works for the promotion and protection of human and civil rights of the assisted persons. Part of the Italian Social Assistance and Integration Programme for Trafficked Persons, OTR offers accommodation and protection; social, health, psychological and legal counselling and assistance; accompaniment to social and health services; vocational guidance and training; on-the-job training programmes and direct insertion into the labour market. It also manages awareness-raising activities, community work, and development of social inclusion policies, training modules, research and publications.

Organization for Security and Co-operation in Europe (OSCE)
The OSCE is the largest regional security organisation in the world with fifty-five participating states from Europe, Central Asia and North America. It is active in early warning, conflict prevention, crisis management and post-conflict rehabilitation.

OSCE - Anti-Trafficking Assistance Unit
OSCE Secretariat, Press and Public Information Section
Kärntner Ring 5-7, 4th floor, 1010 Vienna, Austria
info@osce.org; www.osce.org/cthb

In 2003 the Anti-Trafficking Assistance Unit was established in the OSCE Secretariat to support the OSCE Special Representative. The Unit cooperates with other OSCE institutions, units and bodies as well as with OSCE participating states and various international and non-governmental organisations.

OSCE - Office of the Co-ordinator of Economic and Environmental Activities (OCEEA)
OSCE Secretariat, Press and Public Information Section
Kärntner Ring 5-7, 4th floor, 1010 Vienna, Austria
info@osce.org; www.osce.org/eea

As part of its comprehensive approach to security, the OSCE is concerned with economic and environmental matters, recognising that cooperation in these areas can contribute to peace, prosperity and stability. The OCEEA has developed an Anti-Trafficking Programme on Public-Private Co-operation in the Prevention of Trafficking in Human Beings.

Reaching Out Romania (ROR)

Pitesti, Romania

reachingoutrom@yahoo.com; www.famnet.ro

Reaching Out Romania is a non-governmental organisation based in Pitesti, Romania. Its objective is to provide rescue, safe housing, food, medical care, counselling and reintegration to trafficked victims, who often are children between 13 and 18 years of age. ROR's shelter is the only shelter in Romania that provides long-term assistance to trafficked persons returning to Romania.

Self-Empowerment Program for Migrant Women (SEPOM)

120 M 15 Sankhongluang St., Muang Chiang Rai 57000, Thailand

Sepom2002@yahoo.com

SEPOM is a support group of and for formerly trafficked women to Japan and their Thai-Japanese children based in Chiang Rai, a province in the North of Thailand. SEPOM's staff consists of volunteers and formerly trafficked women. SEPOM focuses on improving women's capabilities, raising their awareness of becoming victims of trafficking and supporting their rehabilitation into the community. Victims receive psychological, social and legal support.

The Prince of Wales International Business Leaders Forum (IBLF)

15-16 Cornwall Terrace, Regents Park, London, NW1 4QP, United Kingdom

itp@iblf.org; www.iblf.org

The IBLF was formed in 1990 by the Prince of Wales as an international, business-led, non-profit membership organisation focused on responsible business and development. The IBLF has action-orientated initiatives in over 50 countries, including the least developed and emerging economies that make a significant impact on education, health, environment, enterprise, business standards and performance. The Youth Career Initiative is a programme of IBLF.

United Nations Children's Fund (UNICEF)

Regional Office for CEE/CIS and the Baltics

Palais des Nations, CH-1211 Geneva 10, Switzerland

www.unicef.org/ceecis

For nearly 60 years UNICEF has been the world's leader for supporting children, working on the ground in 157 countries to help children survive and thrive from early childhood through adolescence. The world's largest provider of vaccines for poor countries, UNICEF works to advance the Millennium Development Goals by supporting child health and nutrition, quality basic education for all boys and girls, access to clean water and sanitation, and the protection of children from violence, exploitation, and AIDS. UNICEF is funded entirely by the voluntary contributions of governments, businesses, foundations and individuals.

References

Adepoju, Aderanti (2004): Review of Research and Data on Human Trafficking in Sub Saharan Africa, presented at the International Expert Meeting on Improving Data and Research on Human Trafficking organised by IOM and the Government of Italy. Rome.

Ahlemeyer, Heinrich (1996): Prostitutive Intimkommunikation. Zur Mikrosoziologie heterosexueller Prostitution. Stuttgart.

Alt, Jörg (2003): Leben in der Schattenwelt. Problemkomplex Illegale Migration. Karlsruhe.

Amnesty International (AI) (2000): Sierra Leone: Rape and Other Forms of Sexual Violence Against Girls and Women. AI Index: AFR 51/035/2000. (http://web.amnesty.org/)

Anderson, Bridget/ Rogaly, Ben (2005): Forced Labour and Migration to the UK. London.

Ban Ying (2003): Information for Domestic Workers Working for Diplomats. Berlin.

Barahona, Milagros (2003): Informe de Taller sobre Trata y Tráfico de Personas. Managua.

Blackett, Adelle (1998): Making Domestic Work Visible: The Case for Specific Regulation, Labour Law and Labour Relations Branch. Geneva.

Bundesministerium für wirtschaftliche Zusammenarbeit und Entwicklung (2004): BMZ Concepts No. 128. Development policy action plan on human rights 2004 – 2007. Every person has a right to development. German development policy approach to respecting, protecting and fulfilling political, civil, economical, social and cultural human rights. Bonn.

Castle, Sarah / Diarra, Aïsse (2003): The International Migration of Young Malians: Tradition, Necessity or Rite of Passage? London School of Hygiene and Tropical Medicine. London.

Center for Strategic and International Studies(CSIS) (2005): Barracks and Brothels: Peacekeepers and Human Trafficking in the Balkans. Washington D.C. (http://www.csis.org/ruseura/pubs/0502_barracksbrothels.pdf)

CNN (28 November 2000): Russian grandmother wanted to sell child for organs. (http://archives.cnn.com/2000/WORLD/europe/11/28/russia.children)

Comisión de Jefes, Jefas y Directores/as de Centro América y el Caribe (2004): Acuerdo 004/04 – Trata de Personas y Tráfico Ilícito de Personas. Managua.

Coomaraswamy, Radhika (1997): Report of the Special Rapporteur on Violence against Women, Its Causes and Consequences. United Nations Economic and Social Council, E/CN.4/1997/47. Geneva.

Coomaraswamy, Radhika (2000): Report of the Special Rapporteur on Violence against Women, Its Causes and Consequences, on Trafficking in Women, Women's Migration and Violence against Women. United Nations Economic and Social Council, E/CN.4/2000/68. Geneva.

Cyrus, Norbert (2005): Human Trafficking and Exploitation in Germany. Geneva.

D'Cunha, Jean (2002): Trafficking in Persons: A Gender and Rights Perspective. Expert Group Meeting on "Trafficking in Women and Girls", 18-22 November 2002. EGM/TRAF/2002/EP.8. New York.

Derks, Annuska, (2000): Combating Trafficking in Southeast Asia: A Review of Policy and Programme Responses. IOM. Geneva.

De Stoop, Chris (1992): They are so sweet, Sir. Manila.

Deutsche Gesellschaft für Technische Zusammenarbeit (GTZ) GmbH: Sector Project against Trafficking in Women (2004): Armed Conflict and Trafficking in Women. Eschborn.

Deutsche Gesellschaft für Technische Zusammenarbeit (GTZ) GmbH: Sector Project against Trafficking in Women: www.gtz.de/traffickinginwomen

Deutsche Gesellschaft für Technische Zusammenarbeit (GTZ) GmbH (2003): La Lucha contra la Trata de Personas en Centro América y el Caribe. Un Manual para Instituciones Policiales. Eschborn.

Doezema, Jo (2002): 'Who gets to choose? Coercion, consent, and the UN Trafficking Protocol'. In: Masika, Rachel (ed. 2002): Gender, Trafficking and Slavery. Oxford, pp. 20 – 27. (http://www.walnet.org/csis/papers/doezema-choose.html)

Dormaels, Arne / Moens, Bruno / Praet, Nele: 'The Belgian Counter-trafficking Policy'. In: Van Den Anker Christien' (eds. 2004). The Political Economy of New Slavery. Houndmills, Basingstoke, Hampshire, pp. 75 – 90.

El-Cherkeh, Tanja / Stirbu, Elena / Lazaroiu, Sebastian / Radu, Dragos (2004): EU-Enlargement, Migration and Trafficking in Women: The Case of South Eastern Europe. Hamburgisches Welt-Wirtschafts-Archiv (HWWA) Report. Hamburg.

European Commission, Directorate-General Justice, Freedom and Security (2004): Report of the Experts Group on Trafficking in Human Beings. Brussels.

Federal Criminal Police Office (2004): Situation Report Trafficking in Human Beings 2003. Wiesbaden.

Gallagher, Anne (2002): 'Trafficking, smuggling and human rights: tricks and treaties'. In: Forced Migration Review (FMR), Volume 25, February 2002, Oxford, pp. 25 – 28.

Global Alliance Against Traffic in Women (GAATW) (2000): Human Rights and Trafficking in Persons: A Handbook. Bangkok.

Goyal, Madhav et. al. (2002): 'Economic and Health Consequences of Selling a Kidney in India'. In: Journal of the American Medical Association, Vol. 288, No. 13/ 2002, pp 1589-1593.

Graaf, Ronald de (1995): Prostitutes and their Clients: Sexual Networks and Determinants of Condom Use. Utrecht.

Gramegna, Marco A. (2004): Migration and Trafficking in Persons. Paper issued at the First Meeting of the Alliance Against Trafficking in Persons, 23 July 2004. Vienna.

Gronow, Jane (2000): Trafficking in Human Beings in South Eastern Europe (SEE). An Inventory of the Current Situation and Responses to Trafficking in Albania, Bosnia and Herzegovina, Croatia, The Republic of Yugoslavia and the Former Yugoslav Republic of Macedonia. UNICEF Area Office. August 2000. Sarajevo.

Gronow, Jane (2002): 'HIV/AIDS and Trafficking'. UNICEF Internal Strategy Document. Sarajevo.

Howe, Christiane (2004): ‚Bilderwelten-Innenwelten, Ergebnisse der qualitativen Studie über Kunden von ausländischen Prostituierten.' In: Dokumentation der Fachtagung von context e.V.: Prostitutionskunden – sich auszutauschen, um Standpunkte zu verrücken. Frankfurt/ Main, pp. 31 – 45.

Human Rights Watch (HRW) (1996): Shattered Lives. Sexual Violence during the Rwandan Genocide and its Aftermath. Kigali/Washington D.C. (http://www.hrw.org/reports/1996/Rwanda.htm)

Human Rights Watch (HRW) (2002): Hopes Betrayed: Trafficking of Women and Girls to Post-Conflict Bosnia and Herzegovina for Forced Prostitution. Volume 14 No. 9 (D). New York. (http://www.hrw.org/reports/2002/bosnia/)

Interamerican Development Bank (IDB) (2003): Workshop Report on Anti-Trafficking Initiatives in Asia, Latin America & Caribbean and the US. Washington D.C.

International Criminal Tribunal for the Former Yugoslavia (ICTY) (2001): Prosecutor v. Dragoljub Kunarac, Radomir Kovac, and Zoran Vukovic. Case No. IT-96-23-T & IT-96-23/1-T. February 22, 2001.

International Human Rights Law Institute, De Paul University, College of Law (2002): El Tráfico de Mujeres y Niños para la Explotación Sexual Comercial en las Américas. Chicago.

International Labour Office (ILO) (2002): A Future without Child Labour. Geneva.

International Labour Organization (1930): ILO Convention 29: Convention Concerning Forced or Compulsory Labour. Geneva.

International Labour Office (ILO) (2004): Human Trafficking and Forced Labour Exploitation: Guidelines for Legislators and Law Enforcement. Geneva.

International Labour Office (ILO) (2005): A Global Alliance Against Forced Labour. Geneva.

International Labour Office (ILO) (2005a): A Global Alliance Against Forced Labour. Global Report under the Follow-up to the ILO Declaration on Fundamental Principles and Rights at Work. Geneva.

International Labour Office (ILO) (2005b): Trafficking for Forced Labour. How to Monitor the Recruitment of Migrant Workers. Training Manual. Geneva.

International Labour Office (ILO) (2005c): Human Trafficking and Forced Labour Exploitation. Guidance for Legislation and Law Enforcement. Geneva.

International Labour Office (ILO) (2005d): Employers' Handbook on Trafficking and Forced Labour Exploitation (draft). Geneva.

International Labour Organization, IPEC (ILO/IPEC) (2004): Trafficking in Children for Labour and Sexual Exploitation in Moldova. Results of a Rapid Assessment Survey. Chisinau.

International Labour Organization, IPEC (ILO/IPEC) (2004): Trafficking in Children for Labour and Sexual Exploitation in Ukraine. Results of a Rapid Assessment Survey. Kiev.

International Organization for Migration (IOM) (2002): Position paper on HIV/AIDS and Migration. Eighty-fourth Session, MC/INF/252. Geneva. (http://www.iom.int/DOCUMENTS/GOVERNING/EN/Mcinf252.pdf)

International Organization for Migration Counter-Trafficking Service (IOM) (2004): Changing Patterns and Trends of Trafficking in Persons in the Balkan Region. Assessment carried out in Albania, Bosnia and Herzegovina, the Province of Kosovo, the Former Yugoslav Republic of Macedonian and the Republic of Moldova. Geneva.

Italian Department for Equal Opportunities (2005): Art. 18 D.lgs 286/98 – Testo Unico delle disposizioni concernenti la disciplina dell'immigrazione e norme sulla condizione dello straniero, mimeo. Rome.

Jana, Smarajit et al. (2002): 'A Tale of 2 Cities: Shifting the Paradigm of Anti-trafficking Programmes'. In: Masika, Rachel (ed. 2002): Gender, Trafficking and Slavery. Oxford, pp. 69 – 79.

Joint Council for the Welfare of Immigrants (2004): Statement (in response to the Morecambe Bay Tragedy, where 21 migrants died picking cockles). London.

Kern, Dominique (2000): Don Juan: Face-to-face Freierbildung – Ein Projekt der HIV/Aids-Prävention für Sexkonsumenten. Evaluationsbericht. Strasbourg and Zurich.

Kohler, Franz (1997): Freier und HIV-Risiko: eine Literaturanalyse über ungeschützte Sexualkontakte zwischen Sexkonsumenten und Prostituierten in der Schweiz. Zurich.

Kohler, Franz (1998): ‚Recherche Niederlande, neue Erkenntnisse und Konsequenzen für das Projekt Don Juan'. Bericht. Zurich.

Langanke, Harriet (2004): Internet, Freier und Frauenhandel. Recherchen zur Frage, ob und wie Freier via Internet zum Thema Frauenhandel angesprochen und sensibilisiert werden können. Eschborn.

Latin American Institute for Human Rights (ILADH)/State Program to Combat Trafficking (2005): Working Papers and Interviews. Recife.

Limanowska, Barbara (2002): Trafficking in Human Beings in South Eastern Europe. Current Situation and Responses to Trafficking in Human Beings. UNICEF/UNOHCHR/OSCE/ODIHR. Sarajevo. (www.seerights.org)

Limanowska, Barbara (2003): Trafficking in Human Beings in South Eastern Europe. Update on Situation and Responses to Trafficking in Human Beings. UNICEF/UNOHCHR/OSCE/ODIHR. Belgrade. (www.seerights.org)

Limanowska, Barbara (2005): Trafficking in Human Beings in South Eastern Europe. 2004 Focus on Prevention: in Albania, Bosnia and Herzegovina, Bulgaria, Croatia, the Former Republic of Macedonia, Moldova, Romania, Serbia and Montenegro and the UN Administered Province of Kosovo. UNICEF/UNOHCHR/OSCE/ODIHR. Sarajevo. (www.seerights.org)

Local Governments for Sustainability (ICLEI) (2000): Guide to Implementing Local Agenda 21. Freiburg.

Médecins sans Frontières (MSF) (2005): The Crushing Burden of Rape: Sexual Violence in Darfur. A briefing paper for the International Women's Day 8 March 2005. (http://www.msf.ca/press/images/070305_darfur_sexualviolence.pdf)

Minnesota Advocates for Human Rights (2003): Developing an Advocacy Strategy. (http://www.stopvaw.org/Developing_an_Advocacy_Strategy.html)

Moens, Bruno (2002): Country report Belgium. Report prepared for Anti-Slavery International. Human traffic human rights: Redefining victim protection. London, Antwerp.

North Atlantic Treaty Organisation (NATO) (2004): Policy on Combating Trafficking in Human Beings. EAPC (C) D (2004) 0029. 8 June 2004. Brussels. (http://www.nato.int/issues/trafficking/index.html)

North Atlantic Treaty Organisation (NATO) (2005): Combating Trafficking in Human Beings. (http://www.pfp.ethz.ch)

The other NATO training modules can be obtained at the NATO Headquarters: Blvd Leopold III, 1110 Brussels, Belgium. (natodoc@hq.nato.int)

Organization for Security and Co-operation in Europe (OSCE) (2003): Consolidated Summary of the Second Preparatory Seminar for the 11th Economic Forum. The National and International Economic Impact of Trafficking in Human Beings. Ioannina, Greece, 17-18 February 2003. (SEC.GAL/56/03/Corr.1, 28 March 2003). Vienna.

Organization for Security and Co-operation in Europe (OSCE) (2003): Summary of the OSCE Economic Forum on Trafficking in Human Beings, Drugs, Small Arms and Light Weapons: National and International Economic Impact. (EF.GAL/13/03 Rev.1, 11 June 2003). Vienna.

Organization for Security and Co-operation in Europe (OSCE) (2003): Action Plan to Combat Trafficking in Human Beings. PC.DEC/557, 24 July 2003. Vienna.

Organization for Security and Co-operation in Europe/Office for Democratic Institutions and Human Rights (OSCE/ODIHR) (2004): National Referral Mechanisms. Joining Efforts to Protect the Rights of Trafficked Persons. A Practical Handbook. Warsaw.

Pag Asa (2003): Jaarverslag 2002. Brussels.

Payoke (2005): Jaarverslag 2004. Antwerp.

Pearson, Elaine (2002): Human Traffic, Human Rights: Redefining Victim Protection. Anti-Slavery International. London.

Pesquisa Pestraf-Brasil (2002): CECRIA Centro de Referencia Estudios e Ações sobre Crianças e Adolescentes Brasil. Brasilia.

Petrini, D. / Prina, F. / Virgilio, M. / Bertone, C. / Ferraris, V. / Orfano, I. / Aràn, M.G. / Oberlies, D. (2001): Article 18: Protection of Victims of Trafficking and Fight against Crime (Italy and the European scenarios). On the Road Edizioni. Martinsicuro.

Proyecto de Promoción de Políticas de Género (2004): Género y Seguridad Ciudadana. Módulo de Capacitación Regional. Managua.

Raymond, Janice (2001): Guide to the New UN Trafficking Protocol. Coalition Against Trafficking in Women. North Amherst, MA. (http://action.web.ca/home/catw/attach/Guideun_protocol ENG.pdf).

Rizvi, Sylvia (2000): 'Die Kampagne *Männer setzen Zeichen*'. Beiträge zur feministischen Theorie und Praxis. Köln.

Rohter, Larry (2004): 'Tracking the Sale of a Kidney on a Path of Poverty and Hope'. In: New York Times, 23 May 2004.

Savona, E.U. / Bella, R. / Curtol, F. / Decarli, S. / Di Nicola, A. (2004): Trafficking in persons and smuggling of migrants into Italy. Final Report. Transcrime/University of Trento – Direzione Nazionale Antimafia. Trento.

Scheper-Hughes, Nancy (2000): 'The Global Traffic in Human Organs'. In: Current Anthropology. Vol. 41, No. 2/ 2000, Chicago, pp. 191 – 224.

Scheper-Hughes, Nancy (2004): 'Parts Unknown: Undercover ethnography on the organs-trafficking underworld'. In: Ethnography. Vol. 5, No. 1/ 2004, Thousand Oaks, CA, pp. 29 – 72.

South East European Regional Initiative aGainst Human Trafficking (SEE RIGHTs) (2001–2005). www.seerights.org

Surya (2005): Rapport d'activité 2004. Liège.

Swami, Praveen (2003): Punjab's kidney industry. In: Frontline, Vol. 20, No. 3/ 2003.

Tallis, Vicci. (2002): Gender and HIV/AIDS. BRIDGE Report. Institute of Development Studies. Brighton, UK.

United Nations Children's Fund (UNICEF) (2003): Guidelines for Protection of the Rights of Children Victims of Trafficking in South Eastern Europe. (http://www.seerights.org)

United Nations Children's Fund (UNICEF) (2003): Child Trafficking and HIV/AIDS. Internal Document. New York.

United Nations Children's Fund (UNICEF) (Undated): Principles for ethical reporting on children. (http://www.unicef.org/media/media_tools_guidelines.html)

United Nations (UN) (2000): Protocol to Prevent, Suppress and Punish Trafficking in Persons, Especially Women and Children, supplementing the UN Convention against Transnational Organized Crime. (http://www.unodc.org/unodc/en/trafficking_convention.html)

United Nations Development Programme (UNDP) (2003): Gender Issues in Ukraine: Challenges and Opportunities. Kiev.

United Nations Development Programme (UNDP) (2005): Bulgaria: (http://www.undp.bg/en/pb_sust_human_development_perspective.php)

United Nations General Assembly (2002): Resolution adopted by the General Assembly, 'A World Fit for Children,' A/RES/S-27/2, pp. 17 – 20. New York. (http://www.unicef.org/specialsession/docs_new/documents/A-RES-S27-2E.pdf)

United Nations High Commissioner for Human Rights (UNHCHR) (2002): Recommended Principles and Guidelines on Human Rights and Human Trafficking. UN document E/2002/68/Add.1.

United Nations Office of the High Commissioner for Human Rights (UNOHCHR) (2002): Recommended Principles and Guidelines on Human Rights and Human Trafficking. Text presented to ECOSOC as an addendum to the report of the United Nations High Commissioner for Human Rights (E/2002/68/Add.1). Vienna. (http://www.unhchr.ch/huridocda/huridoca.nsf/e06a5300f90fa0238025668700518ca4/caf3deb2b05d4f35c1256bf30051a003/$FILE/N024016.pdf)

United Nations Special Rapporteur Report to the Commission on Human Rights (2000): Contemporary Forms of Slavery: Systematic Rape, Sexual Slavery and Slavery-Like Practices During Armed Conflict. E/CN. 4/Sub.2/2000/21. 6 June 2000.

US Department of State, Bureau for Public Affairs (2004): Trafficking in Persons Report 2004. Washington D.C.

Vandekerckhove, W. / Pari, Z. / Moens, B. / Orfano, I. / Hopkins, R. / Nijboer, J. / Vermeulen, G. / Bontinck, W. (2003): Research based on case studies of victims of trafficking in human beings in three EU Member States i.e. Belgium, Italy and the Netherlands. IRCP, University of Ghent. Ghent.

Vermot-Mangold, G. (2003): Trafficking in Organs in Europe. Council of Europe Parliamentary Assembly, Document 9822, 3 June 2003.

Weissbrodt, David/ Anti-Slavery International (2002): Abolishing Slavery and its Contemporary Forms. Geneva.

Wennerholm, C. J. (2000): Trafficking in Women and Girls and HIV Prevention. Conference Presentation, "Together Against AIDS", Malmo, Sweden. (http://www.qweb.kvinnoforum.se/misc/TRAFFICKING%20-HIV%20PREV-text.rtf)

Wijers, Marjan / Lap-Chew, Lin (1997): Trafficking in Women: Forced Labour and Slavery-like Practices in Marriage, Domestic Labour and Prostitution. Foundation Against Trafficking and Global Alliance Against Traffic in Women. Utrecht.

Winter, Reinhard (2000): Die Hotline für Männer. Terre des Femmes Zeitung. Tübingen.

Winter, Reinhard (2004): 'Präventionsarbeit und –ansätze in der Jungen- und Männerarbeit'. In: Dokumentation der Fachtagung von context e.V.: Prostitutionskunden – sich auszutauschen, um Standpunkte zu verrücken. Frankfurt/ Main, pp. 21-30.

Women's Consortium of Nigeria (2000): Research Report on Trafficking in Women in Nigeria. Lagos.

www.aids.ch, www.context-cps.de, www.frauenrechte.de – see for background information on trafficking and addressing clients in prostitution.

www.jnet-trafficking.org – see for the articles produced through the MADI training for journalists.

Zimmerman, C. / Yun, K. / Shvab, I. et al (2003): The Health Risks and Consequences of Trafficking in Women and Adolescents, Findings from a European Study. London School of Hygiene and Tropical Medicine, London.